Hyper-civiliza

An answer to ET conta

Dan D. Farcaș

Published by Flying Disk Press in 2018

Flying Disk Press
4 Saint Michaels Avenue
Pontefract
West Yorkshire
England
WF8 4QX

CONTENTS

Flying Disk Press

INTRODUCTION

The idea of a powerful presence above us is a haunting concept, and for thousands of years the minds of human beings have struggled with this idea. Most people are aware of this, either through their culture, education or religion, some through ufology and others through fairy tales, or even the science fiction seen in movies and on TV and so on. There are also countless testimonies about strange manifestations that can be attributed to such a presence; and in the latter years of the twentieth century as information transparency increased, they have become more and more visible especially via the internet. The reported cases have too many common features to be considered as just the simple products of human imagination. This is not just wishful thinking; something truly strange is happening all around us.

Science will say that these testimonies – even if they are in their millions – do not prove anything, because they talk about miracles or magic and that is impossible according to the known laws that govern the Universe. To challenge these laws, testimony must be backed up by testable hard evidence. If required they should be observed by sceptics and possibly experimented with in laboratories in a repeatable manner, but unfortunately this is not always possible.

Religions recognise the existence of a superior power, as well as testimonies based on miracles and Divine revelations, but here we encounter another problem. Each of the different religions is convinced that it, and only it, is the one which holds the ultimate truth on the nature of the superior power above us. But there are over ten thousand religions in the world, one hundred and fifty of them having at least one million followers each. And the "ultimate truths" of some of them sometimes fundamentally contradict those of others. The dispute to prove who is right has lasted for thousands of years and although it has been bathed in the blood of millions of martyrs, no agreement has been reached regarding who is right. And there is no sign that, in the foreseeable future, a solution will be obtained that everyone will accept. On the contrary.

To the above is added the additional problem that science vocally denies what religions support. The European philosophy of the last few centuries has found a palliative solution to overcome this contradiction, by claiming that there are in fact two distinct realities that exist in two worlds. One is an "imminent" material one, in which science is the appropriate method and another is "transcendent", immaterial and spiritual, which is the domain of religion and philosophy. This is obviously a provisional solution, because the miracles, which all religions embrace, are happening in the material world, so the two worlds cannot be broken apart. The truth is that we live in a unique and indivisible reality that embraces both the material and the immaterial.

This book is an essay, which aims to respond to the problems outlined above using the hypothesis of *'hyper-civilizations'*. This explanation, although not the only one, seems to me the most rational because, based what we know today, it can clarify many disputed phenomena and it is also difficult to dismiss. The basic idea behind this hypothesis has been debated by many people, but, as far as I know, this is the first time it has been assembled into its main issues as a coherent whole.

The arguments contained in the following pages address the concerns of both sceptics with a scientific background and those who accept the reality of the mysteries that surround us. It also addresses both the uninformed reader and those already familiar with the issues raised. But it is addressing, in a very special way, those who feel that they care about the future of our earthly civilization. The main prerequisites are for the reader to be willing to accept that reality may sometimes be very different from what they believe it to be, or as it is described in school books, and also that no one holds the ultimate answer.

I'd like to express my gratitude to friends who, through long discussions, helped me to crystallise the ideas outlined here and to the ufologists and thinkers from various domains who provided many of the facts and arguments used in my exposure. Special thanks goes to the veteran UK UFO researcher Philip Mantle, for his initiative in publishing a book about hyper-civilizations, and for his editorial effort, including the hard work required in transforming my raw text in to readable English.

THE FERMI PARADOX

The Drake equation

It is said that in 1950, Enrico Fermi, the Italian physicist who discovered nuclear fission, was talking with his colleagues about the existence of other civilizations in the Universe. He noted that if there are such civilizations, then some of them must have appeared long before mankind and their representatives would have had enough time to explore our galaxy and reach Earth. Therefore, we ought to have been visited long ago and many times over, but there are no signs of such visits. Fermi summed up this fact using the rhetorical question: "They should be here, but we don't see them anywhere. Where are they?" Since then this problem has been known as "the *Fermi Paradox*".[1]

In the following pages I will try to present some possible answers to this question, as well as some other enigmas which are connected with it. But before that, I ask the reader's permission to present some details, perhaps a bit technical, without which these answers could not be properly understood. At the same time I am asking for the understanding of the informed reader, for whom these things are perhaps superfluous.

We all live on a tiny, blue, cosmic island that we call the Earth; it is one of many heavenly bodies orbiting around the Sun. The Sun, in turn, is just one of about 200 billion stars contained in a spiral conglomerate called a "*Galaxy*", or in our case the "*Milky Way*", and on clear nights we can see it above us in the sky. To understand the dimensions of only the part of universe, which is accessible to our instruments, we should note that in it there are at least 150 billion other galaxies similar to ours. And there could be other worlds beyond this universe. These values are confusing, therefore I advise the reader to be careful considering the kind of numbers we will use in this book, because the human mind cannot fully comprehend such great values, and the sheer scale can lead to confusion.

According to some estimates made by astronomers, in November 2013, in our galaxy alone, there would be about thirty two billion planets on which there may be life. But for the overwhelming majority of them, life is only at the microbial level. It is estimated that on several thousand of these planets, life could reach the diversity of the Earth's biosphere. But only in a very small number of these worlds beings would emerge who are smart enough to build a technological civilization similar to the one we live in, with Internet, space craft, genetic engineering and nuclear capability etc.

At the end of the 1950s, following the launch of the first artificial satellites, many people wondered how many advanced civilizations existed in our cosmic neighbourhood. Could we get in touch with some of them using radio waves? In September 1959, physicists Giuseppe Cocconi and Philip Morrison suggested in an article[2] that civilizations will look for contact in a radio frequency around 1420.4 MHz, which is the radiation emitted naturally by interstellar hydrogen, and at the same time is a frequency with minimal 'jitter'. This 'jitter' is caused by electromagnetic interference and crosstalk with the carriers of other signals

The first program to search for such extra-terrestrial signs was called "OZMA" and was conducted between April and July 1960 by astronomer Frank Drake of Cornell University (Ithaca, New York) with the 26-meter dish at the Green Bank Observatory radio telescope (West Virginia). It was directed to the two closest Sun-like stars: *Epsilon Eridani* and *Tau Ceti*. But nothing special was received.

---

[1]   Webb, 2002
[2]   Cocconi, 1959

Then, in 1961, Drake convened a meeting with ten specialists at Green Bank to discuss the issue of communication with other cosmic civilizations. As a prerequisite for the discussion, Drake proposed a formula designed to estimate how many civilizations that communicate using radio waves, might exist in our galaxy. The equation looked like this:

$$N = R \times fp \times ne \times fl \times fi \times fc \times L$$

In this equation, N is the number of civilizations. It would be equal to the number (R) of stars born in one year in our galaxy, multiplied by the fraction of them possessing planets (fp), also by the average number of planets (ne) that can support life near such a star, by the fraction of those planets (fl) on which life develops abundantly, by the fraction (fi) of them on which intelligent, civilised life, has developed, by the fraction (fc) of intelligences coming to communicate by radio signals and, finally, by the average value (L) of the length of time over which such civilizations release detectable signals in space.

The scientists present at Green Bank estimated the minimum and maximum values of these factors then multiplied them. In the pessimistic version, N equalled twenty civilizations, and in the optimistic one, fifty million. The truth could be somewhere between them, but where?

From then until today the values of those first estimates have changed dramatically. With more recent estimates, the value of N lies between a minimum of two and a maximum of two hundred and eighty million, which is a larger value than the original one. Pessimists should not forget, of course, that these values were only calculated for our galaxy; therefore, for the entire observable Universe these values should be multiplied by about one hundred and fifty billion. So, no matter how rare, there should be some advanced civilizations in our Universe and beyond.

The idea of searching for extra-terrestrial civilizations in this way is not new. In 1896 Nikola Tesla was conducting experiments to "listen" to the Cosmos (more precisely the planet Mars) using radio. In 1899 he had the impression that he had received something, but the signals were not convincing. On August 21-23, 1924, when Mars was closer to Earth than ever, in the United States a "National Day of Radio Silence" was established, where, for thirty six hours, all transmitters stopped broadcasting for five minutes in each hour. A naval radio receiver was lifted three kilometres above the ground with the help of a dirigible, to try and capture any signals. The contribution of the United States Army's chief cryptographer was also provided in case any potential Martian messages should be received and require to be deciphered. Prior to that, Guglielmo Marconi had made similar attempts while on board his yacht, the "Electra". It is said that some unexplained signals were received, but they were not repeated.

The SETI projects

Drake's trials have triggered the *Search for Extra-terrestrial Intelligences* (SETI) projects – a systematic scrutiny of the sky using radio telescopes. Most projects were based in the U.S., using, for example, the Arecibo Observatory (in Puerto Rico). Its antenna is capable of detecting a radar signal from a distance of sixty light-years away. Over a period of time similar projects have also taken place in at least five other countries, including the USSR (Nikolai Kardashev, V. A. Troitski). More recently, instead of large, expensive and hard-to-reach radio telescopes, it is preferable to build dedicated networks of dozens of smaller parabolic antennas working simultaneously. One example is the Allen Telescope Array (ATA), 470 km northeast of San Francisco. This networking method can also help eliminate many of the parasitic signals often caused by unwanted electronic oscillation in an electronic or digital device.

Over the years, some promising signals coming from the cosmos have been received, but they have been either found to have an ordinary explanation, or they were inconclusive and have not been repeated. The most interesting was, on August 15, 1977, when an observer near Columbus (Ohio) received a signal thirty times stronger than the ambient background noise from the constellation of Sagittarius and it was on a narrower frequency band than any earthly transmitter. The signal appeared and disappeared several times, and then it stopped completely. It is known as the *"wow"* signal, because this was the handwritten word on the computer printout that showed the signal in a graphic form.

The workload increased exponentially as other frequencies were taken into account, as well as other stars further away in the Galaxy. Since 1984, coordinating efforts in this regard has been done mainly through the SETI Institute in Mountain View, California, a non-profit organisation that has benefited from the participation of a large number of scientists, including Carl Sagan, Jil Tarter, Seth Shostak and others.

The Institute collaborated with NASA and benefited from the generous support of the U.S. government, until 1993 when this ceased, after which it was mostly supported by private funding. In 2015, the Russian entrepreneur Yuri Milner, through the Breakthrough Foundation, made a $100 million donation to fund the most advanced radio and optical observations for ten years using the world's largest radio telescopes, creating a SETI program more ambitious and robust than ever before. The amount allocated provides thousands of research hours per year to two of the world's most powerful radio telescopes in the U.S. and Australia: Green Bank Observatory in West Virginia, the largest orientable telescope on the planet and Parkes Observatory in New South Wales. The telescopes are going to scan the entire Milky Way, including the core, and also the closest one hundred galaxies. California's Lick Observatory will also conduct a comprehensive search for possible laser optical transmissions coming from other planets. The new project will also dramatically increase the computing capacity for processing the collected data.

Edward Snowden, the former National Security Agency (NSA) employee, suggested that extra-terrestrial messages might exist, but they could be so well encrypted that people who try to eavesdrop on them will get the impression that they are hearing nothing but noise. Seth Shostak, director of a research centre at the SETI Institute, said that they are not looking for a message, but a signal to prove that there is a transmitter. Doug Vakoch, another researcher at the SETI Institute, underlined that telecommunications are changing rapidly. For example – he said – not long ago, we were extremely noisy; we had a lot of TV and radio transmitters that broadcast their energy in all directions. More recently though, using fibre optics and satellite communications, there is much less leakage into space.

Researchers have not only tried to listen, but also send messages to the cosmos. For example, in 1974 a 1679-bit message was transmitted from the Arecibo Observatory in Puerto Rico for three minutes, in the hope that, over a few hundred or perhaps thousands of years, it will be received by other civilizations and it will send a reply. For the same purpose, on the *Pioneer 10* and *11* and *Voyager 1* and *2* space probes, plates were fixed and engraved with drawings and symbols. They have almost left the Solar System and are travelling through the cosmos in the hope that, over tens of thousands of years, they will encounter some intelligence.

Among other things, the researchers in charge of the SETI projects wondered with all seriousness, what to do if someday we obtain scientifically certain evidence of the existence of an extra-terrestrial civilization near us.

In 1960, the Brookings Institution in collaboration with NASA's Committee on Long-Range Studies, made a first report in this regard, highlighting the potential dangers of meeting a civilization superior to us. In 1989, a subcommittee of the SETI Committee of the International Academy of Astronautics produced a document called "the declaration of principles for activities following the detection of extra-terrestrial intelligence" (short: SETI Post-Detection Protocol), including measures to be taken in the case of the discovery of a non-earthly civilization. The protocol was submitted to the UN Committee on the Peaceful

Uses of Space and revised several times, mainly with contributions from John Billingham, Michael Michaud and Jill Tarter.

A preliminary version of the Protocol and its amendments stated that, if an undeniable signal from an alien civilization were to be received, the discoverer would disclose that fact, discreetly, to the other observers participating in SETI-type projects for independent opinions and signal monitoring. Only after a general confirmation will the discovery announced to the authorities and the public. The response to the sender of the signal (providing the message was decrypted and understood) will be discussed and approved by the UN General Assembly, on behalf of all mankind following global consultations.

The NSA (National Security Agency) reacted immediately to this proposal, considering it unacceptable that the United Nations, or an international group of astronomers, would represent the Earth in communications with other worlds. If the representative of another world asks to be led to the leader of our planet – they said – this leader should be the President of the United States as a logical consequence of U.S. military and economic power. From the very first moment of a possible contact – they added – the United States must supervise, monitor and control exclusively all communications with other planets.

The fear of invasion

Some experts considered it is foolish both sending messages to the Cosmos and waiting for a possible message in return. It could be – they said – that the signals might be bait, sent to all the corners of the Galaxy by an aggressive civilization. If we respond, aliens will know (over thousands of years?) that here is an inhabited planet and they will come to invade us. Other speculation even said that, for an advanced cosmic race, we could be regarded as a primitive form of life, maybe regarded as living toys or guinea pigs for experiments, or even culinary delicacies such as domestic animals are to us. One possibility might be that, under the guise of technological aid, for example in biochemical experiments, "they" will place their own forms of life here on Earth.

These views, relevant to the next chapters, must be placed in the context of a general *fear* of a possible alien invasion. This apprehension was consistently maintained, for more than a century in science-fiction novels, stories and films, beginning with "*The War of the Worlds*" by H.G. Wells. As well as in this novel, the "aliens" portrayed in films such as "*Alien*", "*Independence Day*" and "*Signs*", etc. are monstrous, merciless invaders, without any respect for human beings.

As an example, in a 2011 article by Seth D. Baum, Jacob D. Haqq-Misra (both from Pennsylvania State University) and Shawn D. Domagal-Goldman, of the Planetary Sciences Division of NASA, it was speculated that the aliens could come to eat us, to enslave us, or simply to exterminate us. Extra-terrestrials may choose to destroy mankind as a preventive measure, in order to protect other planets, knowing that an aggressive civilization such as ours, that expands very quickly, is prone to destroy other lifeforms to make room for its development.

In April 2010, late British physicist, Stephen Hawking, joined this bizarre speculation, saying that human beings would be better off doing everything they can to avoid contact with extra-terrestrial civilizations, adding that "if aliens visit us, the outcome would be much as when Columbus landed in America, which didn't turn out well for the Native Americans."

Also, in 2015, following the generous sponsorship of SETI projects by Milner, Stephen Hawking repeated his fears, but this time more moderately, saying: "It is important for us to know if we are alone in this darkness." But "A civilization that would read a message of ours could be billions of years more advanced. And if so, it will be much stronger than us and can see us as no more valuable than we see bacteria."

The cultural shock

Is this fear unjustified? Let us think, however, what would happen if someday we were receiving a sign that definitely came from another civilization? Undoubtedly, there are many who will say that this would be the most important event in the history of mankind. But if we took a poll, we would discover that this opinion only belonged to a small minority. In fact, most of us are accustomed to the assurances we have received from wise men for thousands of years that the whole Universe has been created for us and we are the only intelligent mortals within it. We are happy with this situation and would not be anxious to change it.

As early as the late 1940s, the U.S. governments repeatedly commissioned polls to estimate the impact of an official statement about the discovery of extra-terrestrial civilizations. The results were daunting. If people had learned of the coming of aliens, they were prepared to either exterminate the invaders with guns, or to consider that the visitors were the incarnations of the Devil.

As I have already mentioned, at the end of the fifties the Brookings Institute undertook a study paid for by NASA, to identify the long-range goals of the United States' future space program and their impact on American society. The results of the research included a commentary on the implications of the discovery of extra-terrestrial life and intelligence. It was established that the reactions of both individuals and government representatives depend not only on the social and cultural environment they are part of and their religious beliefs, but also on the nature of the discovery itself. The discovery of inferior forms of life, or even of "subhuman intelligence", could easily be assimilated by society. Instead, the discovery of a form of intelligence superior to ours would be followed by profound effects.

If, tomorrow, scientists presented unchallengeable evidence that there is a superior intelligence near us and that it is capable of intervening in earthly activities, the situation would become dramatic. In the history of earthly civilization, there have been many cases where societies that were very sure of their place in the Universe, disintegrated when they were overwhelmed by a superior culture, one which promoted different ideas and lifestyles. And the surviving societies were forced to radically change their system of values and behaviour.

Carl Gustav Jung (1875-1961), one of the founders of psychoanalysis, illustrated our eventual encounter with a more evolved cosmic civilization through the words: "The reins would get out of our hands, we would find ourselves without dreams, we would discover that our intellectual and spiritual aspirations are so overcome that they would leave us completely paralysed."

Traditional religions, the most abiding pillars of morality, would see their sacrosanct dogmas threatened. Some believers would be obliged to accept that there are different paths toward Divinity and toward other hierarchies of intelligence in the Universe than those that are spoken of in their holy books. Others – especially the case of the fundamentalists – will find it difficult to believe that everything related to "aliens" is not the "work of the Devil", against whom they must fight by all possible means, and these fundamentalists have considerable influence, especially in politics,

Science would have to admit that very few of the things that are today the pride of various research institutes would still be worthwhile. As a consequence, people could lose confidence in all science, including what is taught at school. Many theories, laws and statements such as: "Nothing is faster than the speed of light" could no longer be sustained.

If an official statement were made about contact with aliens, if we knew there were infinitely better technologies near us, the economy would collapse, stock markets would close, many businesses would stop with possible global effects that are impossible to predict.

The army in particular would be confronted with an extreme problem, because the discovered civilization would probably be considerably more technologically advanced than we are, so we would have little chance in the event of a military confrontation. And if such a civilization only came to Earth to impose universal love and peace, it would still be extremely serious. As psychologist Scott Mandelker PhD noticed: "Peace is a terrible threat to the status quo: peace will cause the armies to leave their weapons, the police to restrain from law keeping; the whole economic system will have to find other bases than the war. For those in power, peace is dangerous".

Physicist and ufologist Stanton Friedman stated several times that if an official statement was made on contact with aliens, the congregations of churches and the occupants of psychiatric hospitals would increase. He added, however, that there would be also some people who would be overjoyed. They would forget their national affiliations and consider themselves as "citizens of the Earth". It would be a blow to nationalism, national states and politicians; and it is a change that no government could allow.

In short, if officials discovered the existence of an alien civilization, they would hide this information with the utmost rigour. The ordinary human would not object, because they too does not like to see his reference systems overturned. They would be delighted if a government assures them that we are alone in the Universe, or that other civilizations are so far away that there is no possibility of an encounter. Therefore everybody is happy, because nothing threatens our traditional world view. People tend to believe in what makes them feel comfortable. The unknown scares us, while the image of a simple, fully explainable world makes us feel safer and more relaxed.

This bias is not new. The renowned American author Charles Fort wrote one hundred years ago, that if some authentic, human-shaped extra-terrestrials descended into New York City and paraded on the streets for hours, sent us their greetings and told us who they were and where they came from, after which they went home, next day someone would not only say that this was a hoax, but it was they who organised it. As a result, the inhabitants of the city would feel relieved, saying that they suspected all along that something was wrong with these aliens.

Self-destruction?

Until now the efforts of scientists to discover signs of an alien civilization have only produced one result: a "gigantic silence". A very old cosmic civilization might manifest itself through "miracles", that is through phenomena that cannot be explained as natural events, and some of these miracles could be of huge proportions. Among other things, such a civilization should be here, now. But, at least officially, we have had no sign of any such presence.

Astrophysicist Vladimir M. Lipunov, of the State University of Moscow, calculated[3] in 1995 that the probability of absence of "space miracles" in our Universe is $10^{-43,000,000}$, i.e. it is equal to zero! In short, such very old civilizations, as well as their miracles, must exist. Nevertheless, nobody has discovered them even after many years of searching. A world without miracles is incredible and yet such a world exists – Lipunov concluded.

The Russian astronomer Iosif Shklovsky, caused a sensation in the 1960s, claiming that the Martian satellites of Phobos ands Deimos could be artificial, but, in 1985, disappointed that "the Universe is silent", he said that the only explanation is that, despite the estimates, we are alone in Universe. This opinion, to which many scientists rallied, was also called the *Solipsist hypothesis*. The more moderate supporters of this hypothesis admit that the probability of their being the only civilization in the Universe is near zero, hence there are also other civilizations, but we are too far away from one another and are unable to get in touch.

---

[3]   Lipunov, 1995

Another hypothesis explaining why we do not see any other civilization in the Cosmos, is that all technological civilizations somehow disappear shortly after they reach a stage similar to the one we are now in. Would such a scenario be plausible?

Unfortunately, since the only example we have at hand is human civilization, we first have to ask whether it would be possible for mankind to disappear in the foreseeable future.

The first cause that comes to mind might be a natural catastrophe. Perhaps this could be catastrophic arrival of a *super-meteor* with a diameter of several kilometres, but such an event occurs, on average, once every hundred million years or so, therefore it is extremely unlikely that this will happen in the near future. But this is not the only danger. In the Universe there are also occasional explosions such as those of the *supernovae* that spread deadly radiation (gamma rays etc.) capable of destroying any superior form of life thousands of light years away. But fortunately these catastrophes are extremely unlikely to happen near us.

The inversion of Earth's magnetic poles is another threat, this occurs extremely irregularly, on average once every 250,000 years. If it were to happen, over several decades the planet's magnetic field, which protects us from dangerous cosmic radiation, will drop to just ten percent of its normal value. The number of cancers would greatly increase, and many species would consequently disappear, electricity and transmission networks would be severely affected, but civilization as a whole would not be destroyed. It seems that we should most be afraid of the eruption of a "*super-volcano*". The last such eruption that of the Toba super-volcano in northern Sumatra, which occurred 73,500 years ago and its dramatic effects on climate have been felt for 20,000 years. It is estimated that following this event, the human race was reduced to only a few thousand individuals.

Of course, we still don't know the entire list of threats of this kind. However, the fact that evolution of life on Earth has unfolded unswervingly for billions of years, despite all the natural disasters produced in the meantime, gives us hope that earthly civilization could escape, even if only partially, should such misfortunes occur.

The really great dangers capable of threatening the human species with extinction come from human activities. Due to industry and transport, etc., the carbon dioxide levels in the atmosphere have greatly increased. A consequence of this is the increasing "greenhouse effect", where heat coming from the Sun is not reflected back into outer space. For this reason, over the past thirty years the average global temperature has increased by 0.5 centigrade. Pessimistic forecasts say that if the process continues, the increase could be 2.7 degrees by 2100. The consequences will be very hot summers, capricious winters, storms of unprecedented violence, glaciers at the poles melting and mountain ridges, cultivated lands and savannah turning into deserts and so on. The complete melting of the polar ice caps could lead to global ocean levels rising by up to 115 meters, leading to the drowning of whole countries plus the loss of all major coastal cities. But the history of global climate change shows that in this "game" there could be also other, natural partners much stronger than the human species, so these predictions have to be accepted with some reserve.

In an interesting work[4], Joel Levy draws attention to other dangers that may cast doubt on the future of mankind. Antibiotic abuse will create super-bacteria against which we will have no cure. Chemicals or nano-technologies, which we believe today are useful and safe, could manifest – when introduced into medicines, cosmetics, food and supplements, etc. – over time this may produce harmful, irreversible effects for future generations; such as happened with DDT and thalidomide.

---

[4] Levy, 2005

Many are afraid of the kind of experiments being conducted in huge particle accelerators, which could produce – as some think – a "black hole" capable of swallowing the Earth. There is very a small chance that this scenario will materialise, but we do not know whether more powerful accelerators would not create more dangerous "monsters", which at present we do not even suspect.

Others believe that there are other dangers if artificial intelligence got out of control. Stephen Hawking was most concerned about the potential dangers of "powerful autonomous weapons". He has recently warned that artificial intelligence will be either the best, or the worst thing that happened to mankind. By the end of 2015, Hawking had added his name to a coalition of over 20,000 researchers and experts, including Elon Musk, Steve Wozniak and Noam Chomsky, who were calling for a ban on any autonomous weapons systems that could be used without human intervention. As the founders of this initiative have said, our robots are now very submissive, but what if we remove too many of the restrictions that limit their actions?

But the real danger comes from genetic experiments. Obtaining some advantages from these (for example, creating "super-cereals", "super-fruits", "super-vegetables", "super-cattle", etc., but also "super-men" and "super-women", and using them as models for the entire population), could be followed in the next few generations by an irreversible degeneration of the human species. But out-of-control genetic experiments could also create new viruses or other varieties of microorganism, for which humans have no immunity and for which there would be no cure.

While on the subject of dangers that could bring about the end of our civilization, we must not omit the explosive combination of: demographic growth, and the tendency of all the inhabitants of the globe to aspire to "Western living standards", the policy of spheres of influence, military interests and religious, nationalist, or ideological fanaticism, which together will lead, in our century, to wars and migrations of monstrous proportions, as well as to increasing terrorist attacks.

If only 10% of the world's nuclear arsenal was used in a war (possibly triggered by a mistake), very few people would survive (maybe none); in the best case scenario, civilization would be set back by hundreds of years, the sky would remain dark and the average temperature would drop by between five to twenty degrees, creating a decades long "nuclear winter" that would drastically reduce food supplies. If, with the end of the Cold War, this danger has diminished it has not completely disappeared. It is sufficient to know that there are dictatorships willing to maintain their power at any cost, or terrorist groups who would not care if, in the name of a creed, all humanity would be exterminated (saying that "the Lord will distinguish between the good folk and the evil ones"). What happened on September 11, 2001 was the symbolic signal of the entry into the present century, prefiguring the ever-increasing horrors that we can expect.

It is worth remembering that the dangers mentioned above: the genetic experiments, the nuclear weapons and even the aircraft with which you can destroy emblematic buildings and so on, are inventions of the twentieth century. Twenty-first century science and technology will discover (alongside countless wonderful achievements) other, more effective methods of destruction, against which nuclear weapons or artificial pandemics will seem like children's games. But if we can overcome these trials, the twenty-second century then the twenty-third will come and go, until the "ultimate weapon" is finally discovered. It is then possible that the survival of our race will depend on the speed with which we can colonise the outer space so that if, for example, the Earth is completely destroyed or is transformed it into a globe of fire, we at least have distant space colonies to migrate to along with whoever is left and who are hopefully much wiser.

Degradation?

Some have speculated that there might be another explanation for the "gigantic silence", namely that any civilization once it has reached its peak will necessarily degenerate.

On the one hand, we can think of a biological degeneration. For example, the ancient ancestor of Europeans, traditionally called the "Cro-Magnon man", were 1.80-1.90 cm in height and had a brain of 1600 ccm in capacity, while ours only has a capacity of 1350-1400 ccm and we are also somewhat shorter.

The explanation is that in nature only the fittest and best adapted to the environment survive. The others are eliminated before they have descendants and in the beginning this rule was also true for human beings. During our prehistory the number of individuals grew very slowly, because only the most vigorous and intelligent succeeded in reproducing. But more recently our civilization, which has provided care for everyone, has changed this trend and this will continue.

On the other hand, the progress of science and technology provides people with an increasingly comfortable existence requiring less and less effort. Appliances, robots and all kind of machinery will take over much of the work previously done by people. In the first phase this means additional opportunities for self-development and creation; but later it could lull of all humanity in a "paradisical" state. In 1980 Frank Drake even said that maybe the colonisation of outer space is not mandatory as we are tempted to believe. Perhaps the cosmic civilizations that preceded us have comfortably installed themselves around their native stars, without having any interest in wasting their energies on travel into outer space and other stars.

CONCLUSIONS

The Universe, even the part that we can see with our instruments, is huge and in it there are an unimaginably large number of places where not only life, but also a civilization similar to ours could emerge and develop. The calculations say that some of these civilizations must have appeared a long time ago and their representatives would have had enough time to reach the Earth and reveal themselves through displays of astonishing technology. However, if they have there is no sign of them.

We may wonder if it is true that all civilizations will either self-destruct or disappear for other reasons after having reached a level of evolution similar to what we have here on Earth. Or is there another explanation for this absence?

THE CHANCE OF INTELLIGENCE

The Universe and the Solar System

The speculations we have considered so far have not helped us to find a response to Fermi's paradox. A basic rule of analysts is that if they have not found a response to a problem, they probably did not gather enough data, so they need to continue investigating deeper into the details. Following this recommendation, I once again ask for the reader's permission to examine in greater detail the evidence we have at our disposal.

At the time of writing, scientists are convinced that the Universe was born around 13,798 $\pm$ 0,037 billion years ago by the explosion (also called the "*Big Bang*") of an incredibly small object called a singularity. The same event would also have created *space* and *time*. The fragments resulting from this explosion continue today to move away from each other, taking increasingly complex shapes.

Shortly after the "*Big Bang*" the Universe was mostly composed of hydrogen, and gravitational forces gathered it together into agglomerations. At the core of the larger agglomerations, pressure and temperature triggered thermonuclear fusion transforming the hydrogen into helium, which released an enormous amount of energy. This is how the first stars lit up.

When the "fuel" that sustains the thermonuclear fusion is consumed, stars die, often through a gigantic explosion (a phenomenon observed today that we call "novae" or "supernovae"), expelling most of its substance into the space, in the form of huge clouds of dust and gas. The remaining part of the star turns into a small, dark, celestial body.

Within these 'first generation star' as described above, not only helium but also some other chemical elements are also created over time, like carbon and oxygen, etc. The final explosion generates energies large enough to create heavier elements, including complex molecules that could not be produced inside the star.

After a while, the cosmic clouds born out of these explosions gradually condense into "second generation" stars. Some of these stars also explode at the end of their life cycle. In the places where the clouds form, stars of the "third generation" light up. Our Sun is such a star. Orbiting this type of star there are also solid, rocky planets containing practically everything that exists in the periodic table of elements, as well as large quantities of water, methane and many other simple compounds. Our Earth is such a rocky planet.

The life-span of a star depends on its size. The bigger the star, the less time it has. The Sun is fortunate because it has a "life expectancy" of around ten billion years. Of these it has consumed almost half, so it still has a long life ahead. Astronomers know that towards the end of its life the Sun will begin to swell, gradually becoming a huge globe that will swallow nearby planets, perhaps even the Earth, then will expel a great deal of its matter, with the remainder collapsing into its nucleus. If it were only five times larger than it is, the Sun's life would have been only sixty million years, and that is almost 20,000 times shorter. Near such a star life would have had no chance of success and, of course, it would not have produced a technological civilization.

The Sun appeared, according to the latest estimates, 4,567 billion years ago. From a cloud of stones, dust and gas still circulating around the new star, in a process called 'accretion', several planets were born, among which, about 4.54 billion years ago, was the Earth. At first our planet was a burning globe, shattered by an uninterrupted bombardment of celestial bodies, both large and small, that fell onto its surface, as our planet acted like a 'gravitational vacuum cleaner'. At some point there was a terrible impact and the Earth almost broke into pieces and then was rebuilt again, part of it breaking away to form the

Moon. As millions of years passed, the bombardment gradually reduced as the immense boulders orbiting around it reduced in number. The surface of the Moon is covered by craters caused by the impact of such meteorites. We see these craters clearly, because on the moon they can survive for billions of years. Although the Earth received a much greater bombardment, the traces of the craters formed have been erased, with a few exceptions, because of the actions of weather, sea, vegetation, crustal movements etc. In fact, even today meteorites still fall, albeit much more rarely and less violently. Now, on average, some two hundred and thirty meteorites fall on the Earth on a daily basis. These can weigh anything from a few grams to several kilograms

Birth of life

To estimate the chances of life and the civilizations that could have developed in the universe, at present we only have our planet as an example and possibly that of our close neighbours that we can examine using telescopes and probes. What did we discover? First, in the newly-born Solar System there was unexpectedly large amount of water. Even today, comets and meteorites are mostly made of ice. The water, gathered from the meteor bombardment, accumulated both inside and on the surface of the globe and at one point it completely covered both the Earth (and its neighbouring rocky planets, Mars and Venus), with oceans and perhaps polar caps.

Life has developed on Earth thanks to liquid water. Of course we are speaking about a specific form of life that is based on carbon, DNA and proteins. As we know nowadays, this form is the only one capable of providing the complex biosphere that eventually produced the human species. Some believe there might be other life forms based on silicon. However, molecules built from silicon chains are much shorter and their chemical reactions are far less energy efficient. An important argument against this variant is that Earth is, literally, a typical silicon planet (we have much less carbon). And for 4.5 billion years the conditions required to produce a silicon-based life form have been present. But no silicon compounds as complex as those of carbon have been found and, of course, no signs of a silicon life form either.

Four point five billion years ago the Earth's surface was still to a large extent an ocean of liquid magma; but after about just one hundred million years, the planet started to form a solid crust, oceans and an atmosphere. Many experts believe that life arose shortly after this. However, due to the constant impact of large meteorite and other deadly conditions, life may have appeared on the Earth several times, been destroyed and then reappeared time and time again.

For billions of years until now, the Earth's crust was in constant motion. The tectonic plates slid on a magma bed, broke up and slipped into the depths, from where other matter welled up. Despite all of these movements, some small crust fragments have remained on the surface for billions of years. To their surprise, palaeontologists have found, even on the oldest fragments, primitive traces of life. In ferrous rocks in North Quebec, microfossils of at least 3.77, but possibly even 4.28 billion years old, have been found. The structure of primitive creatures suggests that they developed near hydrothermal springs. In West Greenland, in 3.7-billion-year-old sedimentary rocks altered by metamorphism, (the alteration of minerals or geologic texture) graphite deposits have been found, which are believed to have been created by living beings. In October 2015, scientists announced that in Western Australia, "traces of biotic existence" were found in 4.1 billion years old rocks. These are only some of the examples that will continue to be supported by other finds and breakthroughs.

As one of the researchers involved said, "If life appeared so quickly on Earth, then it could be something common in the whole Universe". This hypothesis is shared by practically all scientists. For example, Carl Sagan and Stephen Hawking said more than once, that it is unlikely that life could not exist in places other than the Earth.

These statements are based on physical laws, which seem to be the same everywhere in the unimaginably large expanse of the observable Universe. As recently as thirty years ago, using spectroscopy astronomers identified the presence of water, carbon dioxide, formaldehyde, ammonia, acetaldehyde, methyl alcohol and benzene etc in space. An amino acid, glycine was also identified. Many other organic molecules were recently added to this list, including glycol aldehyde, and polycyclic aromatic hydrocarbons, etc, all of them considered as being important building bricks of life.

If all of these compounds have been detected at such a distance, it means they exist there in huge quantities. For example, near the centre of our galaxy a cloud of alcohol and other organic substances was found. Its mass is five hundred times greater than the mass of the entire Solar System. Based on these findings, some scientists have even questioned whether some extremely primitive components of life have been synthesised at the very core of such clouds and, spreading in all directions, have reached the Earth as well.

Therefore, the possibility cannot be entirely dismissed that extremely primitive forms of life have been born in the clouds of organic matter in outer space, or in the atmosphere of planets otherwise unfit for evolved life. It was even said that the synthesis of the bricks of life could begin at around ten to seventeen million years (i.e. in a very short time) after the Big Bang. These primitive forms could travel for millions of years through space from one star to another "infecting" any suitable place. Experiments conducted in spacecraft have shown that bacteria, a relatively evolved form of life, can survive for a long time in outer space. Experiments in 1998 at the University of Berkeley (California) have proven that the DNA molecules survived for over thirty-five years in a vacuum at room temperature, suggesting that at the temperatures in outer space it could exist indefinitely, for example within small fragments of rock protected from harmful radiation.

So, almost certainly, complex organic molecules already existed in the protoplanetary disk, made of dust grains that roamed around the Sun before the birth of the Earth. And in the same way as they reached Earth, these molecules will have reached many other corners of the Solar System.

The idea that life was brought to Earth from somewhere else in the Universe was started by the Greek philosopher Anaximander, in the sixth century before the Christian era. In the 20th century, supporters of this hypothesis, which they called "panspermia", were chemist Svante Arrhenius, astronomers Fred Hoyle and Chandra Wickramasinghe, the biologist Francis Crick, and the chemist Leslie Orgel. Panspermia proponents are convinced that microscopic forms of life are conveyed on meteorites, asteroids and other bodies, throughout the Universe. For example, a meteorite that fell in 1969, near Murchison, Victoria, Australia, contained over ninety different amino acids, including nineteen of those found in earthly life. Comets and other icy bodies on the periphery of the Solar System also contain large amounts of complex carbon compounds. Such bodies fell like rain on the Earth during the first phase of its existence.

It seems therefore, that the Universe is teeming with very primitive forms of life, travelling for millions of years through space and "infecting" any suitable place. Some even think that this process also explains some of the strange epidemics that we face periodically. Therefore, it appears that regardless of its origin, life could manifest anywhere in the Universe, providing there are favourable conditions and it will continue to spread and evolve as long as these conditions are maintained.

But life could also be born of dead matter, even on Earth. The first experiments that attempted to replicate this process, were conducted by Russian biologist Alexander Oparin (in 1924) and British geneticist J. B. S. Haldane (in 1929).[5] In 1952, American chemist

---

[5]   Dyson, 1999

Stanley Miller, led by Harold Urey and then, in 2009, by Jeffrey L. Bada, who was a disciple of Miller, managed to produce under laboratory conditions that imitated the Earth's environment four billion years ago, several dozen amino acids, the essential bricks of life. However, for the present we do not know how proteins, complex organic molecules, bacteria and other living beings emerged from these basic amino acids. But scientists say that if the germs did not come from the Cosmos, it is likely that the first bacteria appeared, either in the depths of Earth, or near the sulphurous springs at the bottom of the ocean. Some also believe that the mould on which the first life forms appeared was clay.

Life, once it has appeared, can adapt to unimaginably harsh conditions. Bacteria capable of multiplying at minus seventy degrees centigrade were found in Antarctica. Also, twelve thousand years old samples of ice from the same source extracted from a depth of hundreds of meters contained bacteria that could be brought back to life. On the Earth, in the sulphurous springs on the seabed, *"extremophiles"* have been discovered. These are bacteria that can survive at temperatures of one hundred and twenty degrees centigrade and at pressures of over two hundred atmospheres. Some other bacteria can live in brine, acids and inside nuclear reactors, and also at an altitude of eighty kilometres and at a temperature of minus one hundred and ninety-six degrees centigrade

So, at first there were only some very complicated molecules, born here and coming from other parts of the Universe (or perhaps even planted here by some intelligence?). They had two main attributes: on the one hand they could attract some atoms from around themselves, increasing in size this way; and, on the other hand, when a molecule became very large it split into two molecules of the same kind, each continuing to grow and multiply again and again. These miraculous molecules were not all identical; when they split, small "transcription errors" occurred, a kind of *mutation*. As in gaming, most of these random mutations were fatal, but from time to time there were also some lucky mutations. Thanks to them, some molecules fared better than others, which helped them to have more descendants. In other words their success was due to the fact that they gained a better knowledge than their competitors of the environment they lived in.

During an unimaginably long evolution, in which these seeds of life have become more and more complex, this knowledge has been coded to a great extent (but not exclusively) in what is termed 'genetic information', especially in nucleic acids of the RNA or DNA type in the form of what are called *genes*. The genes of an individual encode and transmit their characteristics (appearance, behaviour, life expectancy, etc.) to their offspring. A virus has several genes; a bacterium, such as "Escherichia coli", has about four thousand genes, the yeast six thousand, a wine midge thirteen thousand, a worm about nineteen thousand while a human has about twenty-five thousand genes in their DNA. There are also some creatures apparently more biologically complex than humans: a poplar tree has forty-five and rice fifty thousand genes.

In the same way as mentioned above, genes transmitted from parents to their offspring may undergo mutations: random changes caused by many factors such as radiation or contact with certain chemical compounds, etc. These changes are, in the overwhelming majority of cases, harmful; for example normal parents can have handicapped children; some of the handicaps can make life impossible. Of the approximately five billion species which are estimated to have ever lived on Earth, over 99% no longer exist today, which is the result of this unstoppable mechanism of selection and adaptation that acted, day by day, for around four billion years in all corners of the Earth. The immensity of this evolutionary process exceeds the imagination of the human mind. In such situations we can easily fall prey to the temptation to resort to readily accessible explanations to explain the miracle of the world that we see around us.

In order to understand the immense pressure exerted by the process of natural selection a digression could be useful. Any species has the potential to multiply far beyond the resources at its disposal. If, for example, the growth rate of the human population from the middle of the 20th century remained unchanged, then, in about three thousand years (an insignificant time compared to the periods mentioned above), the total mass of the human race would be equal to the mass of the Earth (!)... Other creatures are much more prolific than humans, but despite this, in the past before the human intervention, over thousands and thousands of years the number of specimens of a given species remained roughly the same, and only the best adapted survived.

Evolution of the living world.
The course of evolution of life on Earth was not at all simple. Three point eight billion years ago the meteoric bombardment slowed, after which a long-term oscillation between glacial and greenhouse threats followed. Four billion years ago, on Earth, the surface temperature was close to that of boiling water. If this point had been reached the oceans would have evaporated and the clouds would have amplified the greenhouse effect, the heat would have increased to two hundred and ninety degrees centigrade and life, if it had not completely disappeared, would never have gone beyond the stage of microorganisms,

The atmosphere of the primitive Earth contained nitrogen, carbon dioxide and sulphur dioxide. About three point five billion years ago, when the average temperature had dropped below seventy degrees centigrade, the lottery of mutations gave birth to a chlorophyll-like pigment called Cyanobacteria, which became capable of photosynthesis and, profiting from this advantage, multiplied because of solar energy and gradually consumed the carbon dioxide in the atmosphere, and in doing so released oxygen. For nearly one billion years this gas oxidised most elements on the surface of the Earth, especially iron. This stage finished about two point five billion years ago, after which the oxygen began to spread in the oceans and the atmosphere.

By reducing the amount of carbon dioxide, the greenhouse effect diminished, and the temperature fell dramatically. In a short time a first severe ice age began, which lasted, with some interruptions, until about six hundred million years ago. Life survived this ordeal well, but not without great changes. The enrichment of the atmosphere and oceans with oxygen had even more dramatic consequences than climate cooling. Oxygen is a killer of any unprotected living organism. Only the bacteria that hid themselves in anaerobic environments, or had a protective membrane survived. There have also been bacteria that have been sheltered inside membrane-providing cells, which provide various services. Some of these types of symbioses learned to "breathe" and took advantage of the fact that oxygen-provided reactions could provide fast movements. This process of recombination of various types of bacteria culminated with the emergence of the so-called *eukaryotic cell*, in which the DNA, with the genes of all the components, was brought together in one place: the nucleus. This innovation proved so successful that it spread across the globe and eliminated its competitors. As a result, today all animals and plants are composed of this type of cell.

At the beginning eukaryotic cells lived alone then in colonies, where component specialisation was becoming more and more accentuated. The next step was to transform these colonies into *pluricellular beings*, this happened about one point seven billion years ago, although cells with differentiated roles had still existed two point one billion years ago.

At first, cells "understood" each other by a means that we still do not fully understand, but which ensured the unity of living beings. This basic communication system still functions in all of us. But, as these beings got bigger, the coordination of the component cells, especially for rapid reactions, became more and more problematic. At this stage, the next formidable "invention" of the living world gradually emerged: the *nervous system*.

19

Another very important turning point was *sexual reproduction*, which began about one point two billion years ago. All animals, plants, and fungi that reproduce sexually are the successors of one successful eukaryotic cell that benefited from this lucky mutation. Sexual reproduction brought a tremendous advantage, among other things, in the fight against parasites and against the risks of unfavourable mutations.

Seven hundred and twenty million years ago a new Ice Age began, perhaps the worst in the history of the Earth, it was a severe winter that lasted for eighty million years. Some even say that, especially in the last five million years of that era, the Earth and the oceans were almost entirely covered by ice, which sometimes reached a kilometre in thickness. The equatorial regions beyond the polar circle resembled those we now have; geologists call this period the "Snowball Earth". At the same time the percentage of oxygen in the atmosphere began to increase steeply and five hundred and seventy million years ago, for the first time it reached twenty-one percent (its present level), preparing the way for large animals with lungs and gills, etc. About the same time the evolutionary process produced a small worm, it was the first creature to have a right and left side, plus a front and a back. This innovation was so successful that relatively quickly from this worm, through successive mutations, all the other animals with external and internal skeletons appeared..

Today archaeologists can precisely determine from the layers of rock deposited on the Earth's crust, era after era, all these events as well as those that followed. They also have several methods accurate enough to date the age of each rock plus the remains of former living creatures. About five hundred and forty two million years ago a process called the "Cambrian Explosion" was triggered. In "just" twenty to twenty-five million years, the ancestors of all animals that exist today appeared. Over the next seventy to eighty million years, the rate of diversification accelerated so that the variety of species in the world began to resemble those of today. For the first time, beings with skeletons left remnants that were visible to the naked eye in the rock layers. These fossils appeared so suddenly and so abundantly in the geological strata corresponding to that era, that Charles Darwin himself said that the phenomenon is the most serious argument against his theory of evolution.

The first vertebrates appeared five hundred and twenty five million years ago, and the first fish five hundred million. The oldest terrestrial plants date back to about four hundred and fifty million years ago and their appearance was the result of microorganisms that existed there millennia before. Then, at least three hundred and fifty million years ago, the first beings began to walk on dry land.

The evolution of life was profoundly influenced throughout this period by dramatic planetary events. The variation of the Earth's orbit around the Sun produced a cycle of glaciations. These glaciations could have been caused by an increase in volcanic eruptions that threw dust into the stratosphere, or perhaps by the Solar System passing through a cloud of cosmic dust. The fall of large meteorites could also lead to devastating effects. Maybe it was also the explosion of "supernovae".

On many occasions, events like these have led to the extinction of many temporarily successful species with others taking their place. In the last half billion years, palaeontologists have noted five great extinctions. The first, and perhaps the most violent event, happened between four hundred and fifty to four hundred and forty million years ago and it was accompanied by an Ice Age. At that time most living things disappeared, including sixty to seventy percent of all species. But shortly after the Ice Age was over, the land became covered with forests and insects. The second extinction, about three hundred and seventy five to three hundred and sixty million years ago, had multiple causes and destroyed a third of all life, especially marine life. But after this episode, three hundred and fifty million years ago, the first vertebrates begin to walk on land and thirty million years later, the entire surface was dominated by the ancestors of the quadrupeds, they were animals that looked like crocodiles or varanid lizards.

Two hundred and fifty two million years ago a third major extinction took place. For palaeontologists it marks the border between the Paleozoic and the Mesozoic era. In this cataclysm, fifty percent of the animal families and ninety to ninety six percent of the species living in the seas disappeared. The causes were again multiple. Among other things, all the tectonic plates were then crowded into a single supercontinent, called Pangea, which had many desert areas. The winners of this extinction were the ancestors of the dinosaurs, some of which later reached fifteen metres in height, fifty metres in length and one hundred tonnes in weight. But next to them, two hundred and twenty five million years ago, mammals first appeared as nocturnal insectivores that mostly lived underground. Their descendants became the ultimate winners.

The fourth major extinction took place two hundred and one million years ago. The cause of this may have been an asteroid, or perhaps the intensification of volcanism, but most probably both. This event caused seventy to seventy five percent of all species to disappear, including many dinosaurs, but fortunately not the first mammals. The surviving dinosaurs resumed their dominant position until sixty six point two million years ago, when – together with three-quarters of plant and animal species – they were permanently wiped out, their only surviving descendants being the birds.

This fifth great extinction, which marked the border between the Mesozoic and the Neozoic (or Cenozoic) era, has the best documented cause. A giant meteorite, with a diameter of ten to fifteen kilometres struck the Earth at a speed at least ten times higher than that of an artillery shell. The moment the base of the meteorite reached the ground its tip was still in the stratosphere at the same height as modern intercontinental airplanes, but in just one second it had already sunk into the Earth's crust.

Following the impact, which took place in the northern Yucatan peninsula near Chicxulub, the tectonic plates dislocated intensifying the volcanic activity throughout the globe. It is estimated that the tsunami produced was one kilometre in height. For a few months dust, smoke and the ashes of immense fires created a permanent night on the entire surface of the Earth. The temperature fell, vegetation and phytoplankton in the oceans was reduced to almost zero, which first led to the extinction of herbivorous dinosaurs and then the carnivores. When the sky cleared, because of the greenhouse effect the average temperature climbed fifteen to twenty degrees centigrade above normal; this was a situation that lasted for several hundreds of thousands of years.

Only a few species, unpretentious and well-sheltered, survived including small mammals, birds, reptiles and amphibians, etc. In a short period based on the geological clock, the descendants of the humble mammals occupied the Earth, their descendants became elephants and lions, dolphins and whales, horses and wolves, bulls and boars as well as thousands of other species, among which were some arboreal creatures, that a few million years ago began evolving into our human ancestors.

Becoming Human

The distant forerunners of the human species evolved from gibbon ancestors fifteen to twenty million years ago, fourteen million years ago the orang-utans, eight million years ago the gorillas and then the predecessors of chimpanzees some seven and a half million years ago.

Shortly afterwards our ancestors, called *Homo habilis*, walked on two legs and used their hands to make tools in the African savannah. The (accidental?) doubling of a gene, named SRGAP2, has accelerated the growth of this species brain, especially the frontal cortex. About one point five million years ago a descendant of theirs, *Homo erectus*, had an average cranial capacity of eight hundred and fifty cubic centimetres, but he used fire to prepare food, had more complex tools and possibly possessed a rudimentary speech. He was the first hominid to leave Africa, spreading to Asia and Europe. Its main European descendants, the Neanderthal people, appeared one hundred thousand years ago, they were, robust and had an average cranial capacity of sixteen hundred cubic centimetres, significantly higher than the average of fourteen hundred cubic centimetres of modern humans, but the structure of his brain was more primitive than ours.

About three hundred thousand years ago, in Central or South Africa, a new species, called "Homo Sapiens" separated from Homo erectus. Its representatives were at last the "true human beings". About one hundred and twenty thousand years ago a small group of them passed through the Arabian Peninsula in Asia. Seventy millennia ago their descendants, following the shores of the Indian Ocean, reached India and, fifty millennia ago Australia. Other branches migrated to the Central Asian steppes, giving birth to the Mongolian people. Fifteen thousand years ago a clan crossed the Behring strait and populated America.

Those who, over forty five thousand years ago went to Europe, are traditionally called the Cro-Magnons. They had a brain of over sixteen hundred cubic centimetres and had a robust constitution. Their average height was between one hundred and seventy five to one hundred and eighty centimetres, but some individuals reached two meters. They migrated westward, along the Danube and then the Rhine Corridor. Twenty thousand years ago, after they had eliminated their Neanderthal precursors, they occupied the whole continent.

Then, over millennia and the gradual accumulation of knowledge and technology thanks to libraries, schools, the economy, etc., "homo sapiens", that is 'us', has started using atomic energy, space travel, the Internet and the cloning of living beings. In other words mankind has reached the current level of a "technological civilization". What next?

This has perhaps been a lengthy recap of a much longer history. But I think it will help us to better understand the complexity of how we got here and, by extension, how life could evolve on other planets. As we have seen, the Earth was a planet with a very special history, a special place, where ideal conditions eventually led to the emergence of an abundant biosphere and human civilization. Such fortunate planets are probably very rare in the Universe.[6] However, if an alien had visited the Earth at some random point between the birth of the planet and today, it would have had only one chance out of seven of encountering animals visible to the naked eye, one chance out of twenty thousand of meeting a human being and one chance of four hundred thousand of encountering a settled, albeit primitive, civilization. Finally, if they had sent a radio message to us, they would only have one chance of forty-five million of finding anyone who received it.

I have the feeling that those concerned with SETI projects are not prepared to take this into account. But they are not alone, for the overwhelming majority of people, both "millions of years" and "billions of years" mean very little, because the numbers are so huge. As an example of this thinking, many popular movies suggest that primitive humans were contemporary with dinosaurs; and that was not the case, so in the following chapters it is important that the reader does not fall into this trap.

Life in Solar System

In ancient times, Anaxagoras, Plutarch and Lucian believed there might be people on the Moon. In the Middle Ages, although the Christian church had formally accepted Plato's and Aristotle's views, that there are no other inhabited worlds outside the Earth, scholars such as Buridan, Ockham, or Oresme, argued that this could not be so, because it would limit the creative power of God. After them, in 1440, Nicolaus Cusanus claimed that everything in the

---

[6]   See Gonzalez, 2004 and Ward, 2004

power of the Lord was actually accomplished. The answer of ecclesiastical officials was that although God could create other worlds, he decided to create only one. But with the propagation of Copernicus's vision, which suggested that the Earth and the Sun are not the centre of the Universe, Giordano Bruno, Kepler, Campanella and others have argued – even more fiercely – the hypothesis of the plurality of inhabited worlds. In 1600 Bruno was burnt at the stake for suggesting such a heresy.

Subsequently, with the gradual understanding of the immensity of Universe and our peripheral status in this immensity, many individuals such as Huygens, Fontenelle, Locke, d'Alembert, Berkeley, Buffon, Herschel, Kant, Lomonosov and Gauss etc. have claimed the existence of alien civilizations. As astronomy advanced, scientists became aware that, according to probability which I have already mentioned, it is almost certain that life and intelligence in present elsewhere in the endless cosmic expanses. Nowadays some religious authorities have begun to wonder why, if God has created such a huge and diverse Universe, is there only one species of intelligent beings and does the rest only comprise of desolate planets?

Of course, they only considered the observable Universe. However, it is worth mentioning that, since ancient times, Leucippus, Democritus and Epicurus supported the existence of other inhabited realms that are invisible to us. This point of view resembles today's hypotheses of other dimensions, parallel universes, multiverses and other realms based on as yet unknown laws of physics.

Today we know that in our Solar System, outside the Earth there is no hope of finding evolved beings, quite apart from advanced civilizations. The planet Venus is, in its volume and composition, very similar to Earth. However, being closer to the Sun the temperature at the surface of Venus was, from the outset, a little higher. It seems that two point five billion years ago, while at the same stage as the Earth, life also existed there as microorganisms in the depths of its vast oceans. Unfortunately, these oceans gradually evaporated because of the heat. This resulted in a thick blanket of clouds, which further accentuated the greenhouse effect and increased the temperature. The planet developed into a vicious circle from which it could not escape. Nowadays, on Venus the layer of clouds stretches in a compact mass from thirty to eighty kilometres in altitude (on the Earth they rarely climb more than ten kilometres), the clouds are formed mainly of drops of sulphuric acid. Under these clouds the temperature is over four hundred degrees centigrade, both at the poles and at the Equator. The atmosphere consists of ninety-six percent carbon dioxide and three percent nitrogen. Under these conditions complex life as we know it is virtually impossible.

The most "classic" planet for hosting life would have been Mars. There is evidence that it also had a warmer and wetter past. The images obtained by the Martian probes revealed polar caps and the dry whites of former rivers. In 2013, the Curiosity Rover found the dried bed of an ancient freshwater lake which could once have been hosted microbial life. But, over time, the water evaporated and scattered into space along with most of the gas, because the gravity of the planet was too weak to hold them.

At present, the Martian atmosphere is one hundred and seventy times as rarefied as that of the Earth, which, together with the low temperature, means that any small amount of liquid water (possibly brine) would have only two forms, it would either freeze or evaporate almost instantly. It is also known that on Mars there are large underground caverns of volcanic origin; it is speculated that some microbial life might have retreated here. The methane gas detected in the atmosphere of Mars could be proof of this, and unfortunately for the present that is all the information we have.

The other planets are even more inhospitable. In the 1960s and 1970s, some scientists, including Carl Sagan, speculated that, hypothetically, very primitive organisms could live in Jupiter's atmosphere. This hypothesis seems unlikely so far, given the intense radiation and other unfavourable conditions that seem incompatible with life. The same holds true for Saturn.

Surprisingly, however, a primitive life could exist on several large satellites of Jupiter and Saturn, but if so it is most likely to be only microorganisms.

How many cosmic intelligences could there be?

After reviewing the history that preceded the emergence of human civilization on Earth and the chances of life in the rest of the Solar System, we can return to the question: in how many other locations in our galaxy could these circumstances be repeated?

In an article published in November 2013[7], a group of astronomers have estimated, based on new data from the Kepler Space Quest and on statistical calculations, that about one in five stars of the Sun type possesses an Earth-like planet placed in the "habitable or goldilocks zone", that is neither too close nor too far from the central star. In our galaxy alone there would be about eleven billion potentially habitable Earth-like planets, orbiting around stars similar to the Sun. The authors of the article observed that life could also exist around another types of stars, namely red dwarfs, which raises the number of living planets to forty billion. The nearest habitable planet could most likely be at a distance of about twelve light-years from us. But we should not forget that in the overwhelming majority of these planets, life can only exist at the microbial level. Even on the most inviting planets, as was the case with our Earth, for almost four billion years a potential cosmic visitor would only have encountered algae and bacteria.

Here on the Earth we also benefited from countless other favourable circumstances besides those shown above. Our planet has virtually all existing chemical elements (most of them are indispensable for the human body) and gravity capable of retaining the water and the atmosphere (as opposed to what happened to our neighbour, the planet Mars). On many occasions and for various reasons the biosphere of our planet has been close to returning to the bacterial stage, or even of completely disappearing.

It seems that for a technological civilization it is necessary to have four billion years of relatively quiet evolution. Fortunately, for over 4 billion years, the Earth had been kept inside the habitable zone and its orbit around the sun is almost circular, so that on its surface there was always liquid water (unlike Venus, which became a hell because of the greenhouse effect). There was always just enough water, neither too much nor too little. If the surface of the Earth were perfectly smooth, it would have been completely covered with a two point seven kilometre deep ocean. By comparison Europa, a satellite of Jupiter which is a little smaller than the Moon, is uniformly covered by a one hundred kilometre deep ocean of liquid water.

Inside Earth there were enough radioactive elements to maintain internal heating, which produced, among other things, plate tectonics and therefore mountains and very long and varied shores. Also important was the special composition of the crust allowed it to bend and break. As a result of this almost thirty percent of the surface of Earth is not covered by water and there is an ideal proportion between land and oceans, plus the continents also have a fairly uniform distribution.

Also important was the fact that a day was twenty-four hours long, ensuring that the temperature differences between day and night were reasonable. Equally important was the tilt (twenty three percent) of the Earth's spin axis, which ensured a beneficial succession of the seasons. In both of these happy conditions an important role was taken by our natural satellite – the Moon – which is the largest satellite in the Solar System relative to the planet it orbits, also produces tides that are important to both the oceans and the land. It also

---

[7]   Petigura, 2013

effectively "massages" the crust frees and balances, little by little, the telluric energies that could otherwise become devastating. The lunar tides were also responsible for stabilising and slowing the Earth's rate of rotation.

Our fortunate position also seems to have been contributed to by the planet Jupiter, which has a mass three hundred and eighteen times greater than that of the Earth and has acted as a "gravitational vacuum cleaner" freeing the space around it by attracting many asteroids and meteorites that could have otherwise badly affected us. If Jupiter were not in its present position, the number of asteroids falling on Earth could have been ten thousand times greater, which would have threatened the development of an advanced life form. But if the giant planets Jupiter and Saturn had been much larger or closer to the Sun, they could have destabilised or even destroyed the Earth.

The shield provided by the Earth's magnetic field, created by the iron and nickel at the core of our planet, has protected us from dangerous cosmic particles and this shield is not found on all planets. We were fortunate in other ways too, such as the fact that we did not encounter a rogue planet entering the Solar System that could disturb the Earth's orbit and pull it out of the favourable zone, or that the Sun was not part of a double or multiple star system.

There is also the already mentioned "galactic habitable - or goldilocks - zone". The Earth was in such a zone, not too close to the galactic centre, where the violent supernova explosions would sterilise the planet too often, preventing or slowing down the evolution of life and it was also not too far on the outskirts, where there are not enough heavy elements to create Earth size planets.

Undoubtedly, very few planets in the Galaxy were as lucky. So, although we initially considered eleven billion possible Earth-like habitable planets, an extremely conservative calculation tells us that in our galaxy alone there might exist very few places on which a technological civilization similar to Earth's could emerge. Maybe there are hundreds of them, but it is not impossible that we are also alone. This is the so-called *"Rare-Earth Hypothesis"* of Peter D. Ward and Donald Brownlee.[8]

As an example, Guillermo Gonzalez and Jay W. Richards estimated that in our galaxy there could be 0.01 technological civilizations[9] that have a probability of only one per one hundred galaxies.

We must not forget that in our observable Universe there are around one hundred and fifty billion galaxies, but these do not resemble each other. At an estimate, perhaps only two percent of galaxies are sufficiently "metal-rich" to ensure the existence of Earth-type planets.[10]

Something else to keep in mind – other upcoming cosmic civilizations may currently be in very different stages of evolution. Some may still be in the same phase we were in billions of years ago when bacteria were created. Others might have overtaken us long ago. If so, how many of them are still using spaceships and communicating through radio waves? This could be the first clue in answering Fermi's paradox.

CONCLUSIONS

The progress of life on Earth, from the cooling of the crust and the appearance of the oceans until today, has been an extremely convoluted adventure taking place of over four billion years. During this time, the Earth has overcome several critical moments that could have stopped evolution. Animals visible with the naked eye (and not only microorganisms)

---

[8]   Ward, 2004
[9]   Gonzalez, 2004, pp. 338-339
[10] Gonzalez, 2004, pp.289-290

existed only in the last seventh part of this journey. And a cosmic traveller who might have come to our planet at a randomly chosen moment, would have had only one chance out of one million to meet a being that could communicate.

The conditions that have secured the evolution of life and intelligence on Earth are very rare. It can be estimated that in our Galaxy there may be now, at most, a few hundred planets on which a technological civilization was born in the past, or on which one will be born in future. Some of them could be very old. Most probably such civilizations emerge in the Milky Way only once every few million years. Therefore, it is extremely unlikely that on any of these planets evolution will be at a level similar to ours. This could be one answer to Fermi's paradox.

HYPER-CIVILIZATIONS

Conquering cosmic space

So far we have considered the history of life and intelligence on Earth, but in order to understand what a cosmic civilization might be, one that we might eventually meet, there are much more important next steps in our evolution. Again, we cannot speculate on this subject based on anything other than the example we have at hand – our civilization. But, although have some reliable data from our past, for the future we have to rely on some forecasted trends and try to extrapolate from them as much as we can.

If, fifty years ago we were asked what the future holds for us, we would have answered without hesitation it was the colonisation of the cosmos. At the beginning we would colonise the Solar System then the Galaxy and so on. Even if our enthusiasm for this has fallen away slightly, the idea has not entirely disappeared. For example, physicist Stephen Hawking said in a public lecture held at the University of Cambridge in November 2016, that efforts to conquer outer space are essential for the future of mankind as, "I do not think we will survive for another thousand years, unless we escape beyond our fragile planet". He alluded to the fact that the only way to safely escape our extinction due to the tendency to self-destruct, is to set up colonies somewhere else in the Solar System where at least a part of our species and of our civilization might continue to exist.

Colonisation of the Solar System would also have other advantages. On other celestial bodies there are abundant mineral resources and the colonisations would not displace other populations or destroy ecosystems as has occurred in the past. There is ample room to live (at least theoretically) on the Moon, Mars, large asteroids and some of the satellites of Jupiter or Saturn. It is already known that in these places there sources and basic conditions such as water, solar energy and various other materials.

Although the enthusiasm of humanity's move away from the Earth has declined considerably over the last decades, it is still hoped that in the second half of our century there will be inhabited bases on the Moon and on Mars and then on some asteroids on which rare metals suitable for mining are found. Even if these celestial bodies are not habitable as such, they will be able to host small surface or underground bases. Bases on the Moon will likely be installed at the polar zones, where the temperature varies less and where there is also water in the form of ice. Since the very low gravity of the asteroids could have degenerative effects on human beings, people could only stay here for short periods, while the majority of the work will be left to robots.

Of course the ideal solution, at least in more remote locations including planets beyond the Solar System, is that the settlers would have occupations as similar as possible to those they followed on Earth. To this end, plans for conquering outer space required so-called *terraforming* actions. The word was invented to describe the transformation of an environment on an inhospitable planet so that it could accommodate life, particularly for human beings partially or ideally over its entire surface.

The first terraforming target could be the planet Mars. At the moment, the atmosphere of this celestial body is so rare that a human could not survive in it for a minute. It would be necessary to construct factories to produce oxygen and water from the minerals found on site, first for large greenhouses on the surface and then to enrich the atmosphere as a whole. Gradually, lichens, mosses, ferns and alpine shrubs could be acclimatised to produce biomass and even oxygen at the surface of the planet, However, these projects would take many centuries or possibly millennia, but do not forget that on Earth and under much more advantageous conditions, this process lasted for billions of years.

With *Venus* – the only other planet that might prove suitable could pose even more complicated problems. In 1975 Carl Sagan proposed to systematically and continuously sow the upper layers of the Venusian clouds with algae capable of reducing carbon dioxide levels and releasing oxygen but using the carbon to multiply. Falling slowly to the surface of the planet, the algae would be destroyed by sulphuric acid, which would in turn be gradually neutralised. The resulting compounds would prepare the ground for future plants. Sadly, we do not currently know of algae that are capable of such performance, although they could be manufactured in the near future by genetic engineering. But in this case too, the terraforming process would take a very long time, at best thousands of years. Unfortunately, Venus presents other, much more difficult issues. The fact that one day and one night on Venus lasts for two hundred and forty three earthly days is just one of them.

Another solution for the colonisation of the Solar System would be the construction of independent space stations, orbiting around the Sun or around another celestial body. There have been several plans and even experiments regarding such bases. There is already a preliminary miniature version – the International Space Station – which is expected to be used in its current form until 2028. There have been discussions about the construction of other structures to replace it afterwards.

Both the bases built on celestial bodies and the space stations will be isolated self sufficient worlds, with greenhouses to produce food, recycling facilities for air, water and waste, etc., but also with an environment that will ensure the emotional stabilityof a relatively small group of people forced to stay together for a very long time. In the case of space stations, artificial gravity must also be ensured, possibly by permanent rotation of the assembly (which will have the form of a wheel or cylinder.).

Colonising the Galaxy

After populating the Solar System, it is assumed that interstellar journeys and the colonisation of the Galaxy will eventually follow, but here we are faced with the problem of the vast distances involved.

The Earth is 150 million kilometres away from the Sun, it's a distance 3750 times greater than the diameter of the Earth at the Equator. If we would manage to scale down the Sun and the Earth's orbit to fit into Trafalgar Square, the nearest star would be about fifteen to twenty times farther from London than Beijing. Using a current spaceship, we can reach the Moon in three days and Mars in eight and a half months, a ship of the same type would require seventy thousand years to travel to the nearest star, Proxima Centauri. This star is about four light years away from us. In other words, the light from this star needs four years to reach us (at a known speed of 300 million kilometres per second).

So, to travel to the stars we need ships using propulsion systems other than those we have used so far in space missions. For the last fifty years, engineers have imagined all sorts of ships with various propulsion systems: nuclear fusion, ionic propulsion, laser beams, antimatter annihilation etc. Travelling to a star these ships were intended to travel the first half of the way by constantly accelerating, with the maximum speed determined by the limitations of the human body and the other of the journey slowing, with a deceleration of the same value. Based on out current technology the duration of a trip to the nearest star would last at least fifty years, so it is clear that these ships would have to be self sufficient, even more than the space stations. There might even be some space travellers who will be born on the ship and will die before seeing anything other than what is within its walls.

In 2002, the anthropologist John H. Moore estimated that a population of one hundred and fifty to one hundred people on such a ship (or space station) could form a stable society capable of surviving for sixty to eighty generations, which is about to thousand years. But – it is claimed – even a much smaller initial population, such as only two women and a sperm bank, would be viable, because it would allow for a negligible inbreeding. Another way suggested in science-fiction, would be through 'cryopreservation', which is of type of hibernation using freezing.

Once a ship of the type mentioned, carried a group of several hundred or several thousand people to a nearby star, travellers would have to find a suitable (almost surely uninhabited) planet. They would need to build autonomous bases and robotised factories using of raw materials mined from the planet and of course also build temporary bases. But there might be planets on which the "terraforming" experience accumulated in the Solar System might apply. Then, in – let's say – another fifty years, three other similar ships could be built and they, along with new generations of pioneers, would continue for a century and multiplying like a chain reaction.

The famous American writer Isaac Asimov believed that it would be a more viable variant on autonomous space stations that would drift through the cosmos, stopping from time to time at planets to "replenish" any necessary substances. At this rate, unfortunately, the Galaxy would be colonised by the human species at a much slower rate and would require generations of people to live in a closed, artificial, environment.

It seems a common-sense scenario that, before these cosmic emigrations, the first explorations of other solar systems would be carried out by robot interstellar probes that will transmit much of the information needed to prepare for human expeditions. These probes would be small and unaffected by the cold and radiation in outer space and every time they descended on a suitable celestial body, they would explore the geology and look for signs of possible life forms then transmit the data to the Earth and, if suitable, would begin basic terraforming actions to prepare the ground for human colonists. Some scholars have even proposed that these robots might even carry human DNA or embryos from which humans could be born, as soon as the conditions on a target planet would permit their survival.

A more worrying idea was that these robot probes might also have self-reproductive ability and as they reach a suitable planet they would extract the necessary minerals, and manufacture various parts and components, then eventually assemble several copies of themselves (including rocket launchers), which, like a chain reaction, would then travel to other possible planetary destinations. The idea of self-replicating robots like these was proposed around 1950 by John von Neumann, who had even created a computer simulation of mutations and variants through which, thanks to a selection process, allowed the automated devices to become more intelligent and powerful. For this reason the devices described above have also been sometimes called, "*von Neumann probes*".

Carl Sagan and William Newman of Cornell University plus many others have drawn attention to the fact that such self-replicating machines could become extremely dangerous. Multiplying exponentially, these mechanisms could, in two million years, convert all the matter of the planets of the Galaxy into copies of themselves. A civilization capable of making these probes would probably be wise enough not to use them, because at some point they could get out of control. If this misfortune were to occur, all civilizations would be forced to exterminate them before they did the same to them.

Using the ways outlined above, in about one to two million years, the human race could explore and perhaps entirely colonise our galaxy, the Milky Way, which is about 100,000 light years in diameter. Of course, this would depend entirely on our enthusiasm for such a project not being lost within this time frame and that, at least in the first phase, we had the necessary funding, which, for the time being does not seem realistic.

Using scenarios of the kind suggested above, some authors have advanced different time frames for mankind to conquer and colonise the Galaxy. Michael Hart of Cambridge University estimated in 1975 that by using vehicles moving on average of ten percent of the speed of light the Galaxy could be colonised in less than a million years. Cosmologist Frank

Tipler proposed a value of one hundred million years; British-American physicist Freeman Dyson and Russian astrophysicist Iosif Shklovsky spoke about ten million years; Polish writer Stanislaw Lem was more optimistic and hoped that only a few hundred thousand years would be enough.

The above time frames seem slightly disappointing; but we must not lose hope. All these predictions were based on the idea that science and technology would stop at their current level. We hope, however, that in the centuries and millennia to come, scholars and scientists will discover many other principles of physics, whereby humanity can overcome the limitations imposed by the speed of light, as well as those of human physiology. In this way our cosmic outlook could become much more optimistic.

The special theory of relativity was first theorised by Einstein at the beginning of the 20th century and then confirmed experimentally. It says that no known form of matter can move faster than the speed of light (300,000 kilometres per second). But this limitation was never accepted as definitive. For more than a century, physicists have constantly sought and proposed variants to overcome this barrier. For example there are the "wormholes" proposed in 1916 by Viennese physicist Ludwig Flamm, and the "Einstein-Rosen Bridge" described in 1930, which are proposals to modify space and time by using the properties of quantum physics.

We could also mention a hypothetical particle (with imaginary mass) that always moves faster than light. This particle was discovered in 1967 by the American physicist Gerald Feinberg, and he called it the *tachyon*. Unfortunately, between the world of these particles (if they exist) and our world, there is a barrier which, at the moment, seems impenetrable. So, at present, despite repeated experiments these particles must remain theoretical.

Another hope for faster than light travels comes from the hypothesis of multi-dimensional space and parallel universes that could provide "shortcuts" between two points in our Universe. We can also consider the possibility of different aggregation states of matter, such as 'dark matter' and 'dark energy' states that are hypothetical form of energy that exist throughtout all of space could avoid the limitations imposed by the theory of relativity.

To show that the speed of light is not a limit, countless practical experiments have been made. In some of them, and under very special conditions, researchers had the impression that the speed of light was exceeded, if only by a little. Unfortunately, each time that the experiment was resumed it was found that the results had been sabotaged by the measuring appliances.

But we should not be discouraged, because all the approaches, speculation and experiments described above are the fruits of 20th century science and, given our ability to learn and develop, the discoveries of the 21st, 22nd, 23rd, century's science will continue to innovate. These discoveries will change many of our preconceptions about the nature of matter, space, time, dimensions and so on. This has always happened, therefore undoubtedly at some point, and probably in an unexpected way, the barrier of the light speed will be overcome.

The Great Filter

Unfortunately, our project of colonising the Galaxy should take into account the fact that mankind might disappear in the meantime. As I have already shown, there is a serious chance that any technological civilization such as ours can self-destruct shortly after it has reached the stage we are at today. This might be due to a combination of super-weapons, environmental pollution, and genetic experiments, etc.

Economics professor Robin Hanson speculated in a book published in 1998, that, as life evolves towards a planetary civilization barriers can emerge. Some can be overcome and some not. He also spoke of a barrier he called "*The Great Filter*", which almost all intelligent species fail to pass. In an interview given in 2015, he said that although the path from bacteria to civilization was extremely difficult, what is still unknown to us are the steps we have not yet gone through and it may well be that our toughest challenges are still to come.

If we succeed in passing this "filter" what comes next? David Grinspoon, an astrobiologist and NASA consultant, has argued more recently that once a civilization has evolved sufficiently (which does not seem to apply in our case!), it will be able to overcome all the threats that would come in its way and perhaps survive for billions of years.

Carl Sagan considered that our aversion toward people who speak another language or have another skin colour, our aggression and obedience to local traditions becomes, not only anachronistic, but also extremely dangerous. Consequently, he estimated that in the long run mankind's chances of survival will be one percent. Of course, he also took into account the way we destroy our environment and other dangerous activities that threaten our future.

I do believe, however, that I will not be considered overly optimistic if I hope that, of the technological civilizations that we have seen so far, at least one in ten was wise enough to survive these 'childhood diseases' mentioned above and remained alive for millions of years.

At the end of the previous chapter we estimated that our galaxy would have room for a few hundred technological civilizations. A tenth of them, only a few dozen (or less), would have the chance to become "long-term surviving civilizations". Certainly, some of these would already have come and gone, but others will appear in the future, so where do we stand?

Astronomy professor Dimitar Sasselov from Harvard University, a famous extrasolar planets seeker with the Kepler Mission, estimated in 2012 in his book "The Life of Super-Earths", that intelligent life is a relatively recent phenomenon in the Universe, so our human technological civilization could be among the earliest. He believes that today, the Universe is at the age where it has reached its maximum capacity to create new stars and new planets, potential hosts of life; and this process will continue for hundreds of billions of years.

Other astronomers think otherwise. The Universe we see is about thirteen point eight billion years old. In the first few billion years there would be no planets on which life or intelligence might appear, but the situation changes soon after that, therefore it is extremely unlikely that the Sun and the Earth was the cradle of the first technological civilization.

Our Sun is about four point six billion years old. But only in our galaxy there are many similar third generation stars with Earth-like planets which are a few billion years older than our Solar System. For example, very close to us (astronomically speaking), at just thirty-seven light-years away there are Zeta1 and Zeta2 Reticuli, two stars of the same type as the Sun, but older than it by one billion years. Or, here is another example: in July 2015, it was announced that an exoplanet, called *Kepler 452b*, and one thousand four hundred light years from Earth, is similar to our planet and it orbits round a Sun-type star, in an area where water is kept liquid. This solar system is also one billion years older than ours. Around of such stars life could have appeared long before that on Earth. This life could also have been be lucky enough to enjoy four billion years of the same peaceful evolution that we have benefited from, at the end of which, in some cases, a technological civilization might have emerged.

In other words, some of those "long-term surviving civilizations" in our galaxy, which I mentioned above, could have reached the stage we are currently at one billion years ago, if not much sooner. Using similar reasoning, a cosmologist, Paul Davies, also believes that there may be civilizations in the Universe that are even older than the Earth's four point five billion years. And Dan Werthimer, a senior researcher on the SETI project said that since some stars are twice the Sun's age and have planets around them, they could host civilizations many billions of years more advanced than ours. We must also remember that astrophysicist Vladimir M. Lipunov, from the Astronomical Institute of the University of Moscow, calculated in 1997 that the probability that there are *not* very old civilizations in the

Universe is $10^{-43000000}$, in other words virtually zero. Therefore some very old "long-term surviving civilizations" must exist.

We have estimated that, even with the technology we currently have, in a few million years we could explore and even colonise our entire Galaxy. But a civilization that has surpassed us by hundreds of millions (if not billions) of years, could have already done this long, long ago. Therefore they should be here, but we do not see them, which brings us back to the 'Fermi paradox', so it seems that we're still caught in the same vicious circle.

At the beginning of the previous chapter I mentioned that in such situations, past experience teaches us that we probably did not gather enough data and did not provide sufficiently precise definitions of what we were looking for, and worst of all, did not examine the details closely enough.

The first thought that comes to mind in this respect is that maybe, our definitions are not correct. For example, to recognise whether or not the members of an ancient, space-going civilizations are here, we should first be sure that we can recognise them. In other words, after a difference in evolution of hundreds of millions of years do they even look like us? Do they use the same kind of vehicles and do they still communicate using radio waves?

Obviously the answer is not easy, because it is virtually impossible to imagine what would have become of a civilization that, after reaching our level, passed through "The Great Filter" and continued to progress, not for hundreds, not for hundreds of thousands, but hundreds of millions of years. The only thing we can assume is that such a civilization may have evolved into something else entirely, something beyond anything we can imagine, might this now be a hyper-civilization.

How would they look?

What would these representatives of a hyper-civilization look like? Experts' opinions are increasingly inclined towards the idea that intelligent beings in other corners of the Universe, at least those in our evolutionary stage, might be physically similar to us. In a book published in June 2015[11], Simon Conway Morris, a palaeontologist at Cambridge University, argued that life on other Earth-like planets should follow a similar developmental path to ours. This theory, known as *convergent evolution*, observed that there are species here on Earth that exist far apart and have evolved independently, yet developed similar features, characteristics and physical attributes, in order to solve similar problems which they encountered in their environment. A good example is the eye. It has been found that over time this organ has evolved independently in more than fifty different animals, but ultimately reached the same structure in all of them – the optimal one. 'Evolution is far from being a random process' – said Morris – 'And if the results of biological evolution are, at least in general, predictable, then what is valid on Earth will be valid everywhere in the Milky Way and not only there'. The professor added that on every Earth-like planet, predators such as sharks, carnivorous plants, mangroves, mushrooms, as well as many other beings, should develop in the same way as on our own planet.

An interesting consequence of this mechanism – argues Conway Morris – is that on Earth-like planets there should similarly be almost guaranteed, not just the emergence of life, but also the limbs, brain and the development of intelligence. Features of human intelligence have evolved to other species – for example, octopuses and some birds have a tendency to play social games – and this, as the book suggests, indicates that intelligence is an inevitable consequence of evolution, which would also characterise extra-terrestrial beings.

Professor Morris also says, in his book, that although astronomers continue to discover a growing number of Earth-like planets, surprisingly they have not yet found any sign of

---

[11] Morris, 2015

32

intelligent alien life. He writes that in any habitable area that does not boil or freeze, intelligent life must eventually emerge, because intelligence is a "convergent phenomenon". It can almost certainly be said that the chance for something similar to human evolution to occur there is reasonably high. And given the potential number of planets we now know, there are good reasons to think that, even if the chance would only be favourable in a case of one hundred, there are many intelligences around us that can be similar to us.

But Conway Morris's observations only refers to our level of evolution, arguing that the representatives of an intelligent interplanetary species, when arriving at the stage of "technological civilization", should resemble us in appearance: two hands, two feet, and a head containing a brain, eyes, nose and a mouth placed at the top of the body. Yet evolution does not stop here; e.g. if our civilization survives that long, what will we look like after millions of years, because five hundred and fifty million years ago our ancestors were small worms. It is possible that, at that time in our evolution, somewhere in another corner of the Universe other beings probably looked like us as we are now and had our intelligence and technology. In the meantime we evolved from that worm to our present stage, so we must assume that the other civilizations also evolved. Did they evolve in the same way that we did from worms to humans, or did they keep the same or similar appearance, like "living fossils", such as the *coelacanth*, that, after finding a safe niche in the ecosystem and an ideal shape, remained unchanged for four hundred million years?

However, in the case of our evolution, from now on the blind mechanisms of natural selection will count less, but possible artificial modifications deliberately introduced using advanced technologies could produce changes that we cannot even imagine.

Nowadays the media talk more and more about human augmentation and overcoming, temporarily or permanently, the current limitations of the human body using natural or artificial means at the individual level, but also where these changes could be transferred to any descendants of these individuals, which implies modifications to our genetic makeup. Human augmentation aims to improve memory, communications, perception, thinking, and also physical abilities. These changes can be made by various means, using everything from neuro-stimulators and food supplements, to implants (such as pacemaker), special prostheses such as an exoskeleton, or as we have seen by modifying human DNA.

Futurist and artificial intelligence specialist Ray Kurzweil has expressed his concern that, during the course of our century, some individuals might be forced to use human augmentation to compete, mainly in the army and on the labour market, but also in other areas.

Increasingly sophisticated implants and prostheses will gradually replace or amplify most physical body functions. Human beings will gradually be transformed into "cyber organisms" (*cyborgs*), where biology and technology will work together, but there is no clear definition in which proportions. A cyborg can be considered as anything from as an insulin pump or a pacemaker, to the science-fiction concept of a being that only has a human brain and the rest is a synthetic body commanded by this brain, a bit like the cyborg in Robocop.

Another way to modify and "improve" the human species is through genetics. Examples are embryo selection, where foetuses with potential abnormalities are either eliminated or modified through the recombination of DNA, *in vitro*, into the fertilised egg. At some later time even defective genes could be replaced, so it could become commonplace to add genes that provide certain advantages, which could lead to the eventual cloning of successful specimens. So gradually the human species could change, and taken to a nightmare scenario, people with defects will disappear followed by the handicapped, until everyone is physically perfect and look like movie stars.

But these eugenic actions will lead to the sharp degradation in human biodiversity and neurodiversity. Foolish and selfish short-term goals will generate serious long-term consequences for both individuals and society. The biological power of the human species lies precisely within the great variety of its genetic dowry, which genetic engineering like this would drastically reduce. Besides, it is almost impossible to assess any unintended side effects of such operations.

If in some countries legislation prohibits such manipulation, other countries that are less politically correct, could promote them in order to achieve superiority in world competitions. If these tendencies cannot be resisted it is entirely possible that, by the year three thousand, we could end up with several versions of the human race. These could be specifically designed to perform certain functions, i.e. tradesmen of all sorts, soldiers and even artists etc. just as various science fiction authors have prophesied. As I have already pointed out, species adapt very quickly to the changes imposed on them by their environment. Consider how, after only a few thousand years of selection and specialisation, how many breeds of dogs evolved from wolves.

One objective of improving the human species could be prolonging life expectancy, which could lead to immortality. It is known that the average life span of an individual is not only caused by progressive damage to the cells, but it is a feature encrypted in the genes, just like the number of fingers or toes, or the colour of the skin. By controlling the genes responsible for ageing the "biological clock" of DNA could be changed.

Would this be welcome? If this kind of technology and been achieved in the past, say just four hundred years ago, Isaac Newton would still be the supreme authority in physics, Leibniz in philosophy, Bach in music, Rembrandt in painting, etc. Would this be good, or would it be bad? Perhaps scientific, social and cultural progress would have been slowed by the influence of these giants.

Genetic engineering could also address regeneration, because unlike a lizard or a starfish, in human beings an amputated leg or finger never grows back again. Why? Perhaps in a century, or even sooner, we will able to correct this "omission" of nature, so that we can force the regeneration of the larger portions of our bodies. Eventually perhaps we will be able to replace all our organs with spare parts grown "in vitro". In this way it might even be possible to replace the brain without affecting its knowledge, personality, or consciousness.

Theoretically, regeneration techniques could therefore be another way to create immortal beings. But if this practice were to become generalised, any new-born would be a problem, because resources and space would soon become insufficient. We can even ask if immortality is desirable at the individual level. As an illustration, we can recall tales of people cursed to live forever, wandering vainly in search of peace like the legendary Flying Dutchman,

Intelligent robots

Around us there are more and more robots, meant to replace human beings in repetitive, tiring and dangerous work, increasing productivity and adding value to human life. But much has been said about imagining the future, about the possibility that the robots will overcome humans in all respects and eventually take control of the Earth as a victorious species, subordinating or completely removing *homo sapiens*. There are many who also claim that the first extra-terrestrial civilization that we encounter will be robotic.

In the past sixty to seventy years much has been done to bring robots and the computer technology behind them as close as possible to human behaviour and intelligence. The discipline of artificial intelligence has made important advances in the recognition of shapes and human speech, in automatic translation and the ability to learn from experience and so on. Performance, at least in some directions, has increased exponentially. As an example, in May 1997, the Deep Blue computer designed by IBM defeated the world chess champion, Garry Kasparov, in a six game tournament, and in 2017, the AlphaGo computer program created by Google DeepMind repeatedly defeated several masters in the much more difficult game called "Go 19x19", including the Chinese world champion Ke Jie.

Unfortunately, today the most spectacular versions of autonomous robots are those used on battlefields. Individuals such as Stephen Hawking, Elon Musk and Bill Gates have repeatedly called for several limiting the use of these 'artificial soldiers', or completely banning this type of robots deliberately made to ("autonomously"?) kill people.

To prevent unpleasant surprises and to regulate the freedom of action of these machines, in 1942 a science fiction short story Isaac Asimov proposed the three "laws of robotics" namely: (1) A robot may not injure a human being or, through inaction, allow a human being to come to harm. (2) A robot must obey the orders given it by human beings except where such orders would conflict with the First Law. (3) A robot must protect its own existence as long as such protection does not conflict with the First or Second Laws. But eventually Asimov wrote a novel about a robot which, although complying with these laws, unwittingly killed a human being by being directed to carry out a series of successive actions which resulted in the death of the victim. It did this because the machine could not see the eventual outcome of its actions, because none of them individually contravened any element of the programme.

Despite the concerns, top IT experts do not believe that, in a foreseeable future, artificial intelligence will be a serious competitor for the human species. Since the 1970s, the German-American computer scientist Joseph Weizenbaum has written that artificial intelligence, will by definition, not be able to emulate human values and human empathy. He was deeply disturbed by those who believed that the human mind was a computer program. A number of other specialists later highlighted key differences in this respect: robots and computers have no self-determination and can only operate using human input. They do not have their own interests, ambitions or goals, and only fulfil the tasks assigned by their user. So, by definition, they do not possess the mechanisms needed for the supposed action of taking over from humans and dominating the world. They are not aware of the fact that they could do so, nor do they have the free will to take decisions in this direction. They can only mimic these attributes, sometimes in a very convincing way, but always under the control of a hidden human operator.

The computer and the human mind, even though they seem to compete, are, in fact, extremely different and in many ways complementary. The computer performs sequential logical and arithmetical operations with enormous speed, while a human has a pluralistic way of thinking, which simultaneously takes into account various factors which seem to contradict each other. The computer makes logical, rational, choices based on mathematical calculations with "utility functions", but only human beings can make decisions based on various opinions, which are frequently unclear, often change and are influenced by values that do not have a common denominator. The free will of a person is always accompanied by a responsibility that the machine cannot have. As a result of its activity, the computer can only recombine prefabricated elements, sometimes in a positive way and sometimes not, but only human beings can create something utterly unique.

There are many similar arguments and as a consequence, the possibility of a machine acquiring self-awareness such as we find in some science-fiction films or novels, is not foreseeable at present. In other words computers think in straight lines, but human beings do not. Of course we cannot rule out that in the very distant future computers or robots will appear that operate on other principles. For example, they may possess a brain similar in how it functions to a human one, but this would present other problems. But even then in some respects human superiority will not disappear. I will present some arguments in this respect in the last chapters of this book.

Moving into virtual reality

In the foreseeable future, however, there is an excellent chance for human and computer collaboration. One of the most dynamic dimensions of this collaboration is virtual reality. Starting with computer games, in this new artificial world there are houses, streets and objects as well as artificial beings, and sometimes they are difficult to distinguish from real ones. A popular variant is one called Second Life, in which the user can build and introduce a version of his or her self, in other words the user's alter ego, which is called a 'resident' or an 'avatar'. Certain accessories can be added, like shoes and a more or less complete suit, allowing the person to fully enter the virtual world, where they can have the almost perfect illusion of a real-life visit. They will be able to "touch" a virtual object and the special sensors in the glove will make them feel cold, solid or heavy and so on. Gradually, these accessories will become simpler and more comfortable. It is thought that in over fifty years a large part of the population will spend most of their existence in such virtual worlds, for work purposes, or for leisure. For example, people from different countries will be able to visit a virtual Champs Élysées, which is almost indistinguishable from the real one, or a realistic Niagara Falls can be reproduced in the same manner. They will find other visitors there who entered in the same manner, and with whom they can interact. They will also be able to meet friends or business partners who may be elsewhere and negotiate with them, the possibilities are infinite.

In 1997 an English researcher estimated that information used by a human in a lifetime, in the form of words and formulae etc. is between thirty to one hundred gigabytes; images should add up to about one million gigabytes. If the current trends continue, a regular, high-end server will have this capacity by around 2030. At some point in the near future, researchers dream of adding all the thoughts and images that have passed through a human mind during its lifetime to the above data. In doing so they will have copied the entire life of a human being, both physical and mental, on to a computer hard drive. Techniques to achieve this are already in place and need only be improved. Moore's Law, which predicted the doubling of equipment performance every eighteen months, has accompanied the progress of computer technology over the last half century. Even if it reaches a limit, no doubt new methods based on other principles will be discovered allowing this to continue.

At the centre for Innovation in Neuroscience and Technology at Washington University, in St. Louis, a team of researchers led by neurosurgeon Eric Leuthardt, used low voltage electrodes to identify the locations on the brain responsible for the creation of about forty common English words. On this basis a program could be created to "read" the phrases pronounced by someone as they thought about them. The method could be useful for patients with speech problems.

Another path is the one called "thought identification". Since 2009, researchers Marcel Just and Tom Mitchell of the Center for Cognitive Brain Imaging of Carnegie Mellon University in Pittsburg, have tried to identify the configurations of neural activity in the brain of subjects taking part in the experiment when they saw a particular object, thought of the object, or heard the name of the object. They used functional magnetic resonance imaging to measure brain activity and detect changes associated with blood flow. In this way the researchers could later tell what the subject was thinking.

In 2012, computer scientist Ivan Martinović, of Oxford University, also presented the results of some research using EEG electrode headphones like those used for video games, to map the brain activity of some subjects when they have been given numbers, names and certain symbols. Kevin Warwick of the University of Coventry experimented with completely copying a conscious mind from a brain on to a non-biological substrate. He said that "the brain and the body of a person need not necessarily be in the same place". The results of this experiment are at present unknown.

In the 1960s, Spanish neurologist Jose Delgado, a professor of physiology at Yale University, became famous by inventing and experimenting with a device called a 'stimoceiver'. This device, the size of a medium coin, was implanted in the brain of animals, to control their electroencephalographic waves (EEG) and in this way managed to control their activity.

Delgado first experimented on cats, then on bulls and chimpanzees. He managed to command several bulls fitted with implanted stimoceivers to raise their legs, bend their heads down, walk in circles or bellow. In 1965 he became famous by defeating a renowned and ferocious bull in the arena. When the angry animal headed for him, Delgado pressed on a remote control and the bull – that had an implanted stimoceiver – stopped. With another push of the remote the bull began to spin in a circle.

The professor also implanted devices in some twenty-five schizophrenics, epileptics, and depressed individuals to improve their behaviour. But in the 1970s the public began to react with increasing nervousness to the idea of mind control using implants. As a result the neurophysiologist returned to Spain and continued with less controversial research.

These researches continued discreetly in other laboratories. Recently, Mark Zuckerberg the CEO of Facebook, said that specialists in this organisation were working on a brain-computer interface allowing people to directly communicate with a computer using only the power of mind. Elon Musk, a co-founder of Pay-Pal and well-known businessman, also believes that in the future people will have to become cyborgs "If they do not want to become irrelevant". As artificial intelligence systems develop, in 2017 Musk said that people will have to compensate for their biological weaknesses by integrating their brains with computers. In this way, people will benefit from a higher processing power and will be better able to compete with robots in the competition for jobs. To this end in 2016 he invested in a company named Neuralink, which is dedicated to connecting people's brains to computers using special implants. In this way – Musk said – people will be able to become experts in, say, botany or anatomy in a matter of seconds or minutes. They will be able to assimilate large amounts of information in a very short space of time and will be able to download, using external support, their thoughts, knowledge and memories that could be stored in order to be accessed in the future.

We can forecast that, in this way, there will also come a time when technology will alow every human being to be meticulously recorded their entire life, including every word, image, thought and gesture etc. After the body had died, the individual could then be reconstructed using artificial intelligence techniques into a virtual reality world where they could manifest in the form of an "avatar". In this way, the individual could theoretically continue their existence in an immaterial "parallel world".

If a scientist had been recorded for posterity in the same way, as an "all-encompassing avatar", they would also remain accessible in virtual reality after their death. We would be able to meet them here, for example to ask some questions about their work. A "knowledge base", containing all the known hypotheses that the scholar had worked in his life, plus an "inference engine", would ensure (using an enhanced "expert system" technique) that the "avatar" would respond to new ideas and questions in the same way that they would have done in reality. In a foreseeable future, this "knowledge base" could be extended with the thoughts he has had but had not yet formulated into words.

But nobody prevents us from hoping of more. Perhaps in a very distant future, scientists will give this kind of virtual personality a portion of autonomous will and initiative and perhaps even a spark of its original consciousness, i.e. the ability to realise who the person was and what objectives they pursued. There could be people who would like to continue, in this way even indirectly, the activities that were interrupted by death.

The principle of minimal intervention

The suggestions given above regarding our future unfortunately only encompass a few centuries, and at most a millennium. But when we talk about the huge gap between our level of evolution and that of a hypothetical hyper-civilizations, we are not talking about a few millenniums, but tens or hundreds of millions of years. In this time frame some interplanetary consciousness have probably discovered laws of nature other than those we are aware of, plus other dimensions and properties of reality etc.

The speed with which their information circulates will certainly be much higher than that of light. Perhaps space and time no longer have the same relevance for them; maybe they have become spiritual beings of a subtle nature and they live simultaneously in various realities. Perhaps they no longer exist as individuals but as parts of kind of a Universal Consciousness residing in another realm. Or, it is not completely impossible that our material world is actually just a sort of huge virtual reality (with one pixel equal to one quantum?), created by these beings, as in the "Matrix" movies. But almost certainly their concept of reality will go far beyond anything we can imagine.

J. Allen Hynek (1910-1986) was an American astronomer, university professor and a brilliant Ufologist. For twenty one years he acted as a scientific advisor on UFO studies undertaken by the U.S. Air Force and in later years he conducted his own independent UFO research and developed the most commonly used UFO classification system.

At the first International UFO Congress held in Chicago in 1977, J. Allen Hynek said: "I hold it entirely possible that a technology exists, which encompasses both the physical and the psychic, the material and the mental. There are stars that are millions of years older than the sun. There may be a civilization that are millions of years more advanced than man's. We have gone from Kitty Hawk[12] to the Moon in some seventy years, but it's possible that a million-year-old civilization may know something that we don't... I hypothesise an 'M&M' technology encompassing the mental and material realms. The psychic realms, so mysterious to us today, may be an ordinary part of an advanced technology."[13]

Even at the slow pace of currently envisioned interstellar travel, the Milky Way galaxy could be completely explored in a few million years. But a hypothetical hyper-civilization may have developed a much more efficient means for interstellar travel. Once again, if they exist, they must be here.

What attitude would such a hyper-civilization have toward us? A 1998 survey for the Planetary Society suggested that 86% of Americans who believed in alien civilizations, were convinced they were friendly. Prominent figures of research on this subject, such as Philip Morrison, the late Carl Sagan, and Ronald Bracewell were of the same opinion. They argued that a civilization which survived a crisis similar to that which humanity is experiencing both currently and in the immediate future must be a peaceful civilization.

The 20th century will remain in the conscience of our descendants as one of the most bloody in all mankind's history, a century of world wars, Nazi and Communist extermination camps and many other such horrors. However, the 20th century was also extremely important. At the beginning the great powers were competing to include the last "backward peoples" into their colonial empires and these empires were almost completely disintegrated. In 1950 the hunt of lions, tigers, elephants, whales, etc. was a thriving industry, but by 2000 the ecological movement made this kind of hunting or wearing the fur of endangered species unacceptable and safaris became photographic trips. If, in the past, the conquerors tried to forcibly "civilise", the inhabitants of newly discovered territories, we currently cherish and protect the alternative visions of native tribes.

---

12 Town in North Carolina, where the Wright brothers did their first controlled flight.
13 Fuller, 1980, pp. 164–165.

Nowadays, if anyone found a location untouched by human beings, it would be immediately declared a reserve; and tourists would be forbidden, and even the well known naturalists would not be allowed to smooth the path of a new-born turtle to the sea. In the same way we begin to understand that it is correct and necessary to protect the habitats of tribes that live far from technological civilization.

Although it is very dangerous to speculate about the goals and values of an intelligence that has surpassed us by millions of years, the tendencies above make it reasonable to advance the assumption that a hyper-civilization will respect an ecological principle, protecting any living being – anything that is called life – particularly human beings with their diversity of appearance and thought. And this protection has as an important added dimension, the principle of minimal intervention in the natural course of evolution.

CONCLUSIONS

If a technological civilization has overcome the "Great Filter" and did not self-destruct, then it could survive for millions, if not billions of years. During this time, it would surely turn into something else, something that went beyond what we could imagine, but to which we could still give a name, that of a hyper-civilization.

What features might be possessed by the inhabitants of a hyper-civilization, what might they look like? Judging by the tendencies of our own future evolution they could travel through the cosmos without limitations imposed by the speed of light and perhaps even control the laws of time, space, dimensions and types of matter etc, concepts that are now unimaginable to us. Maybe they could become immortal, either biologically or by moving into a virtual reality or in some other form. They would be peaceful and cherish any new civilization that exists in the universe and with only minimal intervention in its evolution.

THEY ARE HERE, BUT WE CAN'T SEE THEM?

The cultural hypnosis

In his notes about his voyage aboard the vessel, The Beagle, Charles Darwin recounted that the natives on one of the islands he visited in Tierra del Fuego paid no attention to the ship anchored off the shore. Apparently, they did not see it at all, probably because they could not associate it with anything in their experience. However, they showed an interest in the boats in which the crew came ashore, because they looked somewhat like their pirogues.

Alexander von Humboldt wrote in a similar vein when he observed that our perception of the world in which we live can have an effect our culture. There are tribes that live in an always green jungle and do not have a word for "green". Thus they remain "mentally blind" toward the colour green.

An old experiment may help illustrate this. Someone placed some kittens that had not yet opened their eyes into boxes that were painted inside with either vertical or horizontal stripes. When they were released, the unfortunate creatures were no longer able to make sense of anything other than what looked like the vertical or horizontal stripes which had surrounded them while they had been held in the box. There are many other varieties of this phenomenon which ethologists call "imprinting". The interested reader can find other similar examples.

Such things – even though it could be hard to believe – do not happen only in primitive cultures or at animals. No human is protected from the imprinting process. Objects seen and touched, or the sounds heard in early childhood and what infants are taught in the first years of life will accumulate and gradually consolidate in the mind of the child and later the adult and become the landmarks against which he will compare everything the later encounter.

Marshall McLuhan argued (for example in his book "*The Gutenberg Galaxy*") that school, printing and mass media as a whole, are accustoming all members of a community to certain patterns of thought, leading to a "popular mesmerism achieved by uniformity and repeatability", standardising the way in which all of them see the world. This phenomenon, sometimes called, "cultural hypnosis", will determine what details a person will perceive and understand from the surrounding world. At the same time it will make them mentally blind toward other aspects of reality. Often cultural hypnosis can be achieved by repeating some alleged facts millions of times; although there might be no obvious evidence for them. As a result millions of people will blindly accept these statements. Also, in any culture there are taboos that must be avoided, which result in unconscious precautions being taken. In this way, in the midst of various cultures everyone risks suffering from the same kind of blindness and being conditioned into seeing some things in the same way, while other things will ignored and therefore effectively invisible.

In our case, I dare say that the reason why we have not found a response to Fermi's paradox could be the fact that we suffer from such a "mental blindness", making us unable to see the answer that is in front of us. The causes of this are due to common beliefs learned during the first years of life and composed of elements taken from culture, school, religion, popular science, history, science-fiction stories (or films) and so on. They have shaped our minds using templates that only accept a certain narrow view of extra-terrestrials and their possible visits – a vision that I would call "the primitive extra-terrestrial hypothesis" – and at the same time they have made many of us mentally blind and unable to see that that the concept of hyper-civilizations could provide an answer.

It is possible that the above statement is a bit hard to accept for some readers, so I ask their permission to use the following example to illustrate this.

As a first example, I mention that Carl Sagan – who devoted much of his work to seeking extra-terrestrial civilizations and developing ways to contact them – made a calculation to show that a visit to the Earth by an alien ship would be an extremely rare event[14]. He admitted that moving through the stars with ships using twentieth century technology is feasible (though complicated) but he supposed that these ships would be launched randomly, even blindly, to different corners of the universe and the chance that we would be discovered in that way is very small. Therefore – Sagan said – UFOs cannot be ships from other civilizations as they communicate using an extremely high frequency. He simply had not considered the possibility that a civilization that has overtaken us by millions of years could have other means to communicate apart from 20th century technology.

The same type of mental blindness causes many to assume that the eventual arrival on Earth by an alien civilization would only occur after a long and agonising interplanetary journey. The visitors, tired of the long time spent aboard their ships, would be happy to land on firm ground and bring their distant planet's message to us here one Earth. Using the same logic the aliens would land on the lawn of the White House (why would they not – some might ask – land in Red Square, or Tianamen Square, or in front of Buckingham Palace or whatever?) and ask to see the "Great Chief of the Earth" (of course this would be the President of the USA). The same logic suggests they might propose a treaty, either on the basis of equality or for mutually beneficial exchanges. And if neither of these happens – say the followers of this idea – it means that we have not been visited (yet) by a non-earthly intelligence.

The time gulfs

Fortunately, there are also thinkers who consider more realistic scenarios, closer to the hypothesis of hyper-civilizations. In a conference in January 2010, entitled "The Detection of Extra-terrestrial Life and the Consequences for Science and Society", Lord Martin Rees, then president of the Royal Society and astronomer to the Queen, said the existence of extra-terrestrial life may be beyond human understanding. "They could be staring us in the face and we just don't recognise them. The problem is that we're looking for something very much like us, assuming that they have something like the same mathematics and technology. I suspect there could be life and intelligence out there in forms we can't conceive of. Just as a chimpanzee can't understand quantum theory, it could be there as aspects of reality that are beyond the capacity of our brains."

The first of those around one hundred "long-term surviving civilizations", which we believe could exist in our galaxy, might have been around for at least one billion years. The others which followed it in turn became hyper-civilizations on an average of one in many million of years. On a number of some other planet the evolutionary process will produce technological civilizations over the course of many millions of years. So, at this point in the galaxy, on the one hand there are either hyper-civilizations, or on the other hand a promising fauna from which civilizations could be born in a very distant future. Even if the civilization closest to us has attained a level of evolution that surpasses ours by millions of years, this seems to be in an order of magnitude the "normal" distance in time between two neighbouring cosmic civilizations.

In conclusion, although the average distance – in space – between two evolved neighbouring civilizations in our Galaxy is of the order of thousands of light-years, paradoxically, it seems that it is *not these distances that separate us, but those of time*. And it seems that in these immense gulfs of time, maybe hundreds of millions of years, between the

---

[14] Sagan, 1974, pp. 202-203;

early surviving civilizations and humanity, lies the key to answering the problem we encountered at the beginning of this book, as well as many of the others.

And, if someone thinks we were too optimistic, as technological civilizations may arise much less frequently therefore a much smaller number of them could survive for millions of years, may I remind the reader that the estimates above were only made for our galaxy, which is just one of at least one hundred and fifty billions other galaxies which are more or less similar to ours and exist within the universe. So, all of the estimates we have made on the number of hyper-civilizations have to be multiplied by hundreds of millions, remembering of course that for the far away galaxies, the distances become millions or billions of light years. But this may not present a problem to a hyper-civilization.

We have also good reasons to believe that there are other universes, perhaps in "parallel" dimensions, and perhaps existing in other states of matter, or as parts of a "Multiverse" and so on. That is why it is absolutely certain that there are hyper-civilizations in the cosmos.

Our minds are unable to understand the logical consequences of the above. We cannot imagine what differences of millions of years in evolution might produce. The famous science-fiction writer Arthur C. Clarke wrote: *"A sufficiently advanced technology is indistinguishable from magic"*. Hyper-civilizations would certainly have such magical technologies, among which may be the means by which – if they wish – they could get here at speeds much greater than light.

Several of those who have struggled with such problems, such as Carl Sagan, Michio Kaku and others, voiced doubt that an advanced civilization would be interested in us. But the emergence of new civilizations like ours seems to be a very rare event in the galaxy, something that happens only once in millions of years. It is therefore extremely plausible that we are of interest and out of curiosity are monitored. And for that purpose, higher intelligences could have covertly established bases somewhere nearby that operate on the principle of non-intervention and visit us as often as they think necessary.

We understand therefore, that the representatives of a hypothetical hyper-civilization may already be here, but we do not recognise them because of their "magic". We are suffering from the same kind of mental blindness as the natives who saw the small boat, but not the great ship. This mental blindness is reinforced by a widespread system of preconceptions about how a cosmic civilization should look. These ideas are much more deeply embedded in our culture than we believe. In the following I will try to illustrate some of these preconceptions.

The preconception of exponentialist thinking

One of the preconceptions that only served to confuse rather than clarify the awareness of the existence of hyper-civilizations, was the extended use of "exponential growth" in some forecasts. In the 1960s, enthusiasm following the Russian-American competition to conquer space led to all kinds of scenarios and programs being made concerning the future of mankind in outer space. According to some of them, by 2000 we would have colonised the Moon and reached Mars and, shortly after, we would install bases on the main solid bodies in the Solar System, exploit the minerals on asteroids and build orbiting cities around our planet. After that and until the end of the 21st century, travel to other stars would start. Even today many of these scenarios still exist and are seriously considered by some scientists. All these unrealised and continually postponed projects, all suffered from what we could call "exponential preconception".

For example, it was believed that the population of the globe, as well as the needs of each individual, will grow exponentially over time. In order to make room for the newcomers, since our planet would no longer be able to accommodate the number of people, the colonisation of the Solar System, then the Galaxy, then eventually the entire observable universe would follow.

From the middle of the last century, the promoters of exponential cosmic expansion said that around the year 3000, Earth's need for energy would reach an acute crisis and mankind would be forced to consider the use of the full potential of the Sun. It is known that the Earth receives only a billionth of the heat of the Sun, the rest being lost in space. The energy crisis of the year 3000 – it was said – could be solved if we managed to capture the entire solar energy flow. To this end, the English physicist and naturalised American, Freeman John Dyson, FRS, proposed, in 1959, to build a sphere around the Sun at a distance twice as great than that between the Earth and the Sun. This concept, called a *"Dyson sphere"*, was actually first described by Olaf Stapledon in his 1937 science-fiction novel *"Star Maker"*. The sphere would only have a thickness of two to three meters, and it would be made by "dismantling" Jupiter's metal core. It was immediately demonstrated that such a sphere would be mechanically unstable and extremely vulnerable to asteroids and would be subjected to forces that would rapidly lead to its destruction and collapse into the Sun. Dyson immediately proposed a second solution – another "sphere", this time not a rigid one, but consisting of a huge number of artificial satellites rotating around the Sun on different circular orbits, programmed not to collide with each other. Together they would capture virtually all the solar energy and send it to wherever it was required. In this case the spherical swarm of satellites would about one million kilometres thick.

A third type of Dyson sphere was also proposed, consisting of a very thin stationary foil, whose sole role would be to collect energy and direct it to consumers. The sphere would be inflated from the inside using the pressure of the solar particles.

Who would build these spheres? For this purpose it has been proposed to use self-replicating robots organised in assembly lines. These robots could duplicate themselves in an incredibly short time, such as two milliseconds, but this would depend on the cooling capacity of the components. The construction of these systems would require the use of nano-technologies at the molecular level. Such a system could create a Dyson sphere (or something similar) using raw materials from an uninhabited planet in a time frame of anything between a few days and a few decades.

Could it be possible – wondered some astronomers attached to SETI projects – that some ancient civilizations in the Universe have already built Dyson spheres? In this case, a way to search for alien civilizations might be to look for such constructions throughout the cosmos, using astronomical observations. Dyson objects would resemble a protostar, as it would absorb most visible and higher frequency radiation and only let some of the infrared radiation pass through. In this regard Dyson himself said that irregular variations in brightness, caused by the light of the star passing through the curtain cracks, as well as the electromagnetic and radio interference produced by the large-scale electrical operations involved, should be sought.

This concern is, at present, a respectable topic for many scientific events. While looking for exoplanets, in the autumn of 2015 astronomers discovered, for the first time, somewhere between the Cygnus and Lyra constellations, a strange phenomenon that could be – as some of them speculated – a Dyson sphere. The star in question is called KIC 8462852, it is about 1500 light-years away from us and it is hotter and more massive than the Sun. Nobody had a final explanation about what's going on there, but that does not necessarily mean – as astronomers have said – that aliens live there.

Another example of exponential thinking is the prognosis of population growth, which, as has been said, will eventually force us to emigrate to outer space. Indeed, in the middle of the last century the population of the planet tended to double every thirty-five years. If this tendency persists, as we have already mentioned, in about 3000 years the human population would exceed the total mass of the Earth. And if it continued at the same rate, in more than 4,400 years would exceed the mass of the Solar System. In over 7,000 years this would exceed the mass of our Galaxy and in 10,000 years (a very short period compared with the history of life and of the Earth) it would become equal to the mass of the entire Universe. However, demographers, who study the statistics relating to human populations, have now observed that the population growth has begun to slow down and by 2100, or not long after that, the growth will stop. So, using "demographic pressure" as a reason for building "Dyson spheres" or to colonise some distant star systems is very shaky.

Another illustration of exponential thinking is the Kardashev Scale, which was received with enthusiasm by SETI researchers. It was proposed in 1964 by Nikolai Semionovici Kardashev (b. 1932), a Russian astrophysicist, Doctor of Physical and Mathematical Sciences, and deputy director of the Astro-Cosmic centre at the Institute of Physics of the Moscow Academy of Sciences. He called a "Type 1 civilization" or one that uses the power of 10^{17} watts to communicate with other celestial bodies This is approximately the power received by the Earth from the Sun (this is not only the energy used for broadcasts, but the power required for domestic and industrial use etc.). A civilization would be "Type 2" if it used 10^{27} watts for communications, which is about the entire output of the Sun with nothing used for other purposes and a "Type 3 civilization" a 10^{37} watts power, about the power of an entire galaxy. Since, at the time this classification was made, the Earth's most powerful transmitter was the Arecibo (Puerto Rico) radio-telescope with a power of about 10^{14} watts, Carl Sagan calculated that, according to this classification, earthly civilization as a whole was about a type 0.7 civilisation.

We can use the same reasoning for the Kardashev classification of civilizations. If the energy consumed for communications (telephones, the Internet, etc.) increased by only 1% a year, which some would consider to be exceedingly small (which means doubling in just 70 years), we would become a "Type 1" civilization by 2200, after another 2500 years a "Type 2" civilization and by 7200 a "Type 3" civilization. This would use as much energy as released our entire Galaxy and only for communications. I mentioned that perhaps hyper-civilizations have already gone beyond our level not by thousands but by millions of years. Do they use energy from the entire Galaxy, or from the whole Universe to do this? If so, their work should be visible from Earth. But astronomers have not noticed anything like this.

Meanwhile, it has been seen that with the emergence of high-performance devices, although the amount of information has increased, the energy consumed for broadcasts has diminished.

Indeed, practice shows that any exponential growth encounters a limit, usually linked to resources, at which it stops. It is much more reasonable to accept that our predictions, based on the exponential growth of population, energy consumption and so on, have been erroneous and a hyper-civilization looks totally different from Kardashev's "Type 3 civilizations". Would not it be better to think that, unlike the exponential prognosis, beyond a certain point future changes could be qualitative rather than quantitative?

An example of a qualitative change following an exponential evolution was discovered by mathematician and SF writer Vernor Vinge from the San Diego State University in an article published in 1993. He said that the exponential acceleration of technological progress in artificial intelligence and the imminent creation of entities with greater than human intelligence, will lead to a "Technological Singularity". As he said: "From the human point of view, this change will be a throwaway of all the previous rules, perhaps in the blink of an eye".

My own guess is that we will indeed encounter a "singularity", but a much more dramatic one and much further in the future. This will include progress in artificial intelligence and much more. It will change mankind completely into "something else". It will change all the rules and everything around us. It will turn humanity, not into a Type 3 Civilization, but into a *hyper-civilization*.

The temporal provincialism

There is also another inherent deficiency in our way of thinking. Everyone who passes through school will learn that scholars of the past centuries were fumbling around in an awkward and ridiculous manner, talking about the phlogiston, the luminiferous aether, animal magnetism etc, while, behold, we *finally* came to 'see the light', we live in a happy epoch in which we have found the *real* answers to most of the great problems, it is an era where we can decide, among others, what things can exist and what things will never be possible.

If, a century or so ago, we had discovered radio, many would think it always be the best means of remote communication. If, in 1905, Einstein had postulated that the speed of light is the limit, then no other principle of physics would be discovered that avoided this limit and so on. No one thinks that in a few hundred years, our descendants will smile about our most cherished theories, as we smile at some of the theories of Galileo Galilei, or at the representation of human brain made by Rene Descartes, and these are only the most respectable names.

Various authors have called this tendency to explain everything on the basis of what science knows today and to reject testimonies of some events that cannot be explained by what we know as *temporal chauvinism* or *temporo-centrism*. Prof. J Allen Hynek called it *temporal provincialism*. At a symposium on Unidentified Flying Objects organised in 1968 by the U.S. Congress, he said: "I have begun to feel that there is a tendency in 20th Century science to forget that there will be a 21st Century science and indeed a 30th Century science, from which vantage points our knowledge of the universe may appear quite different than it does to us. We suffer, perhaps, from temporal provincialism, a form of arrogance that has always irritated posterity".

This "mental blindness" or "cultural hypnosis" is influencing not only the general public, but also many scientists. The examples are numerous, but it is worth mentioning some of them. Sextus Frontinus, an engineer from the time of the emperor Vespasian, wrote about two thousand years ago that: "there are no more ideas for other new war machines and works; their perfection has reached the limit and I do not see how they could be improved". Leonardo da Vinci was convinced that everything that could be discovered in mathematics had already been discovered by his forerunners. Physiologist Claude Bernard, the parent of experimental medicine, said in the middle of the nineteenth century, "Shut the doors. Nobody will ever equal the giants who invented the steam engine". Napoleon III's experts have shown that all electric motors are actually variants of a *perpetuum mobile*. In 1875, the Director of the United States Patent Office presented his resignation to the Secretary of State for Trade, on the grounds that there was no point in staying in the post, once everything that could be invented was invented. In 1877 the great chemist Marcellin Berthelot wrote: "The Universe no longer has any mystery". In 1895, Professor Gabriel Lippmann (later a Nobel Laureate) advised one of his students who wanted to become a physicist, to give up this idea if he did not want to become a loser. At the time everyone believed that "physics is a completed science", where important discoveries are no longer possible. In 1898, Edouard Branly, one of the pioneers of radio, decided to give up his experiments that he considered to be out of perspective. A few years earlier, physicist Heinrich Hertz (the unit of frequency, cycle per second, was named the "*hertz*" in his honor), wrote to the Dresden Chamber of Commerce that research on the electromagnetic waves he had discovered should be discouraged, as they would not have any practical applicability.

A similar narrow-mindedness has made other eminent personalities of science predict what will never happen. In 1895, Lord Kelvin (Sir William Thomson), president of the

British Royal Society, firmly affirmed that "flying with heavier-than-air aircraft is impossible". So, did Simon Newcomb as well as many other famous personalities. Also, Thomas A. Edison declared in 1897 that although aircraft heavier than air would be possible one day, they would never be more than toys. Lord Kelvin holds a kind of record here, because he also stated that, "the radio has no future" and that, "X rays will prove to be a humbug".

Physicist Robert Millikan, Nobel Prize laureate, said in 1923 that, "it does not seem plausible for man to ever use the power of the atom". Some time before this, Henry Poincare had also stated, that "common sense alone is enough to tell us that destroying a city by disintegrating one pound of metal is an obvious impossibility". Ernest Rutherford, one of the first scientists to create nuclear fission, was asked in 1935 when this process could be used in practice, he replied – "never". In 1932, astronomer F.R. Moulton of the University of Chicago conceived that the fantastic idea of flying to the Moon has no chance of becoming a reality. And so on...

In the same manner, today there is the impression that every strange phenomenon that occurs can be explained using quantum physics or holograms, or, for example, that travelling faster than light will always be impossible.

Without further elaboration, temporocentrism can be added to the greater preconception, called "anthropocentrism", where many people believe, for example, that there is only one religion and this is the ultimate truth and that those who do not ascribe to the religion are worthy of contempt, and a lot worse besides

This conviction, that we are in possession of the ultimate truth, is probably the most important cause of that mental blindness that makes most people unable to accept the reality of unusual occurrences, no matter how much evidence there is to support them.

The preconception of the small differences and the SETI bias

The hypnosis exerted by the culture in which we have grown up has convinced many of us that we are the ultimate creation, i.e. we are the supreme beings in the material Universe, apart from God, but that is part of another reality.

Most of those who accept that there are other civilizations in the Universe are struggling with another difficulty: their inability to show what millions or billions of years actually means. The result is that we still assume, subconsciously, that hypothetical extra-terrestrial civilizations have appeared simultaneously with our own, so they are at about the same level as us (or perhaps just a few centuries or millennia ahead).

Many like to believe that the civilizations that we will meet in Cosmos will use weapons resembling those of the medieval knights (of course oversized and modified with gadgets specific to the 20th century, such as lasers or robots). Many successful films are testimony to that because the producers have understood this "cultural hypnosis". Others imagine that the arrival on Earth of extra-terrestrials – more or less peacefully – should resemble the landing of Christopher Columbus among the natives of San Salvador. Or we can bet on the "Independence Day" movie scenario, where, although the alien ships are much larger and stronger than ours, we have better computer engineers and they will hack the software of the invaders.

I have also met people who thought that if life was created in the Universe at the same time, on millions or billions of planets, at the wave of a magic wand and after billions of years of evolution on some planets, the same magical wand simultaneously created an intelligent being, able to reach, once again at the same time, the same stage of technological civilization. In that case, inevitably, these civilizations will start to send each other radio messages, or start travelling blindly in cumbersome ships across the galaxy, either to fall with joy into the arms of other intelligent beings or, alternatively, with the intention of subjugating them.

If, hypothetically, life had been created simultaneously in the Universe, say four billion years ago and evolved the same way with the same type of DNA, etc, we should accept that there would be an important gap when they arrived at a technological civilization. Even in a marathon where all the athletes start with approximately equal chances, there is a difference of several percent between the first and the last to arrive at the finish line. But in our case, one percent means forty millions of years. Even a difference of one million year involves such a great gap in science and technology that it is impossible for us to evaluate it.

As a typical example of the way of thinking illustrated above, we can talk about the *SETI bias*. In the vision of SETI researchers, even if radio signals take thousands of years to travel from one inhabited planet to another, this will be the ideal solution for cosmic contacts, and it is our duty look for them. Perhaps a native in a remote jungle thinks in the same way when he imagines that his drum is the only possible means of communication, If we ask the tribe's elders if this will continue for many generations, when it becomes necessary to transmit information over vast distances he will think of drums as huge as a house. And if he does not hear the noise of these drums coming from great distances, he will conclude that no one is more advanced than his tribe or that there is no other person beyond the edges of the jungle. "They might not guess a technology beyond their ken."[15]

SETI-type projects are in fact looking for technological civilizations similar to ours that use radio waves for communications. This method was introduced a century ago. Will we use it indefinitely? Will there be no other physical principle in the coming hundreds or thousands of years allowing a quicker means of contact? On the other hand, the chance to find, within a radius of ten thousand light years, a civilization that still uses radio waves for communication is practically *zero*. And if we find one could it be called a conversation it we send a message and receive the answer after thousands of years?

So, we have to agree with the controversial American philosopher Terence McKenna, who said about SETI projects, that this search, waiting for a radio signal from an alien source, is a just as much a culturally viable assumption as exploring the Galaxy for a good Italian restaurant.

In 2005, in a *Coast to Coast AM* interview, Dr. Michio Kaku, physics professor at New York's City College (CUNY), also said: "The Universe might be teeming with signals from aliens and we are too primitive to notice. Hence, I think the SETI people are well meaning, but woefully inadequate. The key problem is that scientists blindly assume that aliens are just like us, only a few decades ahead. We have to expand our minds, to grasp the possibility that they are millions of years ahead."

The preconception of equal rights

Indeed, there is a zero probability that the extra-terrestrial civilizations we might come into contact with would be at about the same level as ours, or even slightly more advanced. Since the 1960s, several authors have pointed out that a difference of millions of years (or even better, hundreds of millions) is as big as that between us and a lizard or a bee. If the representatives of hyper-civilizations are installed around our planet (as is most likely), they can examine us, monitor our evolution and even contact us in some way, but they will never put themselves on the same level as us.

In a 1985 article, Jan Narveson, professor of philosophy at the University of Waterloo (Ontario, Canada), also attempted to assess the differences between civilizations which are very distant and their level of evolution. Let's say, he said, that we contacted some ants and

---

[15]   The example was taken from Sagan, 1974, p. 224

they explained how they build their colonies and they follow their chiefs during their migrations based solely on faith. Would it impress us to the point that we would grant them some rights, Probably not, but we would protect them, which would not exclude some limited experiments.

Indeed, an entomologist who proposed studying an ant colony would try to disturb it as little as possible. He would try to obtain the maximum of information but would not present a letter of accreditation to the ant queen. He will probably take some ants to learn more about their anatomy and physiology, he may also try to see if there are any differences between them, by studying them genetically. If the researcher possesses the proper technology, he will create a few bio-robot ants, which he will send through the colony to observe them. And if a robot ant is destroyed or damaged, although would add to the cost of the research, it would not be anything drastic. The ants would not understand what was happening. Does this scenario not resemble some unexplained phenomena that have happen to us?

A number of scholars are sharing a similar point of view. For example, at the end of 2015 in a phone interview with "The Observer" newspaper, Dr. Michio Kaku declared that: "Some people say if there are intelligent lifeforms out there, and I think there are, how come they don't visit us? Why don't they land on the White House lawn, announce their presence and give us their technology? Well, if you're walking down a country road and you see an anthill, do you go down to the ants and say I bring you gifts, I bring you trinkets, beads, I bring you nuclear energy, take me to your ant queen? ... If aliens are so advanced that they can land on the White House lawn, then we are like ants to them..."

The preconception of invasion

History has taught us that if someone is lurking around, spying on us and bypassing open meetings, it is very likely that after obtaining the information it needs, it attacks us. The alien invasion hypothesis was in fashion in the early 1950s, and with the increase in UFO phenomena it was interpreted as preparation for the imminent landing of an aggressive civilization, which was attempting to test the defence capacity with which the Earth might oppose it.

General Douglas MacArthur, commander of the Pacific Allied Force in World War II and the UN forces in the Korean War, declared to the New York Times after his retirement in 1955: "The next war will be an interplanetary war. The nations of the Earth must someday make a common front against attack by people from other planets. The politics of the future will be cosmic or interplanetary".

Later, as the phenomenon continued with no signs of harm, the invasion hypothesis gradually lost its credibility. But it is understandable that science fiction authors cannot imagine a confrontation between cosmic civilizations unless the distance between them, in terms of science and technology, is between a few hundred to several thousand years. As Carl Sagan noticed in his book "Cosmos": "A standard motif in science fiction and UFO literature assume extra-terrestrials are roughly as capable as we are. Perhaps they have a different sort of spaceship or ray gun, but in battle – and science fiction loves to portray battles between civilizations – they and we are rather equally matched. In fact, in any confrontation, one will always utterly dominate the other. A million years is a great many. If an advanced civilization were to arrive in our solar system, there would be nothing whatever we could do about it."[16]

This belief, that an alien civilization that arrives here will has to be aggressive, combined with the fear that certain signs indicate that the aliens are coming, could be called the *preconception of invasion*. But if we will encounter a hyper-civilization (and it seems this is the only likely scenario), invasion will not even come into question. At the end of the previous chapter, I have shown that several individuals agree on the supposition that an

---

[16]   Sagan, 1980, p.311

aggressive technological civilization, eager for conquest, and does not care about other forms of life, will not pass the "great filter" and will destroy itself. I also argued that hyper-civilizations, i.e. "the long-term survivors", must have peaceful intentions, and obey both the "ecological principle" and the "principle of minimal intervention". They are precisely those who have protected and cherished life and intelligence everywhere from the very beginning. If they had wanted to conquer Earth and maybe exterminate us, they could have done that, much more easily millions of years ago, when they supposedly discovered our existence. Finally, there seems to there are evidence that, since that time, they have always been here. So, in a way the they invaded the Earth a very long time ago

The preconception of aid and education

Similarly there is the preconception of aid. It has two forms: one of them says that if supposed extra-terrestrial (benevolent) visitors arrive on Earth, it would be normal for them to share their science and technology with us; the other is that, in the case of a cataclysm, the aliens will save the "good part" of humanity, the "chosen", e.g. those affiliated to a certain UFO sect, or the 144,000 "righteous beings" and so on.

Given that the Earth is monitored by a hyper-civilization, by virtue of the above mentioned "ecological principle", it is natural that the cosmic "watchers" will distinguish between humans – conscious beings, creators of various cultures, the potential buds of a future hyper-civilization – and other living creatures. But at the same time they will refrain from intervening in our evolution.

A few centuries ago, the "civilising" of some "primitive" peoples has led to the loss of various alternative ways of perceiving reality, thus narrowing our knowledge. We are now making efforts not to repeat this mistake, by protecting and capitalising on the few remaining visions of primitive thinking.

By virtue of the 'ecological principle', a hypothetical 'administrator' could indirectly give us messages about not destroying the biological or cultural diversity of the Earth. But, using the same logic, according to the "principle of minimal intervention", this 'administrator' should not give us, even using vague hints, its own vision of the Universe, or the technologies it possesses, in order not to destroy our natural development. But instead let it mature, so that the entire community of hyper-civilizations can enjoy it. It would not even give us evidence that hit is here and that it is monitoring us, for even one hint would overturn our whole evolution.

The kind of evolution that a hyper-civilization could expect from us is probably a moral one, because that will make the difference between self-destruction and our future as a potential new hyper-civilization. No external intervention could eradicate our aggressiveness, thirst for wealth, power and conquest. If they gave us their technologies, we would probably use them for new weapons that could very well bring our self-destruction. And if we do not annihilate ourselves, with those technologies we could become the greatest danger to peaceful cosmic civilizations. Therefore, the higher intelligences will not give us their knowledge and will not stop the wars or the injustices, because our path can only be found by our own sacrifices and by becoming aware of the bad habits that characterise us.

There are two extra-terrestrial hypotheses

The hypothesis of the extra-terrestrial origin of unexplained events, such as the UFO phenomenon, although it is popular, has often been resisted because it is difficult to accept, taking into account the laws of nature as we currently understand them. But from the list of preconceptions above, the reader should have already understood that we have in fact two very different extra-terrestrial hypotheses: on the one hand, there is the "primitive extra-terrestrial hypothesis" and, on the other hand, the hypothesis of *hyper-civilizations*.

The *primitive extra-terrestrial hypothesis* claims that we could be visited by aliens who have settled here on Earth, coming with ships that have crossed interstellar space. Their intent is to occupy our planet and take advantage of its resources and so on. To that end, they plan to exterminate us, or to turn us into slaves, or, by genetic engineering, combine human beings with their own race. In the science-fiction version of this hypothesis, the visitors usually resemble human beings and even if they are – let's say – one million years ahead of us, their technology is at most a few thousand years more advanced than ours. They communicate through radio waves and have computers like ours. This hypothesis was rightly considered unlikely by such leading ufologists as J. Allen Hynek and Jacques Vallée.

The alternative, the *hypothesis of hyper-civilizations*, is also extra-terrestrial in nature, but it estimates that an encounter with an extra-terrestrial civilization, having more or less our level of development is practically nil, but that we may be monitored instead by *hyper-civilizations*, hundreds of millions of years old, which look and behave quite differently from the aliens depicted by most science-fiction films. This hypothesis is regarded with suspicion, although – as we have argued – it is much more reasonable (though it requires some flexibility and boldness of mind).

Therefore, blinded by a "cultural hypnosis" on the one hand, we have waited for decades for the materialisation of an incorrect scenario, with erroneous characters, and been disappointed that nothing happened as we expect, and on the other hand, we are unable to see that the show is actually playing elsewhere. This "mental blindness" prevents us from seeing that hyper-civilizations are in fact already here on Earth and have been for a very long time and their presence is accompanied by countless "miracles". Indeed, even if some of these miracles manifested before our eyes, we would find them so unexpected and inexplicable that most of us would consider them to be illusions or hallucinations, etc. and try to forget them as soon as possible.

Are there really magic and miracles occurring around us and if so, what could they be? In the following chapters I will try to present some examples of the most important of them.

CONCLUSIONS

The information we possess about the Universe suggests that, around us, there are probably a number of extra-terrestrial "*hyper-civilizations*", some of them maybe more than one billion years old. They are so advanced compared to us that based on our science, philosophy and technology we would consider their actions as magic? If we contact some of them we would not believe our eyes. The explanation is a mental blindness that we all suffer from, because of "cultural hypnosis". This manifests in, among other things, preconceptions such as the small differences in evolution between us and the extra-terrestrials, and the aggressiveness we attribute to them and so on.

Consequently there are two extra-terrestrial hypotheses: (1) the primitive one, implausible though it is, but considered favourably by some scientists and promoted by SF films and literature, and (2), the hypothesis of *hyper-civilizations*, that are capable of explaining many of the events that have been witnessed and indicating a non-earthly presence near us.

UFOs

Unidentified visitors

In the preceding chapters I have argued that it is highly probable that we could be monitored by civilizations hundreds of millions of years old, which we have called *hyper-civilizations*. This hypothesis is theoretically consistent, but the crucial question is whether it is confirmed in practice by some *facts*. If "they are here", do we ever see this "magic" that Arthur C. Clarke was talking about? Do we have any evidence to this effect?

The answer is that such "magic" not only exists, but it manifests itself all over the world and has accompanied the evolution of mankind. And the fact that we refuse to see that magic, simply because we consider it incredible, is the best example of our cultural blindness.

In the following chapters, I will give a number of examples of this "magic" phenomena. In order to prevent 'overload' from the many available examples, I will choose only a few illustrative ones, but I think they will be enough for the reader to understand the vast amount of evidence lying behind them. I will give these examples primarily for those who don't know about the wealth of evidence available, and also for the benefit of those already familiar with the subject.

A first category of this kind of "magic" could be the UFO phenomenon itself. There are hundreds of thousands of reports, many of them official and made by the most credible and qualified observers, including pilots, radar operators, police officers and others who have seen unexplained lights or objects in the sky. There are hundreds of films, radar and video recordings, plus thousands of pictures of these objects. Usually they have been subjected to expert evaluation and it has been proven that are not counterfeits (although there have been some fakes too).

In these reports a number of strange features were repeatedly observed, such as hovering in mid-air, making zigzag manoeuvres impossible for any normal aircraft, it was as if they had no mass, yet they left traces as if weighing many tonnes when they landed. They have emitted strange light beams and sometimes they lifted human beings from the ground, and there were discontinuities in the passage of time, etc. Even if for 80-95% of these reports can be found to have natural explanations (meteorological balloons, Chinese lanterns, fireballs, globular lightning, planets, missiles, aircrafts, drones, satellites, hoaxes, etc.), those remaining defy any explanation.

The scientific world does not accept the reality of the UFO phenomenon. The reason is very simple: the phenomenon does not meet the fundamental criteria of a scientific approach, it cannot be brought into a laboratory to be examined repeatedly and, especially, it does not behave according to the laws of the physics as they exist the beginning of the 21st century. But from this moment on the logic applied becomes bizarre. Instead of saying that science is not capable of examining the phenomenon, many stated that the phenomenon does not exist. And if it does not exist there is no point in wasting time by examining any evidence about it. It's a vicious circle.

But this "mental blindness" is not only caused by the constraints of science, it is part of a much wider system of self-defence, specific to our culture. I will illustrate this by using some examples. In the years 1983-87, on the Hudson River Valley north of New York City, multicolour light configurations, described as being as large as a football field, appeared in the sky. Sometimes they stopped at the height of the treetops and hovered over a motorway full of commuters. This caused a gridlock and terrified those who got out of their cars. There were thousands of written testimonies and hundreds of photos and videos of what occurred. The explanations given by the authorities were ridiculous. It was said that maybe it was an airship, or a formation of light aircraft, although the wind was blowing at 50 km/h and the U.S. Federal Aviation Administration admitted that there was no evidence of airships or light aircraft in the area.[17] With few exceptions, reporting and commenting on such incidents did not go beyond the local press and no authority or media was interested in a more thorough investigation. They were happy to forget what happened as quickly as possible.

A similar case is the one called the "Phoenix Lights". On March 13, 1997, between 19.30 and 22.30, thousands of people reported on a 480 km route stretching from Nevada and Arizona (USA), to Sonora (Mexico), a giant, dark, UFO in the form of a "V", which produced no sound and – according to some descriptions – it bore five spherical lights. The stars disappeared behind the object and reappeared after it passed. Most testimonies came from the city of Phoenix. A private investigation, which gathered testimonies from over seven hundred witnesses, including policemen, pilots and soldiers, ended up being ridiculed.

Things would have stopped here if the case had not been taken up in the national media. For this reason, Fife Symington, a two term governor of Arizona, was forced to order an investigation; then, on June 19, he convened a press conference, and announced that he had discovered the perpetrator, and brought his chief of staff disguised in an alien into the room accompanied by a cop, as if the "alien" had been arrested: his assistants laughed. Symington then announced that he asked everywhere, and no one had an explanation. Surprisingly, in 2007 ten years after the incident when he was no longer the governor, Fife Symington admitted that he had heard the news of the sighting and decided to check it out personally. He said: "I was expecting to see something at a distance, but I was shocked when I saw this object just above my head. It was moving constantly and without noise... There was something not of this world". He explained this late admission by saying that, when you have a high public position, if you start talking about aliens the media immediately ridicules you. You have to be very careful what you say, because the media can completely destroy your credibility.

But the evidence does not stop just at such observations. There have been many cases where a UFO has been seen landing and there have been imprints in the ground, apparently caused by the landing pads of the vehicle or perhaps from drilling that was carried out. There have also been broken branches, dehydrated or even burnt vegetation and sometimes the soil has been burned, or made radioactive. When this occurs, grass grows badly or not at all (or, in some cases, abundantly). Sometimes UFOs leave behind liquid or gelatinous residues. Occasionally, a passing UFO produces so-called "angel hair" – long threads, thin like a spider web – coming from the sky, which has either escaped or been intentionally ejected by the UFO. If the witnesses collect them the threads disintegrate quickly, usually before they can be analysed.

There are many UFO reports of "electric vampirism". For example, the witness drives on a road with a car, a UFO appears above of it and the engine stops immediately, the headlights turn off, the radio and the phones stop working, but after the object moves away it all reverts to normal. There were also unexplainable blackouts in some locations, sometimes covering large areas while UFOs have been reported in the sky. I have examined one such case in Romania.[18]

These unidentified phenomena have often also been *observed by astronomers*, starting with Charles Messier, who saw more black discs flying on the sky on June 17, 1777. But after 1947, when UFOs entered the folk culture as "alien star ships" and science said that such a thing is impossible, any astronomer would have risked his scientific career if he had taken the phenomenon seriously.

Among the last to break this taboo was the astronomer Clyde W. Tombaugh, but he was famous, because he had discovered the planet Pluto in 1930. Tombaugh reported that, on the

---

[17]   Hynek, 1987
[18]   Farcaş, 2016, pp. 70-73

evening of August 20, 1949, he had seen, with his wife and mother-in-law, in the garden of his home in Las Cruces (New Mexico), a formation of six to eight green rectangular lights flying to the south; they flew silently and at a uniform speed. The first impression was that they were the portholes of a huge, dark ship. The astronomer said that the objects seemed to be under control, and they were different from all the other phenomena he previously observed.

J. Allen Hynek (1910-1986) was professor of astronomy at Ohio State University in Columbus, then dean and director of the Astronomical Research Center at the University of Evanston (Illinois). He was also, for 21 years until 1969, U.S. Air Force consultant in UFO projects. At a conference in 1952, he asked forty professional astronomers in private, if they seen UFOs, he promised to assure their anonymity. Five responded positively. The percentage of UFO sightings among astronomers is higher than that of the general public. Also, Stanford University physicist, Peter Sturrock, conducted two major UFO surveys in the 1970's among members of the American Institute of Aeronautics and Astronautics and the American Astronomical Society, unsurprisingly the survey revealed that astronomers also see UFOs.

Hynek was originally used as the "official debunker" of UFO reports, someone who had to find a natural explanation for any such observation. Subsequently, after realising that many of the observations cannot be explained away and, after over 12,000 cases had passed through his hands, becoming convinced of the reality of the phenomenon, he became the first to carry out a scientific analysis, at an academic level, of the UFO phenomenon[19].

Then there is case of Carl Sagan, an astronomer and highly successful author, who publicly said UFOs could be only be a natural phenomenon or a man-made object. But research journalist Paola Leopizzi-Harris said in 2010 that she had been informed in 1984 that Carl Sagan said, in a private conversation to J. Allen Hynek: "I know UFOs are real, but I would not risk my research funding, as you do, to talk openly about them in public."

This official attitude towards the UFO phenomenon is illustrated by another personality in the field. Jacques Vallée (b.1939) who is currently one of the most distinguished personalities in ufology. A former French astrophysicist, naturalised American, Doctor of Computer Sciences, he was a NASA employee for the Mars planet mapping project and is one of the creators of the ARPANET network, the forerunner of the Internet. His interest in the UFO phenomenon began in 1961 when he was working at the Paris Observatory in a team looking at artificial satellites. One night the scientific equipment recorded, on magnetic tape, eleven positions of a flying object that was not a satellite or any other known object. The project manager confiscated the tape and erased it. Asked, he replied that he did this because otherwise the Observatory would have lost the project and its funding and Vallée his job.

There are countless testimonies proving that military and civilian pilots and also astronauts and cosmonauts, avoid talking about the unexplained encounters they have had, because they do not want to endanger their careers.

There are some exceptions, but only after full retirement. One example among many is that of the NASA astronaut Dr. Edgar Mitchel, who stepped on the surface of the Moon in 1971, as part of "Apollo 14" mission. In an NBC interview in 1996, he was asked if he thought it more likely than not, that extra-terrestrials have been to this planet. Mitchel answered: "From what I now understand and have experienced and seen the evidence for, I think the evidence is very strong and large portions of it are classified... by governments".

In many cases, pilots were asked to sign statements that they would keep such encounters secret. I also have had private discussions with several military pilots who brought me

---

[19]   Hynek, 1972

evidence in this regard.[20] But interested readers can find many similar cases in various publications.

The army remains extremely interested

The military became aware of the UFO phenomenon during the Second World War. On February 25, 1942, shortly after 02:00, radar reported that aerial objects were approaching Los Angeles from the ocean. Since only two and a half months had passed after Pearl Harbour and suspecting a new Japanese attack, at 02:25 the alarm signals were triggered. Then in the sky there appeared many red or silvery objects that were rapidly moving up and down. In the middle of them was a large, almost motionless, dark object. According to various witnesses, the objects, which were appearing and disappearing, seemed to hover at a constant height of about 3000 metres. It has been estimated that there were about one million eyewitnesses of this event.

In a report prepared by General George C. Marshall, Head of Staff, for President Roosevelt, it is said, among other things: "Unidentified air-planes, other than American Army or Navy planes, were probably over Los Angeles and were fired on... As many as fifteen air-planes may have been involved, flying at various speeds from what is officially reported as being 'very slow', to as much as 200 Mph... No bombs were dropped... No planes were shot down..."

In World War II, allied aircraft pilots reported unidentified balls of fire or other mysterious aerial phenomena seen flying, over both the European and Pacific theatres of operations. There were hundreds of reports; the descriptions of the phenomena varied, but the pilots agreed that the mysterious lights followed their aircraft closely at high speed. They were eventually named, *"foo fighters"*. It was later discovered that the Germans, Japanese and Russians reported the same phenomenon. Initially, all parties were convinced that they had encountered a new enemy weapon; but no pilots reported having been attacked by them.

In 1946, a wave of UFO observations began over the Scandinavian Peninsula, especially in Sweden. Up until July 30, 1946, six hundred reports were received and by the end of the year the number reached about thousand. Most reports spoke of bright flying objects, or of very short winged aircraft resembling missiles. Objects have also often appeared on radar screens. Their manoeuvres of dropping, reversing and turning at a sharp angle, etc, were impossible for any man-made device. It was estimated that in 1946, in all European countries, there were about 2000 observations of this kind. Until now no one has been able to provide a satisfactory explanation for what happened.

The UFO phenomenon was widely acknowledged after June 24, 1947, when Kenneth Arnold, flying alone with his personal plane over the Cascade Mountains in the state of Washington, saw a formation of four silver objects, followed by five others, flying in the sunlight in two parallel strings. The pilot told the media that they were leaping like a saucer skimming on water. The next day the newspapers were full of news about "flying saucers". Soon, a lot of people began to report similar observations and in June and July 1947, 850 UFO reports were received in the U.S.

In 1947, the 509th Operations Group bombers at Roswell Army Air Field (New Mexico), were the only ones in the world carrying operational atomic bombs. On July 8 at 14:26, the Associated Press broadcasted a press release, approved by the commander of that base, that the U.S. Air Force has captured a flying saucer of unknown origin near Roswell. All the major newspapers in the world published the news. Shortly after, the officials came up with a denial, announcing that it was just a 'special meteorological balloon'. At present there are dozens of books containing the testimonies of hundreds of direct or indirect witnesses of the recovery.

---

[20] Farcaș, 2016.

Some people were talking about a crashed disc and even about some humanoids that were inside it. The witnesses said that the recovered remains were transported and hidden in secret locations. Some ever-changing official descriptions given by the U.S. Air Force to explain what happened were not enough as to remove suspicions of a cover-up.

A few weeks after the Roswell incident, on July 30, 1947, a common FBI/Army Intelligence Report states: "This 'Flying saucer' situation is not all imaginary or seeing too much in some natural phenomena. Something is really flying around". The document continues with the technical description of the observations. On September 23, 1947, after analysing a number of reported observations, General Nathan Twining, the head of the U.S. Air Force Air Materiel Command, at the Wright (after 1948, Wright-Patterson) Air Base, in Dayton (Ohio), sent a letter containing descriptions of "flying saucers to General George Shulgen, the deputy head of the Air Force information service, in Washington", to which he added: "The phenomenon is something real and not visionary or fictitious", making remarks about the possibility of making something similar in the U.S. and about the chances that it is a secret, American or foreign project. At this time, U.S. authorities feared that UFOs could be a new weapon built by the Russians, possibly on the basis of projects seized from the Nazis.

Following this letter, the General Staff ordered the creation, in January 1948, of a UFO special commission called "Sign", to research what the UFOs really were. It was soon replaced by the "Grudge" commission and from the beginning of 1952, by project "Blue Book", under the leadership of Captain Edward J. Ruppelt. For the first time he used the term "unidentified flying objects" (abbreviated UFO). Prof. J. Allen Hynek was hired as the scientific consultant for these projects.

Since 1949, the UFO data gathering was done in accordance with strict military regulations. For example, in the AFR 200-2, entirely dedicated to UFO reporting, it was written that the "interest in unidentified flying objects is twofold: first as a possible threat to the security of the United States and its forces and second, to determine the technical aspects involved". The regulation also stated that, for public consumption, they should release information *only* about cases that were "positively identified as a familiar object".

The Blue Book project was closed in 1969,after having gathered 12618 observations, of which 701 (i.e. over 5%) did not have any rational explanation. The decision was based on the conclusions of an infamous project led by Professor Edward Condon, from Colorado University in 1966-68, which stated that UFOs are of no scientific interest.

After closing project Blue Book, U.S. officials have stated, whenever asked, that the UFO phenomenon is no interest to the army or government and that there will be no other such project in the future. The message for the general public was that UFOs are probably just a benign natural phenomenon and there was nothing to worry about.

But the truth is that to this day the U.S. Army has remained interested in the UFO phenomenon, even when they discovered that they were neither Russian weapons nor weapons of any other power. When the regulation AFR 200-2 was declassified, it was learned that "Air Defence Command – not Blue Book – was responsible for UFO field investigations and that Blue Book did not even get all the reports"[21] Therefore, Blue Book was largely just a screen for the public and the more delicate UFO cases were sent to another destination.

Another proof is in a now declassified memorandum dated October 20, 1969. In it, USAF Brigadier General Carroll Bolender wrote: "Moreover, reports of UFOs which could affect national security are made in accordance with JANAP 146 and Air Force Manual 55-11 and are not part of the Blue Book System... However, as already stated, reports of UFOs

---

[21]   Dolan, 2002, p. 156

which could affect national security would continue to be handled through standard Air Force procedures designed for this purpose."[22]

Even in 2008, the Air Force AFI 10-206 instructions contained clear regulations for pilots, radar operators and other military aviation personnel, regarding what they should do if they encountered unknown flying objects. They were asked to note "altitude, direction of travel, speed, trajectory, manoeuvres, what attracted attention to the object, how long the object was visible and how it disappeared." All these details were to be included in a report to the North American Airspace Defence Command (NORAD). Meanwhile, the term 'UFO' was replaced by: UCT (uncorrelated target) for objects near the ground, UTR (unknown track report) or UCT (uncorrelated events report – reporting an unrelated event) for objects in outer space.

NORAD, with its space detection and tracking system and a naval equivalent, systematically observes unidentified objects above the USA and Canada, which they archive through NUTR (*NORAD Unknown Track Reporting*). UFO Disclosure Advocate Victor Viggiani, speaking in June 25, 2016 at the Alien Cosmic Expo in Ontario, Canada, said that, according to documents, recently released to him, using the Canadian Access to Information Act (AIA), NORAD tracks an average of 1,800 UTRs annually and about 75 times each year, fighter jets have been scrambled for interception. NORAD officials have estimated that 80% of the UTR can later be identified, but about 20% defy any explanation. But "they are, literally, unidentified flying objects and not aliens", they said.

The assertion that after 1969 the U.S. Army was no longer interested in the UFO phenomenon was also recently contradicted by the facts. On December 16, 2017, *The New York Times* announced that The U.S. Defence Department spent $22 million, between 2008 and 2012 on an Advanced Aerospace Threat Identification Program, to investigate reports of unidentified flying objects. The Defence Department has never before acknowledged the existence of such a program. As former Senator Henry Raid said: "The sightings were not often reported up the military's chain of command, because service members were afraid, they would be laughed at or stigmatised". The article was accompanied by dramatic footage showing infrared sensor images of UFOs being pursued by military aircraft.

Everywhere in the world

Officials from other countries also felt that the UFO phenomenon deserves to be studied carefully. As an example, in 1978, Yuri Andropov, a long-time head of the KGB who went on to become leader of Soviet Union between 1982-1984, ordered the launch of the program: "Investigation of unidentified aerial and space phenomena, their possible origin and influence on equipment and staff". The program was included in the 1978 state plan on "Defence Research" and was divided into two parts: the defence Ministry's "*Setka MO*" project, led by Colonel Boris Sokolov and the "*Setka AN*" of Academy of Sciences, led by Dr. Iulii Platov. In this context two research centres, each with a specific objective, were set up. In the next thirteen years, about 3,000 reports were collected regarding about 400 individual events, of which 10% could not be explained even after the careful examination. Early in 1990, Mikhail Gorbachev, then president of the Soviet Union, answered questions from a group of workers from the Ural region, saying: "The UFO phenomenon exists and needs to be treated with seriousness."

Regarding the seriousness with which the UFO phenomenon was treated at the government level, it is worth knowing that in an "Agreement on Measures to Reduce the Risk of Nuclear War between the USA and the USSR", signed on September 30, 1971 by Secretary of State, William Rogers and Foreign Minister Andrei Gromyko, article three

---

[22] Dolan, 2002, p. 362

reads: "The Parties undertake to notify each other immediately in the event of detection by missile warning systems of unidentified objects, [...] if such occurrences could create a risk of outbreak of nuclear war between the two countries." This article has had practical effects.

In many cases military aircraft from various countries have been ordered to track unidentified flying objects, force them to land, or if necessary bring them down, but without any success. I only mention a few well-known cases. On the night of May 20, 1957, Milton Torres (later a professor at Florida International University) executed a flight with a colleague, both piloting an F-86D Super Saber. At one point, they were ordered to fire the missiles they were carrying to shoot in an "unidentified misty and enormous" object above the town of Ipswich. When they were at a distance of 500 metres, preparing to open the fire, in less than a second the object disappeared from the radar screen.

Major George A. Filer III, a U.S. Air Force Intelligence Officer, was stationed at the Sculthorpe RAF base in England in January 1962, when he was sent to intercept an unidentified aircraft stationed just 30 meters above an area between Oxford and Stonehenge. The object, seen on several radars and also with the naked eye, gave a clear and solid echo, like a two kilometres long metallic object. When Filer's plane was eight kilometres from it, it suddenly appeared rise then flare with light, then it accelerated and disappeared.

On the evening of September 19, 1976, officials at Tehran airport detected a bright "rectangular" object. The Iranian Air Force command sent an F-4 interceptor. When it located the UFO on radar and approached it, all its instruments, including communication, lost power. Under these circumstances the pilot was forced to abandon the mission and return to base. The same thing happened to a second interceptor, meanwhile the object, an extremely bright horizontal cylinder about 50 metres long, made various movements that were impossible for any earthly object.

According to military reports, on the night of 19 May 1986, twenty-one spherical objects, each of a diameter of about 100 metres blocking air traffic to major Brazilian airports, were detected by radar and spotted by civilian pilots. To intercept these objects, the Air Force despatched its most experienced pilots in six F-5 and F-103 aircrafts, but without success. The objects were moving at high speed and seemed to jump from one point to another.

Less well known is a case that happened in western Romania, in 1967. One night, two MiG-19 fighters carried out a routine exercise at 12,500 metres. At one point they saw a round, flat, flying object of the size of a football field. They were ordered to launch a rocket in order to force it to land. When one of the pilots wanted to push the trigger, the UFO disappeared instantly and appeared behind the other aircraft. The squadron commander was then given an order to open fire. A pursuit began which ended over Belgrade, the capital of Yugoslavia, but because the aircraft was running short of fuel, it had to return urgently to the Timisoara base,.[23]

The fact that all these incidents occurred many years ago does not mean that they are not still happening; it is only an indication that the secrecy that envelops them is long lasting and, as a rule, the pilots who did speak out were those who had retired from active service.

In 2010, retired Colonel Boris Sokolov said that in ex-Soviet airspace "there were 40 cases where pilots met UFOs. At first, they were ordered to intercept and subdue them. When the pilots engaged in the pursuit, the UFOs accelerated, the pilots lost control and the planes fell. This happened three times and in two cases the pilot lost his life. After that, the pilots were ordered to observe the object, but to change direction and move away."

Many observations, both in Russia and in other countries, also speak of unexplainable objects seen in the depths of the seas and lakes. The objects were moving at impossible speeds for earthly technology and they made sudden manoeuvres that would have killed

---

[23] Farcaş, 2016

living beings. There are also many cases of UFOs that have been seen submerging and emerging from the sea and disappearing into the heights. Russian ufologist Vladimir Azhazha, a former submarine commander, said: "Fifty percent of UFO encounters are related to the oceans. Another fifteen with the lakes. Thus, UFOs tend to associate with water". He believes that the term "extra-terrestrials" given to those responsible for the UFO phenomenon is not entirely correct. "There is no evidence that visitors would come from any other planet. Nobody knows where they come from. It is not excluded that they come from a civilization located in parallel worlds or the ocean. Modern science knows very little about what's happening in the depths of the ocean."

UFOs are visiting nuclear installations

UFOs seem interested in nuclear power plants and nuclear weapons. On the night of July 24, 1984, an ice-cream cornet shaped UFO, as big as "three soccer fields", and adorned with eight dazzling lights, floated for almost a quarter of an hour in a strict no fly zone above the Indian Point nuclear reactor complex on the bank of the River Hudson,. The object hung motionless or moved very slowly despite a strong, gusty wind sometimes reaching 40 to 50 kilometres per hour. Twelve police officers watched helplessly as the object hovered there. Meanwhile, the alarm system and the computers that controlled security and communications for the complex were blocked. The commander of the guard asked the New York State National Guard to send a military helicopter to confront the intruder and was on the verge of ordering the police to open fire, but before hostilities began the object disappeared.[24]

This event in not uncommon and these objects have been seen elsewhere entering the no fly zones around nuclear installations. On the evening of March 4, 1988, at 22:30, a flying triangle was seen hovering near the Perry Nuclear Power Plant on the shores of Lake Erie in the USA. On April 16, 1993 in Bayport (Florida), a policeman followed a giant, triangular UFO moving around the Crystal River Nuclear Power Plant. UFOs have also been seen over nuclear research centres at Oak Ridge (Tennessee), Hanford (Washington) and Los Alamos, near Albuquerque (New Mexico).

Another spectacular visit occurred at Chernobyl nuclear power plant on the day of the catastrophe on April 26, 1986. Three hours after the disaster, a bright globe with a diameter of 6-8 metres, appeared hovering about 300 metres above the damaged reactor, which still on fire. Several specialists who were on the scene, measured the level of radioactivity, which at that time was 3000 miliroentgens per hour. Suddenly, two beams of purple light shot from the hovering UFO to the reactor and remained there for about three minutes. Then the rays gradually weakened in intensity and the globe departed to the north. When they examined the installation, the witnesses were surprised to find that the radiation had inexplicably dropped to 800 miliroentgens per hour. Another bizarre visit to Chernobyl occurred on the evening of October 11, 1991, at 19:46. Also, on March 2 and 17, 1991, and again on October 10, 1991, a luminous triangle, making zigzags impossible for any earthly aircraft, was detected by the Skala radar complex in the Ustinskii Cape area near St. Petersburg, where the "Sosnovii Bor" nuclear power plant is located.

UFOs have visited nuclear facilities in other countries as well. On March 12, 1991, a huge triangular UFO hovered for a minute above the cooling towers of the Tihange nuclear power plant in Belgium and probed the building with a beam of light. In March 2011, UFOs were also seen above the Fukushima (Japan) nuclear power plant, which had been severely damaged during a tsunami.

UFOs also appear to be interested in nuclear weapons. This issue was examined in detail by ufologist Robert Hastings, who organised a press conference on the subject on 27

---

[24] Hynek, 1987, pp.143-152

September 2010, at the National Press Club in Washington DC. Below are just a few of the cases he investigated.

On August 1, 1965, at the F.E. Warren Base (Cheyenne, Wyoming), six objects of unknown origin floated for an hour above the rocket silos. The case was even included in the reports of project "Blue Book". On March 30 and August 25, 1966, UFOs seen with the naked eye produced similar incidents at the Grand Forks Air Base (North Dakota).

Robert Salas, former Lieutenant Major in the US Air Force, told Hastings that on March 16, 1967 he was at the Air Force base in Malmstrom (Montana) acting as the deputy commander of a crew for Minuteman Intercontinental Nuclear Missiles. A few hours after midnight, while on guard at the command point which was twenty metres below the ground, he received repeated calls from the surface security detail, saying they were watching mysterious lights hovering above the missile silos. Salas woke up his commander (who was above ground and off-duty) to inform him, and as he did so, on the side panel next to each missile firing button, the "no go" warning came on, meaning that the missiles could no longer be launched. Reporting the situation to his commander, he was told that a similar phenomenon was happening to another group of missiles and UFOs had also been reported in the area.

Other, similar incidents occurred at Air Force bases located in Minot (North Dakota), Ellsworth (South Dakota), Loring in Limestone (Maine), Wurtsmith (Michigan), etc, and also more recently at Nellis Air Force base (Nevada) and, in 2007, at the Missile Alert Facility near Malmstrom (Montana), and on October 23, 2010 at the Francis E. Warren Air Force Base at Cheyenne (Wyoming).

Journalist Billy Cox ironically commented that: "If the United States had lost operational control of its nuclear missiles from any other cause: sabotage, computer errors, even bad weather or tectonic problems, there would have been hearings, investigative committees, press releases and there even may have been fallen heads. But in this case, it was considered that there was no problem, there were just UFOs".

The phenomenon has been repeated in other countries. "Inspections" of UFOs were also reported over USSR rocket silos at Sverdlovsk in 1959, Voronezh in 1961, and also in 1961, Riabinsk, which is about 267 kilometers north-north-east of Moscow. In 2010, the retired Russian Air Force Lieutenant Colonel Boris Sokolov, told David Ensor, who was the Moscow correspondent for ABC TV News, that on October 5, 1982 he was urgently sent to Ukraine. According to Sokolov, the previous day at a military base near Hmelnitsky, between 16:00 and 20:00, over fifty soldiers witnessed the appearance of a UFO about 250-300 metres in diameter, floating above a nuclear missile base. Meanwhile, the launch ballistic missile codes have been mysteriously altered on all control consoles, the message "prepare to launch" appeared for fifteen seconds, after which everything went back to normal. Colonel Alexander Plaksin (who was the link between the military UFO program and the USSR's academic program) stated that for those fifteen seconds we were on the brink of a nuclear war.

During a 1989 incident at the Kapustin Yar army missile base in the Soviet Union, a dome-shaped craft, seen by multiple witnesses, sent down laser-like beams into the weapons storage area. Similar incidents were also reported at the French nuclear silos of Albion in Provence, and at RAF Bentwaters in England, in December 1980, when a small UFO moved toward the Weapons Storage Area, into which it directed laser-like beams. This is also the location of the iconic 1980's Rendlesham Forest UFO encounter.

Secrecy and debunking

If they could obtain information regarding some non-earthly technology, any government on Earth would keep it top secret in order to secure an advantage over other countries. Even if they did not know how to use this information they would be aware that others might find a use for it, particularly for new offensive or defensive weapons. This is one of the main explanations (and there are several) for the secrecy surrounding the UFO phenomenon.

Here is a single, well documented example to allow the reader to understand this. In 1950, Wilbert B. Smith, an electronics engineer from the Canadian Department of Transportation, was experimenting with magnetic suspension vehicles. Suspecting that UFOs were using this principle to hover, Smith contacted people in Washington whom he learned were studying the UFO phenomenon. On his return, in the top secret memo dated November 21, 1950 (it was declassified a few years later), he wrote that: "The flying saucers exist", the issue is considered to be of "tremendous significance" by U.S. authorities, being the most highly classified subject in the United States government, "rating even higher than the H-bomb".

It was later found that Smith had obtained the information from Dr. Robert I. Sarbacher, professor of physics at Harvard University and scientific advisor to the Military Research Coordination Committee. In Smith's notes he said that Sarbacher told him about UFOs, saying that: "We have not been able to duplicate their performance... All we know is that we didn't make them and it's pretty certain they didn't originate on the Earth... It is classified two points higher than the H-bomb. In fact, it is the most highly classified subject in the U.S. government at the present time." In the early 1980s, Dr. Robert Sarbacher reconfirmed this information to the Ufologist Stanton Friedman, including his knowledge of secret U.S. Government UFO investigations.

The secrecy surrounding the UFO topic was not only for military reasons. On the evening of Saturday, July 19, 1952, the Washington National Airport radar observed a group of seven objects about twenty five kilometres to the south-south-east, flying at a speed of between 160 and 210 kilometres per hour. Later on other objects appeared and they were flying both in formation and individually. They were climbing and descending in zigzags and remaining motionless then shooting off at speeds of up to thirteen thousand kilometres per hour (aircraft of the time could not even get to a tenth of that speed). The airport tower and the Andrews military base confirmed the observation, both visually as an orange fireball, and on the radar. Objects were also seen by civilian pilots. The Air Force sent two fighters to intercept them, but the targets vanished from sight (and the radar) so they returned to their base. Radar signals and visual observations reappeared immediately and lasted until the morning.

Just over a week after their first appearance, on Saturday evening, July 26, UFOs returned. At 21:00, the radar picked up five or six unidentified objects moving at high speed toward the American capital. The control tower at National Airport and Andrews Air Force base confirmed the observations, saying that most of the objects looked "solid" or even "metallic". At one point the mysterious objects even appeared above both the Capitol building and the White House, areas that are for obvious security reasons absolutely forbidden to over flights. Again, at 23:25, two F-94 fighters took off to intercept, but the objects seemed to play with them then simply disappeared.

On July 29, the Air Force convened the largest press conference since the end of the war. Spokesman, General John A. Samford, admitted that officials had many reports of UFO observations and at least 20% of them could not be explained. However, at the end of the press conference, a meteorologist attempted to posit the idea that all the radar signals from the nights mentioned were caused by temperature inversions in the upper layers of the atmosphere. The idea was accepted with enthusiasm by the media, but some officials were not so easily fobbed off.[25]

---

[25]   Dolan, 2002, p. 104-108

Central Intelligence Agency (CIA) Director General Walter Bedell Smith, requested and received on September 24, 1952 a note from H. Marshall Chadwell, Deputy Director of the CIA Scientific Information Office. If a metallic object can be confused with an echo from a temperature inversion – said the note – "we are now in a position where we cannot, on an instant basis, distinguish hardware from phantom and as tension mounts, we will run the increasing risk of false alerts and the even greater danger of falsely identifying the real as phantom."

Chadwell was also worried about the possibility that the Soviets might utilise UFOs as a psychological weapon to induce "mass hysteria and panic". He suggested that in order to minimise the risk of panic, "a national policy should be established as to what should be told to the public regarding the phenomena." On December 2, 1952, the CIA Director received a new letter from the Deputy Director for Information, stating: "At this time, the reports of incidents convince us that there is something going on that must have immediate attention. Sightings of unexplained objects at great altitudes and travelling at high speeds in the vicinity of major U.S. defence installations are of such nature that they are not attributable to natural phenomena or known types of aerial vehicles."

In order to pull a hot chestnut from the fire, the so-called "Robertson Panel", made up of scientists, was summoned to the Pentagon during January 14-17, 1953. For three days, over a total of twelve hours, two films were presented, plus reports on the Russians' interest in U.S. UFO cases, along with maps showing observation locations etc. The Air Force, in good faith, selected 100 of the most thoroughly verified unexplained observations. The panel examined only fifteen of these cases for a few hours, but only superficially. Obviously they could not find a solution to the UFO problem. Although all participants were aware of the popular hypothesis of the non-earthly origin of these objects, they knew equally well that this solution was scientifically impossible and extremely dangerous for their own career, it was also toxic for society in general.

Instead, the Panel concluded: "That the evidence presented on Unidentified Flying Objects shows no indication that these phenomena constitute a direct physical threat to national security". But the big issue remains "the continued emphasis on the reporting of these phenomena. We cite as examples the clogging of channels of communication by irrelevant reports, the danger that false claims could lead us to ignore real indications of hostile action and the cultivation of a morbid national psychology in which skilful hostile propaganda could induce hysterical behaviour and harmful distrust of duly constituted authority."

As a solution, the Panel recommended, among other things: "That the national security agencies take immediate steps to strip the Unidentified Flying Objects of the special status they have been given and the aura of mystery they have unfortunately acquired. That the national security agencies initiate policies on intelligence, training and public education... to reassure the public of the total lack of evidence of inimical forces behind the phenomenon... The 'debunking' aim would result in reduction in public interest in 'flying saucers' which today evokes a strong psychological reaction. This education could be accomplished by using mass media such as television, motion pictures and popular articles."[26]

In short, a real problem was the reaction of the population. As a result, it has been established that a policy of debunking and ridiculing the UFO phenomenon and the people dealing with it, has to be officially carried out and seen by the general public. An excellent analysis made by Terry Hansen shows that this complicity worked very well in the years that followed.[27]

---

[26]   Dolan, 2002, p.122-128
[27]   Hansen, 2000

Following the enactment of the Freedom of Information Act (FOIA) in 1967 and the intensification of actions by organisations such as Citizens Against UFO Secrecy, the policy of discouraging public interest in the UFO phenomenon took new forms: the undermining of some investigators with sensational "disclosures", in reality fakes, by which the person in question is subsequently discredited and through him the whole of ufology. Out of nowhere, a series of fake, but meticulously elaborate documents, photographs, films etc, appeared. They contained a mixture of true and verifiable facts along with fictions about the alien presence on Earth and government collaboration with aliens. In this way, details were 'disclosed' about alleged meetings between American officials and aliens in 1954 at the Muroc Dry Lake Army Air Field in California, and in 1964 at Holloman AFB, White Sands, New Mexico. "Insiders" were talking about secret treaties with different extra-terrestrial powers, and secret underground bases in which the government collaborated with these powers. For example, it was said that at Dulce, in a secret base under Archuleta Mesa in northern New Mexico, thousands of aliens were involved in technology exchanges, and also in sinister experiments on humans and animals, including the creation of mutants or hybrids.

In time it has since come to light that many of these "disclosures", which currently constitute an "urban mythology", were the result of the organised activity of certain government services, such as 'AFOSI' or the Air Force Office of Special Investigations as well as of certain people, some who are well known.

In the same way, in 1989, allegations also appeared that in "Area 51" (officially called Groom Lake), which is a secret U.S. Air Force facility in Nevada, there are captured UFOs and specialists working on putting them back into operation. As an answer, officials were forced to declare that, indeed, the U2, the SR-71 "Blackbird" and the F-117A "Stealth" planes had all been tested at this ultra-secret base, and there were also other, newer, prototypes, but there were no flying saucers. On this occasion there was a suspicion that, in addition to false documents and information, those interested in spreading the disinformation could use brain control methods to induce false memories in some of the supposed witnesses.

All this toxification had a multiple role. If UFOs could be explained as experimental aircraft, the taxpayers would be pleased that there was an official solution to the whole UFO phenomenon, so they would stop asking awkward questions. If, on the contrary, secret experimental planes were assumed to be UFOs and those viewing UFOs could be presented as lunatics, accidental observation of an experimental aircraft could easily be denied. Finally, creating rumours about government pacts with extra-terrestrials, possibly using people who were supposedly psychic, could confuse enemies and create the impression in the general public all those who insist that UFOs are real are delusional. And, eventually using techniques like these, it would become increasingly difficult to distinguish the truth from lies.

Following the same logic, from the former USSR after 1990, data of the same kind emerged. Among them there were also stories about crashed or captured UFOs, and underground alien bases etc. Some of this "hard evidence" could be made professionally for disinformation purposes, but other document and movies, etc. were made *ad hoc* by enterprising individuals who knew they could sell them, for a small amount of foreign currency, to Western fans.

The UFO disinformation phenomenon also existed in other countries. An example is the infamous story of alleged aliens coming from the planet UMMO, which was especially prominent in Spain and France. The story, which first appeared in 1966, was only disproven 2006. In addition to this more and more fake stories, photos, and UFO films were added, most of them made semi-professionally on home computers by pranksters. The result of all these activities is that the fog of confusion is now so thick, that it is advisable to have a thorough knowledge of ufo culture in order to distinguish the false cases from the real ones.

Disclosures and openings

After decades of collecting data on the UFO phenomenon military organisations in many countries have come to the conclusion that this effort has contributed little to achieving their initial objectives. Faced with the demands of civilian groups fuelled by conspiracy theories, the defence ministries in several countries decided to declassify and make most of their UFO archives available to the general public. These documents revealed dramatic military encounters with unidentified objects. The cases have been hidden for a long time; because of the suspicion that UFOs could be an enemy's secret weapons or that they could replicate their performance. UFO encounters also had to be hidden because it was extremely embarrassing for the authorities to admit to taxpayers that some objects were in the skies and that the Air Force was powerless to do anything about them and there was no acceptable explanation regarding what they might be.

As an example, in the United Kingdom, the Ministry of Defence (MoD) had a UFO project that ran from 1953 to 2009 and in that time over 12,000 UFO sightings were logged and investigated. But the MoD announced that, after December 1, 2009, "it is no longer a MoD policy to record, respond to, or investigate UFO sightings", adding that "The MoD has no opinion on the existence or otherwise of extra-terrestrial life. However, over fifty years, no UFO report has presented any evidence of a potential threat to the United Kingdom". In addition, the UFO archives were gradually declassified. Between 2009 and 2013, 52,000 pages of UFO papers have been published. In June 2017, the MoD further declassified a further fifteen UFO files. All of them were submitted to the National Archives. It is presumed, however, that a number of more "sensitive" documents remained secret.

British journalist Nick Pope was civil servant at the MoD, from 1985 to 2006. From 1991 to 1994 his duties included investigating reports of UFO sightings. In 1996, Pope published his conclusions concerning the UFO phenomenon in a book. He said that "something like 90 to 95 percent of all UFO sightings can be explained in conventional terms... Yet allowing for the fact that an estimated thirteen million people have seen 'something', at least 650,000 sightings worldwide remain unexplained. All the Ministry of Defence can say about these sightings is that it keeps an open mind. I suppose this is a fancy way of saying that we have no idea what the objects reported might be."[28]

Pope concluded that "around 80% of UFO sightings were misidentification of ordinary objects or phenomena: aircrafts, aircraft lights, weather balloons, meteors, satellites, bright stars and planets, Chinese lanterns, etc. Some sightings were caused by people seeing secret prototype spy planes or drones. Other cases were hoaxes, or the result of a hallucination or psychological delusion. In around 15% of cases there was insufficient data to make a firm assessment. Finally, around 5% of cases appeared to have no conventional explanation, even after a thorough investigation. Of course, it's important to stress that just because a UFO sighting was categorised as unexplained, it doesn't follow that what was seen was extra-terrestrial. Unexplained means unexplained – nothing more and nothing less"[29]. But even he has no proofs; he also remains open-minded regarding the extra-terrestrial hypothesis.

In an interview with The Huffington Post on August 17, 2011, , Nick Pope admitted that during 1991-94, he also took part in the MoD policy of debunking and ridiculing UFO reports. "While, in public, we were desperately pushing the line that this was of no defence interest, we couldn't say 'There's something in our airspace; pilots see them; they're tracked on radar; sometimes we scramble jets to chase these things, but we can't catch them'. This would be an admission that we'd lost control of our own air space and such a position would be untenable... We are telling the public we're not interested, this is all nonsense, but in

---

[28] Pope, 1996, p.78.
[29] Pope, 2013

reality we were desperately chasing our tails and following this up in great detail." ... "Another trick would be deliberately using phrases like 'little green men'. We were trying to do two things: either to kill any media story on the subject, or if a media story ran, ensure that it ran in such a way that it would make the subject seem ridiculous and that it would make people who were interested in this also seem ridiculous." Pope conceded there's still no evidence confirming alien visits to Earth. "Not just yet – there's no spaceship-in-a-hangar smoking gun. However, there are plenty of sightings that I think show that we're dealing with more than just aircraft lights and weather balloons."

The documents declassified by MoD have confirmed, among other things, some notorious cases such as the 1980 incident in the Rendlesham Forest in Suffolk, about 150 kilometres northeast of London, near two NATO air force bases: Bentwaters and Woodbridge, rented to the U.S. Air Force and hosting an undisclosed number of nuclear warheads. Here, in December 1980, the most spectacular UFO incidents in the United Kingdom occurred, including the alleged landing of a triangular alien vehicle. Lt. Col. Charles I. Halt, Deputy Head of the Woodbridge AFB at that time, personally investigated the incident, filing a report that emerged after a few years. In June 2010, Halt said in an official statement that what he saw at close range was extra-terrestrial in origin.

Another interesting document, that was declassified in 2006, is the so-called *Condign* report, a secret UFO study undertaken by the British Government's Defense Intelligence Staff (DIS) between 1997 and 2000. Project Condign (a randomly generated code word) has over four hundred pages. Its full title is "Unidentified Aerial Phenomena in the UK Air Defense Region". The more appropriate name: "Unidentified Aerial Phenomenon" (UAP) was used here to avoid the pop-culture baggage associated with the term "UFO".

The great advantage of the Condign report is that, being intended only for the military, it does not contain the misinformation commonly served to the general public; and the great flaw is that, in order to keep the secret, the author (whose identity is undisclosed) did not consult with either ufologists or the witnesses to the cases.

Reading this report you can feel that, reading between the lines, the author is puzzled when confronted by such a large amount of incomprehensible material. The study underscores the indisputable evidence for unidentified aerospace phenomena; they have aerodynamic features well beyond those of any known aircraft or missiles, whether piloted or not and the phenomenon has defied any credible explanation regarding its causes.

The study examines and eliminates several hypotheses: experimental military aircraft, unmanned airplanes, gliders and paragliders, helicopters, hot air balloons, captive balloons, meteorological probes, satellites, meteorites, aerosols, lenticular clouds, electric discharges, birds, swarms of butterflies, mirages, other natural or artificial phenomena, including hoaxes. The author of the study believes that some UAPs are caused by poorly understood "plasma phenomena" of a type that has not yet been experimentally demonstrated. But he does not completely eliminate the alien hypothesis.

In France, the Unidentified Aerospace Research and Information Group (GEIPAN) has been active since 1977 (with some name changes) at the National Centre for Spatial Studies (CNRS) in Toulouse. It is the oldest (and, for a long time, the only) official civilian structure of its kind in the world intended for the scientific study of the UFO phenomenon. The management and control of GEIPAN's activities were entrusted to a Steering Committee, consisting of fifteen high-level members representing: the police, civil security, air force, etc., as well as scientific institutions, including CNRS, CNES and Meteo France.

Since March 27, 2007, about 100,000 archive pages of GEIPAN material have been made available on the Internet to the general public. They relate about 1,600 UFO sightings, covering over 30 years of cases on which 3000 reports have been written and involving about 6,000 testimonies. Documents written by the gendarmes, expert reports, witness sketches, video or audio sequences, etc. are included. No file was considered a military secret, the only concern being a respect for the privacy of the people involved. Of the total number of cases and despite the accuracy of the testimonies and the quality of the collected materials, only 28% were considered inexplicable.

In France, in 1999, an important ninety-page document was published, entitled "UFOs and Defence: What Should We Prepare For?" *(Les Ovni Et La Defense: A quoi doit-on se préparer?).* Also named the "COMETA Report", the authors were members of an independent group of former "auditors" at the Institute of Advanced Studies for National Defence (IHEDN), as well as other experts. Before being released, the report was submitted as an open letter to the French President Jacques Chirac and the Prime Minister Lionel Jospin. The study, a result of four years of research, was signed by a number of individuals, including aviation general Bernard Norlain, former director of IHEDN André Lebeau, former president of the National centre for Spatial Studies, aviation General Denis Letty, aviation General Bruno Lemoine, Admiral Marc Merlo, Chief of Police Denis Blancher, Doctor of Political Sciences Michel Algrin, General Pierre Bescond, Army Engineer and by many others.

Among others, the Cometa report states that, "the physical reality of UFOs with unparalleled flight performance on the Earth is 'quasi-sure'. The facts accumulated over the years compel us to consider the alien hypothesis with its various variants. The extra-terrestrial hypothesis, even if it cannot yet be proven, is the only one that can explain all the data currently available and is extremely serious with the possible consequences." As arguments, the report presents remarkable cases from both France and other countries, including military aviation encounters, reports on UFOs over Russian nuclear missile silos and so on. The report also says that preconceptions and fear of ridicule must be overcome, for example through information conferences in major military schools. Measures at the highest government level, cooperation with other countries and with the UN are also proposed.

In the former Soviet space, after 1990 many documents collected within the "Setka" projects, were declassified. Aviation General Igor Maltsev, head of the General Staff of the Armed Forces, made many UFO documents and photographs available to the public. In the April 19, 1990 issue of the newspaper *Raboceaia Tribuna,* he published the synthesis of over one hundred observations reported by commanders of military units. In 1991, General Nikolai Alexeevici Shciam, Vice President of the KGB's Chairmanship Committee, officially made available to the Union of Ufological Associations of the USSR (chairman cosmonaut Pavel Popovici) documents totalling 124 pages collected under the title "Cases of observing unusual phenomena on the territory of the USSR, 1982-1990". The accompanying letter stated that the KGB was not expressly concerned with the UFO study but has received many such reports from individuals and also various agencies. On July 21, 2009, the state-owned Russian news agency RIA Novosti, also announced the release of UFO files owned by the Russian Navy. Many files were compiled by a special group led by Admiral Nikolai Smirnov. It was commented that the unidentified objects were technologically superior to what humanity had ever built.

In Belgium, following the wave of UFOs which began on the evening of 29 November 1989 and extended until 1990, generating thousands of reports, for the first time in the world Defense Minister Guy Coeme authorised the Air Force to unreservedly cooperate with a civil organisation for the study of UFOs, namely SOBEPS. All reports and even an airplane equipped with infrared cameras and sophisticated electronic sensors were made available to them. Colonel Wilfried De Brouwer, chief operating officer of the Belgian Air Force (promoted to General in 1991) convened a press conference on 11 July 1990 as a final conclusion to the subsequent investigations. He acknowledged that the Belgian Air Force was unable to identify neither the nature, nor the origin of the phenomenon. However, they had enough evidence to exclude the following assumptions: balloons, motorised ultra-light vehicles, remote-controlled vehicles, airplanes (including Stealth), laser projections, or mirages.

The declassification of UFO military documents in Spain is irrevocably linked to the name of the ufologist Vicente-Juan Ballester Olmos. In 1990-91, through numerous visits to public relations and flight security offices of the Spanish Air Force, he succeeded in convincing the decision makers that the idea that declassifying UFO information, previously considered "confidential", was helpful. In 1991, documents from many sources were directed to a single information centre and the data collection forms were merged. Also, between 1992 and 1999, eighty four files were declassified and circulated, this included 2000 pages and about 122 UFO events from 1962-1995. In the following years incidents reported by the Air Force were declassified as soon as they were investigated.

In Latin America, perhaps the most spectacular cases come from Brazil. As a result of the pressure exerted through the campaign, "*UFOs: Freedom of Information Now*", led by Adelmar J. Gevaerd, editor of the *Brazilian UFO Magazine* and the head of the Brazilian UFO Researchers' Committee (CBU), on May 20, 2005, the Brazilian Government declared via Brigadier General Telles Ribeiro, head of the Brazilian Air Force Communications Centre (FAB): "We want all the information we have retained in the last decades on this subject to be made available to the public through the UFO community".

On September 30, 2009, the number of declassified pages has already risen to over 4,000. Then interviews were obtained with a retired high rank officer (equivalent to Air Chief Marshal), Socrates da Costa Monteiro, former Minister of Aeronautics between 1990 and 1992. On this occasion details of several unexplained phenomena were disclosed and what followed were declassified a part of the 2000 pages, 500 photos and 16 hours of film on *Operação Prato*, concerning a wave of observations from the last three months of 1977 and the first half of 1978. At that time an area from the Amazon River spill was invaded by UFOs, brilliant objects of various shapes and sizes flying a few feet above the trees and sending strange light beams down to the ground. The objects were zigzagging, stopping, then shooting off at incredible speeds. Many villagers in the Amazon region of Brazil complained that they were being attacked by spheres or bright balls of light and some of them were injured or even killed.

Another set of documents concerned the so-called "*Brazilian Official UFO Night*". Then, on the night of May 19, 1986, twenty-one spherical objects, each with an estimated diameter of 100 metres, were detected by radars and spotted by civilian pilots, they were literally blocking the air traffic above the cities of Rio de Janeiro, São José dos Campos and São Paulo. None of the military aircraft were able to approach the unidentified objects. In a matter of seconds one of the UFOs rose to at an altitude of 180 km above the Atlantic coast in the São Paulo area, then returned to chase the fighters. According to radar records, some of the artefacts instantly accelerated from 250 km/h to 4,000 km/h. "We knew there was no threat. We were convinced that their intentions were to get to know us better... It would have been crazy to try something against them" one of the officers said.

In China, even if we cannot talk about full declassification, the UFO issue is treated with great seriousness. In the "National Society of the Extra-terrestrial Studies", financed by the government, only professional scientists and engineers with published works on UFOs are allowed to be members. Speaking to a panel of six former members of the United States Congress at "The Citizens Hearing" set up in 2013 in Washington DC by Steve Bassett of the Paradigm Research Group, Sun Shili, a retired Chinese foreign ministry official and current president of the Beijing UFO Research Society, said: "After years of research, a large number of Chinese UFO scholars, including myself, are convinced of the authenticity of UFOs and the existence of UFOs and aliens." He also said that extra-terrestrials are living among us.

In August 2010 Prof. Wang Sichao, one of the leaders of the Purple Mountain Observatory belonging to the Chinese Academy of Sciences, said that his 39 years' experience in astronomy convinced him that UFOs are real, aliens visit the Earth on scientific research expeditions and the observatory watched their ships repeatedly at heights of between 150 to 1500 kilometres from the ground. He was also convinced that the visitors are peaceful. In the past 10-15 years, there has been a notable change in the attitude of officials toward the UFO phenomenon coupled with the declassification of large amounts of data. This has also been achieved in other countries, including Sweden, Denmark, Chile, Peru, Uruguay, Mexico, Canada, Australia and New Zealand etc..

CONCLUSIONS

One kind of "magic", through which the hyper-civilizations manifest themselves on Earth could be through the UFO phenomenon. In over 70 years, hundreds of thousands of reports and thousands of photographs and films have been officially gathered from all over the world. The armed forces of all countries have often watched the inexplicable appearances through dedicated projects. Pilots from all over the world have been confronted with them, sometimes with tragic consequences. Tens of thousands of previously secret documents, including photographs and military radar records were recently made public.

The military has always been extremely interested in UFOs. On the one hand, hoping to discover new technical principles for use as weapons, but they kept quiet about "sensitive" cases. On the other hand, because they could not do anything about UFOs and could not explain to the general public what was going on, UFO sightings have been subjected to an official policy of debunking and ridiculing, often with the help of media. Today, scientists, public opinion and "serious" media continue to assert that what we call UFOs are made by us, are badly understood natural phenomena, hoaxes, or simple illusions, as there are no extra-terrestrials near us. It is a natural reaction to defending the safety and tranquillity of our established views about reality. But it is also a typical example of cultural blindness.

ABDUCTIONS

Academics are puzzled

Some scientists said that when searching for extra-terrestrial intelligence we only found a "gigantic silence". If the uneasiness of military about UFOs – described in the previous chapter – seems insufficiently convincing so that we are overwhelmed by the "magic" of an unearthly presence, let's see what we know about another, similar, but even more controversial phenomenon – so-called "alien abductions".

How many people know that in 1992 at the Massachusetts Institute of Technology (MIT) in Cambridge, near Boston, which one of the world's most famous universities, there was a five-day conference dedicated exclusively to the issue of alleged alien abductions? The two co-chairmen of the conference were Professor David E. Pritchard, Ph.D., an atomic and molecular physicist, a recipient of some prestigious international awards and a physicist working at M.I.T. from 1968, and John E. Mack, M.D. (1929-2004), a professor of psychiatry for thirty years at the illustrious Harvard Medical School and a former director of the psychiatric department of the Cambridge hospital of this university.[30]

The conference was attended by several specialists in the field, including David Jacobs, Professor at Temple University, Thomas Bullard Ph.D., Richard Boylan Ph.D., as well as top investigators in the field, such as Budd Hopkins, John Carpenter, Jenny Randles, Linda Moulton Howe and many other researchers and journalists. The participating specialists had about 2000 files concerning abduction cases, all of which had been thoroughly evaluated. In each of them there were abundant details concerning one or more people that had been extracted from their normal environment. This was from the car they were driving, from the place where they were walking or fishing, from their bedroom and so on. They had been taken by non-earthly beings using a 'light beam' that lifted them from the ground, or by some other method. They were taken to artificial enclosure, which could be inside a "spaceship"; here they underwent some often-unpleasant procedures and then were brought back to the place where the abduction began.

What has intrigued the scientists at the conference at M.I.T. was the *great similarity* of the stories of the abducted, as well as the *consistency* of the details in their accounts, despite the fact that they did not influence each other, either directly or through the media (indeed, many of the details had never been published). Among the victims were Protestants, Catholics, Jews, whites, blacks, men, women, young, and the elderly, all with varying levels of education. Those abducted had different professions, were employed or unemployed, married, unmarried, divorced, They came from North and South America, Europe, Africa, Asia and Australia, this diversity accentuated the extraordinary range and mystery of the phenomenon.

Dozens of significant features were found in a large number of the abductions and details from urban folklore about aliens, such as: little green folk, head antennas, laser guns, etc., were *never* mentioned. So, it was hard to talk about media contamination or coincidences. In about 20% of the cases two or more people were abducted simultaneously and their testimonies coincided. There have also been instances of other people witnessing the abduction from a distance, or who found that the person was absent during their abduction.

Not only researchers, but also many victims of abduction attended the Conference at M.I.T. Most of them have been given pseudonyms to protect their identities. The abduction witnesses were worried, confused and not at all eager for publicity. They had, in general, a

---

[30]   An excellent synthesis of the Conference works is in Bryan, 1995.

good reputation in the community where they lived and worked, and they had been hesitant about revealing their incredible stories but wanted to find out what in fact had happened to them.

In an interview with PBS/NOVA about his evolution from scepticism to belief, Professor John Mack said: "When I first encountered this phenomenon, or particularly even before I had actually seen the people themselves, I had very little place in my mind to take this seriously". To convince himself, for nearly four years since 1990 he had examined over a hundred people who said they'd been abducted. Seventy-six of them (forty-seven women and twenty-nine men, aged two 2 to fifty-seven) met the criteria that he had imposed before accepting that there had been an "abduction". At first it seemed that among the abductees, ordinary people were the most common. It was later revealed that this was due to the fact that prominent professional, or political people, hesitated to report their experiences, in order not to be exposed to ridicule and put their careers at risk. The abductees were subjected to tests. No correlation was been found with any particular type of personality or a particular family structure, or with sexual abuse in childhood and so on. None of those examined by Mack had psychiatric problems, except post-traumatic syndrome that was a *consequence* of some traumatic event that had happened to them. None was the kind to invent such stories or to give their dreams or fantasies a reality for gain. Mack noted that these cases cannot be clinically classified. They did not fit anywhere, they were not the result of childhood abuse, nor psychoses, nor neuroses, nor organic diseases of the brain, nor pathological lies, etc.

A repeating scenario

Most alien abductions, sometimes called "Close encounters of the fourth kind", appear to be taking place according a scenario with details that repeat, with small variations, for the great majority of reports or hypnotic regressions records. Among those who contributed to outline this scenario are Thomas Ed Bullard, David M. Jacobs, Edith Fiore and others. According to Bullard, the main steps of the scenario are seizing, examining and conversation with the abductors, visiting the ship, travelling to a non-earthly place, the appearance or manifestation of sacred beings, returning home and subsequent effects. He also identified, in 1996, fifty eight significant details of abduction, which are systematically repeated in the witness reports. In the following, we will extract a number of repeating features from these testimonies, without of course detracting from the phenomenon.

The abductions take place most often at night, from the bedroom, from the car, or from a place under the open sky. Often a beam of light descends from a mysterious ship and lifts the victim. Sometimes the victim is framed by two, three or four alien creatures. The witness sees themselves floating above the Earth then inside an enclosure of some kind, which sometimes is identified with the interior of a spaceship. The victim is stretched on a kind of table or slab where they feel paralysed. There are a few beings around, usually short ones, who carry out medical procedures on the victim, (with or without strange instruments). Often they correct certain health problems. The abductee feels sometimes that they are surrounded by compassion and love, a feeling they return to the abductors. Eye-to-eye visual contact seems to play an important role in this process.

Most of the victims said they were abducted and then examined by the "greys" – creatures around 1.3 meters tall, with telepathic capabilities, huge skulls, large black hypnotic eyes, and with almost no nose and ears and the mouth, just a slit. The limbs of these beings were very thin; their hands can have four, five or six fingers. They wear clothing so tightly fitted that it seemed part of their skin. They did not show signs of sex and they were never seen eating or drinking. Another race, more rarely reported but still quite common, are the "Nordics", with a perfectly human appearance, but are between 2.10 - 2.30 metres tall, with long, often fair or white, hair and usually dressed in white robes reaching to the ankles.

Relatively frequent are "reptilian" beings (muscular, with scaly skin and webs between the fingers, and they have claws and cat-like eyes). There are also "insectoids" (with a grasshopper-like body and head), etc. Sporadically there are dozens of other types of humanoids and pseudo-humanoids, etc., with the most grotesque appearances. Sometimes, the "entities" wear diving helmets, technical devices on the girdle, and boxes or wands that paralyse or annihilate the will of the victim, etc. Thomas Bullard's statistics have established that, for reasons that are not yet clear, that "greys" somehow predominate in reports from North America, "Nordics" in England or Russia and the "monstrous" in South America. However, this is not exclusive.

The entities and UFOs encountered possess capabilities that defy our science. Very often they levitate. They can sometimes go through solid objects, for example through the walls of a house. Apparently, these entities are aware of other laws of nature and forms of matter besides those that are familiar to us. They are also able to hypnotise human beings and communicate telepathically in any language. In some accounts they are described as being deprived of individual will, acting robotically, or only as part of the group they belong to, there is no apparent empathy or understanding of human emotional reactions or feelings.

The "visit" can be combined with other episodes, which vary from one case to case. Eventually, the abducted person is told that they will be taken home. They are not allowed to take any material evidence with them and, before they leave, they are subjected to a hypnotic suggestion that they will not be able to recall – partially or completely – the incident. For this reason, in many cases the abductee will remember, at most, only fragments of the encounter and also find that several hours have passed without understanding how this occurred.

After a while some will spontaneously recall the incident, or while under hypnotic regression, but with varying levels of detail. *Regressive hypnosis* consists of relaxing the conscious mind in order to gain access to information that has been recorded in the unconscious mind, but for various reasons is not accessible in a normal state of consciousness. The method was initially used by the police to help witnesses recall more details of an incident they had experienced, or by physicians help to unlock repressed memories, helping to heal certain forms of neurosis such as post-traumatic stress disorder. In the case of abductions, the purpose was often to supplement the consciously recalled information. With some of the witnesses, hypnotic regression has opened up some memory barriers; in waking state they then spontaneously remembered a lot of other details of the abduction. It is assumed that, however, most victims "completely forget" what has happened; therefore, they will never even know that they have been abducted.

Hypnotic regression has also sparked controversy, as it has sometimes happened when amateur hypnotists and sensationalists, "enrich" these session by using leading questions such as: "have you also seen X?" The hypnotised person will almost certainly agree.

A first case of using this technique was during the investigation of the incident involving Betty and Barney Hill. On the night of September 19, 1961, they returned to their home in Portsmouth, New Hampshire, by car from a holiday in Canada, where they had expected to arrive at 2:30 or 3:00 at dawn. As they crossed the White Mountains chain, they saw closer and closer a light that seemed to pursue them. At one point, the object approached at no more than 30 metres. It was a huge disk with two rows of windows around it. Using binoculars, Barney could see that there were human silhouettes behind the windows. With the feeling of being hunted they fled back to the car and stared it, at one point the two witnesses had the feeling that the object might be just above them. Then they heard a sort of "short, loud, buzz", after which they both felt themselves become terribly sleepy.

They recovered after a few more "short loud buzzes". Barney was at the wheel of the car, but they were nearly sixty miles further south. Neither of them remembered what had happened in the meantime. When they finally arrived home in Portsmouth it was five o'clock, which was about two hours later than expected. How did they lose this period of time?

Ten days after the incident, Barney began to have recurring nightmares. In a dream, he saw humanoids dressed in uniforms and trying to capture him for a kind of medical examination. Next, their health became worse, then, finally, they both decided to see Dr. Benjamin Simon, a noted neuroscientist in Boston. Suspecting that the source of their health issues was a repressed psychological trauma, Dr. Simon proposed separate hypnotic regression sessions with Barney and Betty.

The sessions were recorded, but the contents of the tapes were not disclosed to anyone until all investigations had been completed, not even to those being examined. Both of them reported a great many details and many of them coincided. The sessions revealed that at some point the car engine stopped and six non-earthly creatures forced both of them to go into to the ship that was nearby. The aliens had glossy, pale, metallic-grey skin. They were completely hairless with mongoloid faces, they had big eyes like those of a cat, they also had a lipless mouth and instead of a nose they only had a small excrescence. They were about 1.20 meters high, but one, who appeared to be in charge, was about 1.50 meters.

Both of the Hill's recalled that they had arrived in a room where they underwent a medical examination. Their hair, nails, and skin were harvested with the help of strange devices and then more complex procedures also took place. At the end of the operations the two were told that they would not be allowed to remember what had happened and that they could not take anything with them as evidence. And if they did remember anything it would be heavily distorted. The being in charge told them – "you will be so confused with these memories that you will not know what to do with them".

The case of Betty and Barney Hill was highly publicised. The two have been subjected to a multitude of tests, but no one has been able to question their sincerity or mental health. From the very beginning one the first academics involved was Ronald Leo Sprinkle, who was professor of psychology at the University of Wyoming, in Laramie, and used scientific instruments during the evaluation. Interested in ufology, in 1968 he subjected a policeman, Herbert Schirmer, who was a victim of an alleged abduction to regressive hypnosis. In 1984, Sprinkle had already personally studied over 200 cases of abductions, and by 1994 more than 300. A remarkable practitioner in the field of hypnotic regression, he applied this method, not only to UFO abductions, but also to other areas of the paranormal as this related to memories of supposed past lives. He sought significant correlations between UFO abductions and other paranormal experiences. In all cases his scientific belief was "to continue to explore while we continue to doubt".

As early as 1981, the professor was convinced that the phenomenon was part of a "plan", belonging to intelligent, benevolent beings, representing "extra-terrestrial" and/or "ultra-terrestrial" civilizations, having technology and ethics that greatly surpass earthly ones. They remain "invisible to the human eye and to the dominant culture, unless they want themselves to be seen." The purpose of this plan was to assist in allowing humanity to develop and eventually transform human beings into "citizens of Cosmos."

Leo Sprinkle gradually became convinced that he was also the victim of alien abductions (as well as other famous investigators and authors such as Whitley Strieber, Raymond Fowler and others). Of course, this conviction did not help him in his university career. For this reason, since 1989 he remained only as a consultant and a professor emeritus in the same university.

Maybe the personality most involved in studying the abduction phenomenon was Budd Hopkins (1931-2011). In 1978, when he was already a recognised painter and sculptor, a young man named Steven Kilburn asked him for help in solving a "missing time" issue he had experienced when driving a car at night on a certain section of a road. After this event, he experienced psychological issues was in a very bad state. Hopkins consulted several physicians, including a New York psychotherapist, Dr. Aphrodite Clamar, who specialised in hypnosis treatments, to help investigate the case. The hypnotic regression carried out on the young man revealed a history of UFO abductions, all with sexual connotations. Shortly afterwards other, similar cases emerged involving credible people from all social backgrounds. Budd Hopkins was surprised that, under hypnosis, all of the witnesses recounted abduction stories that appeared to be created from the same mould. He was the first to understand that many cases where someone saw a light or a mysterious object in flight and then discovered that they had "inexplicably lost" an hour or two, this actually represented a UFO abduction that had been carefully erased from the memory of the victim by the abductors. In many cases these signs were accompanied by concrete physical evidence attesting to the phenomenon: such as unexplained traces on the body of victims or on their clothes.

Hopkins was also the first to notice that most abductions are repeated. They can begin around the age of five or six or even earlier and can continue throughout their lives. Sometimes, generation after generation, whole families seem to have been pursued in this way. At his death in 2011, Budd Hopkins had well over 1,000 cases that he had examined personally, which included 700 possible abductions.

Abductions during childhood are significant because in these cases there is much less chance of possible contamination, confusion or misleading intentions. A two-and-a-half year old girl was horrified when she saw the alien portrayed on the cover of the book "*Communion*" by Whitley Strieber. She exclaimed, "There you are Mummy! This is the man who takes me with him to see my doctor; the one who undresses me". When Hopkins was asked to evaluate the case the little girl offered to show him the scar she had – three marks under her navel – a common sign in other abductions. In 1990 Hopkins drew up a "colouring book" containing ten images, all similar in size and depicting: Santa Claus, Batman, a clown, a policeman, a little girl, a ninja turtle, a little boy, a witch, a skull and also the head of a grey alien, as described by most of the abducted. When browsing the images, a small boy when he came across the latter, exclaimed: "So, you know my friends!"

Other investigators added other features of the abduction phenomenon to the findings above. One of them is a concept known in psychoanalysis, the so-called *screen memory*. This is a false memory replacing the memory of a distressing event. In cases examined by Prof. John Mack, after careful investigation he revealed that screen memories such as a series of motorcycles, a forest, a conference room, a cathedral interior, Jesus in a white robe, an angel, a five metres tall kangaroo, etc. were actually UFOs or aliens. In other, similar cases some people saw a monkey, an owl, a deer, a "devil" and so on; a person said that a wolf entered her bedroom and gazed into her eyes.

Another interesting feature of UFO encounters is the so-called "*Oz Factor*", a term proposed in 1983 by Jenny Randles, who is one of the most respected British researchers and authors on UFOs and paranormal phenomena. The term designates a kind of altered state of consciousness commonly found by ufologists, and also in cases of related phenomena such as manifestations of sacred figures such as the Virgin Mary. Sometimes the witness feels a sense of extreme isolation, or have the impression that they has been transported from the real world into a land with different rules, such as world of the Wizard of Oz. For example, they suddenly find that their surroundings have changed – there are no cars to be seen and there is no sound and everything is moving very slowly or seems frozen. People affected by this factor see things that people around him do not, (e.g. UFOs) and, subjectively, sometimes time appears to pass at a different rate.

Post-effects of abduction

At the end of abduction the aliens subject their victim to a hypnotic suggestion to forget the incident. Because of this the terrifying recollections of the abduction are not erased from the memory of the victim but remain in the subconscious. Because they still exist, over time the abducted person may develop symptoms of neurosis, such as fatigue, depression, insomnia, nightmares, anxiety, aggression, confusion, phobias (for example an unexplained fear of darkness, of certain objects, or of certain places, linked with the abduction) and so on.

Those who consciously recall the incident develop a fear of abduction. This can cause disturbed sleep, or a compulsive tendency to repeatedly check all door and window locks and can include fear of being alone. Sometimes victims experience an unexplained fear being looked at directly in the eyes. These symptoms may appear suddenly after the abduction, although the person in question behaved normally prior to this.

The victim may become obsessed by image of an animal (for example, an owl – a "screen memory"), this can sometimes develop into a state of panic. A patient of Prof. Mack, who was abducted while she was young girl, developed a phobia regarding her dolls. She demanded that they were destroyed because she was convinced that they moved around her bedroom during the night.

All of these effects together form what has been called the *Post-Abduction Syndrome*. It can be partially healed through raising awareness of what has happened, possibly involving a hypnotic regression conducted by a specialist.

UFO abductions cannot be proven by hard evidence in a way demanded by science and necessary to convince sceptics. Some have reported that they tried to take objects from the "ship" with them as a proof of the abduction, but that was impossible.

Still, there are some features that can apply as "physical evidence". John Mack observed that: "The abductee may be witnessed to be actually missing for varying periods of time, although this is not common. Independent corroboration, in my experience, especially on the part of someone not directly involved in the encounter is quite rare. The experiencers sometimes report that, during the abduction, implants are inserted under the skin or into one or another orifice and they may feel certain that these represent some sort of tracking or monitoring devices. Several of these have been recovered surgically and analysed. But the evidence regarding the composition of the implants – whether or not they have bizarre physical or chemical characteristics suggesting non-earthly origins – has been inconsistent."[31]

In a PBS/NOVA interview, John Mack mentioned once again: "UFOs are in fact observed, filmed on camera at the same time that people are having their abduction experiences. People, in fact, have been observed to be missing at the time that they are reporting their abduction experiences. They return from their experiences with cuts, ulcers on their bodies, triangular lesions, which follow the distribution of the experiences that they recover, of what was done to them in the craft by the surgical-like activity of these beings".

The victim of abduction can find, for example, strange drawings on their skin, such as triangles or strange signs in the form of a diamond, or a chessboard, etc. Sometimes there are impressive bruises or scars, like a round, deep scoop mark with a diameter of up to one centimetre. There are also two to ten-centimetre cuts and also multiple puncture marks. All these marks appear overnight with no apparent cause and there is no bleeding.

Another kinds of evidence is where the person in question finds clothing that bears marks and stains that could only have been made outside their home. Although as a rule, at the end of the abduction, the victim is brought back to the place where they were taken, sometimes there are also "errors". For example, a woman who was abducted from her bedroom was returned in the middle of a forest a mile away, forced to return home in her bare feet, her soles were badly cut.

Patty Layne, who was also examined by Dr. Jacobs, found after returning that she her nightgown was inside out, although she always was careful when she was asleep that this could

---

[31]   Mack, 1999, pp.14-15.

not happen. Another victim was returned to bed with wet pyjamas, and their socks, which were only worn in bed, were muddy. Another remembered that her nightdress was placed on a chair by the bed. Another abductee, Karen Morgan, had a dental prosthesis that the abductors removed, but they did not put it back so in the morning she found it on her abdomen. Others have woken in bed in unusual positions. In one case two brothers who "dreamed" that they were taken by little creatures woke up morning in one another's bed. Sceptics may well wonder if there are some connections between these cases and sleepwalking. On the other hand one could reply by asking if some supposed cases of sleepwalking were actually abductions?

On the morning after some abductions the victims found strange spots on their pillows, nightclothes and bedclothes, etc. Although at first glance they appeared to be blood stains, they were caused by an unknown substance that defied analysis and had a slightly different colour from that of the blood. The victims had no wounds or scratches to warrant the blood stains. It was supposed that the marks may have come from disinfectant liquids in which the victims were sometimes bathed during their abduction.

To these traces can be added: nasal bleeding, ruptures of the eardrum, leakage and other unjustified vaginal problems, injected eyes and impaired vision the following morning. There was also a feeling of fatigue and pain when waking up, plus other symptoms, all of which occurred at the same time as the supposed abduction and for which there was no other explanation. There are also many cases where the abduction was followed by the inexplicable healing of various conditions.

Messages and spiritual transformation

A dramatic consequence of many abductions is what Professor Mack called "*ontological shock*". For example, a person who is convinced that mankind is alone in the Universe, or that they are watched over by a heavenly God, might be forced reconsider these beliefs and admit that there are other intelligences that dominate us as they wish by using a far superior technology without asking our permission,. Not a few of the abducted said that they had the feeling of contact with a "higher cosmic consciousness". Some of them even felt the need to join or even form sects of likeminded people who worship extra-terrestrials. There are people who, after being abducted, become emotionally isolated and get a sense of alienation from those around them, or have the feeling that they are somehow "different" than other people and start to have family problems: sometimes they just wonder if they have gone crazy.

Many of those abducted, including some I met in Romania, reported that the aliens showed them apocalyptic events: "Scenes of the Earth devastated by a nuclear holocaust, vast panoramas of lifeless, polluted landscapes and waters and apocalyptic images of giant earthquakes, firestorms, floods and even fractures of the planet itself are shown by the aliens. These are powerfully disturbing to the abductees, who tend to experience them as literally predictive of the future of the planet."[32] Sometimes, these highly emotional displays are shown to very sensitive people and they are told that the Earth belongs to more than just human beings and the visions that depict an imaginary the end of the world are reminiscent of the Book of Revelation.

Some people have said that – during their abductions – they have been shown everything from romantic, sexually charged images to very ordinary things. They had the impression that the aliens watched their reactions to these images very closely. More generally, the testimonies speak of procedures, conscious or unconscious, of indoctrination and suggestion as well as both extracting and introducing information into their brains, possibly using devices connected to the brain. Dr. David Jacobs also talked also about a procedure he called a

---

[32] Mack, 1995, p.25.

"mind-scan"[33]. Some people remembered that they were told that the information received during abduction was either secret (I have also investigated such a case), or that the subject would only remember it "at the right time".

As Mack remarked, after the abduction the witnesses suffer a dramatic spiritual change. They realised that human beings are not the 'lords of the Earth', but children of the cosmos who must find their way to live in harmony with all manner of creatures on the Earth and elsewhere.[34] As an interesting aside, many of the abductees become highly concerned with pacifist and ecological issues and acquire a deep sense of love for the planet Earth and all the creatures on it. It is often a love that is accompanied by a revolt against the destruction that our species has caused to the environment.

As Jacques Vallée mentioned in a 2014 interview for *Ovnis-Direct.com*: Dr. Carl Jung didn't miss the cultural and psychological impact of the 1950s "contactees" when he noticed their appeal to powerful archetypes when they said they were in permanent contact with extra-terrestrials. For instance, twenty years before the ecologists, contactees were among the first to mention the risk of dangerous pollution of the planet.

A huge genetic experiment?

It is estimated that about half of all abduction cases also have upsetting elements suggesting that an important objective of the aliens could be a huge genetic experiment involving the human species.

My apologies to the reader for some of the details that will follow, but I only summarise the essential elements of this process as they are described in reports concerning a large number of cases. The reader can easily find many other details in books and articles by Budd Hopkins, David Jacobs, Raymond Fowler and others.

The victim of the abduction is stretched, paralysed, on a flat surface and is surrounded by alien beings. If the victim is a man his semen is harvested by a mechanical device, sometimes like a bell, or sometimes it is through sexual intercourse with a non-earthly female being. From women, an egg is harvested during ovulation. For this purpose, either a flexible tube is inserted into the vagina, or the abdomen is pierced in the umbilical area using a probe sometimes described as a large "syringe". The procedure can be painful, but it seems that the aliens have procedures (perhaps similar to hypnosis) that quickly blocks any discomfort.

The harvested egg is placed in a container that is quickly removed from the room. Some of the victims reported that aliens told them that the operation is for an *in vitro* fertilisation, possibly associated with exchanges in genetic information. The fertilised egg will then be implanted using similar procedures, into the uterus of a 'carrier mother'. Often, this is the same person from whom the egg was harvested.

Since the recollection of these operations is erased from the conscious mind of the victim, after a while they will notice that they are pregnant, but without understanding how, and sometimes despite the fact that during that period they did not have sexual intercourse.

Six to twelve weeks after the abduction, the 'carrier mother' is again subjected to an embarrassing procedure – the embryo extraction. Some witnesses spoke of a long, black device with a "cup" at the end of it, which draws out the foetus using suction while the "patient" is stretched out on the operating table or placed on a special chair. The embryo is immediately placed in a liquid inside a kind of silvery cylindrical container, which is connected to many life-sustaining devices.

The abductions are always carefully erased from the victim's conscious memory. Therefore, if the woman had previously discovered that she is pregnant (for example, using

---

[33] Jacobs, 1999.
[34] Mack, 1995, p.407.

the usual tests), after this last procedure she will find that the pregnancy has inexplicably disappeared. There have also been reports of cases in which the person concerned did not want a child and decided to abort and the doctor who carried out the procedure found that there were no foetuses. In other cases the foetus was removed by a doctor and it was the turn of the aliens to be frustrated.

If we believe these stories, we might wonder how many similar events go unnoticed, or are considered as mere disturbances or delays in the menstrual cycle, or how many mysterious false pregnancies could be explained by abduction? Physicians say that in some cases, during the first few weeks a pregnancy could be "reabsorbed" by the mother's body through natural processes. However, this process is only a hypothesis, as a half-reabsorbed foetus has never been found during an autopsy. So far, not only the abortions carried out by aliens, but also the phenomenon of "reabsorption", remain as unproven theories.

Sexually related procedures are accompanied by intense feelings of shame, embarrassment and humiliation, especially in the case of adolescents where it can be accompanied by negative effects on their subsequent psychosexual development even though they are consciously unaware of what happened. Women who have undergone such reproductive experiments may subsequently exhibit an unnatural coolness towards their children.

As I have already mentioned, according to the information received from several witnesses, the aborted hybrid foetus is immediately immersed into a vessel, described either as a "big jar" or as a "silver cylinder" which is filled with a gelatinous or water-like liquid. The foetus is than attached to other nearby devices. One of the witnesses remembered that before being placed in the container a foetus had electrodes implanted in its head and had been subjected to certain operations on its eyelids and sexual organs,.

The containers could be, as some authors suggest, "*artificial wombs*", in used to mature the hybrid foetuses aborted in these genetic experiments. Many abducted people said they saw "on board the ships" rows with tens or hundreds of such translucent containers in which foetuses floated. Other witnesses reported that, during their abduction, they saw rooms where foetuses were lying in a liquid or dry environment, in drawers serving the role of *incubators*. Other witnesses talk about rooms where there were up to a hundred small children, being cared for by feminine, non-earthly beings. The little ones had a dull and sickly appearance and were lying on a variety of beds or transparent boxes, all of which were placed in rows.

A few years after the "birth" of the small creatures (that is, their extraction from the container when they could survive on their own), there is another strange phase called the "*presentation ceremony*". The same woman – from whom the egg was taken and who was also the carrier mother – is once again abducted and she is confronted with the little hybrid beings, which are more-or-less like earthly children, but extraordinarily placid and seemingly super-intelligent. The woman is told that they are her children, who "need their mother" and she is then invited to embrace them to convey the affection specific to maternal love. After this human contact the hybrids seem to "look better". On departure the mother is told that, unfortunately, the children cannot go with her because they would not survive in earthly conditions.

No matter how much like a hallucination the above scenario looks, its details have been confirmed by hundreds of people all over the world and the reader can find the details, along with names, places and times many of the books about Ufology already mentioned plus other sources. It is unlikely that all of these accounts have been caused by media contamination and I personally have obtained reports of events like these occurring in Romania.

Budd Hopkins and especially Prof. David Jacobs were convinced that these testimonies are evidence that a central objective of various UFO visitors is a huge program of hybridisation of the human race.[35]

Other ufologists have noticed that signs of such procedures can even be found in the oldest traditions. Is it not somehow – they asked – an ongoing process, started hundreds of thousands of years ago? Even some palaeontologists have wondered if human evolution was faster than natural mutations would have allowed. They asked themselves if there was there any external intervention to improve the human race? This possibility could put an end to the contradiction between creationism and evolutionism. According to the intervention hypothesis, mankind could indeed have been created by a cosmic intelligence, but not starting from nothing, but by gradually improving already existing creatures. It is somehow continuing this intervention today using the genetic experiments or hybridisation described by the alleged victims of UFO abductions?

Auxiliary human reserves?

On the evening of July 4, 1989 in Kiev, in the "Hydropark" on an island in the Dnieper river, two women and a child, Vera Prokofievna Ignatenko and Alexandra Stepanovna, plus her six-year-old daughter, met three extremely tall individuals in an alley. These beings had bright eyes and long blond hair and were dressed in a sort of silvery nightgowns. They closely resembled one other as if they were triplets. The women asked if they are foreigners, and they replied in Russian, but with a strange accent, that they are extra-terrestrials, and that they regularly selected people Earth people to take with them to their planet, which was, according to them,' beyond the power of understanding of the witnesses'. Now – they said – they would like to take them...

As proof they showed a giant silver barrel with a circular antenna above it which was sitting in the bushes nearby. The women were terrified and wanted to scream and flee, but they felt paralysed and by a stinging sensation that affected their whole bodies. Eventually they managed to say they wanted to stay on Earth, that they had families, children and responsibilities. The three beings seemed to have been persuaded, saying: "Well, we will not take you with us; we will find others". They climbed into the barrel, which in a few seconds, took off and disappeared.

Interestingly, on the same evening another family called, Iskuskov reported independently that in the same area they saw beings with the same appearance. At the time the event received unexpectedly good media coverage. In fact in this location of the former USSR, there are several stories about similar abduction attempts, so we might wonder how many "permanent abductions" have been successfully completed.

Ukrainian ufologist Anton A. Anfalov said that Lieutenant Colonel (ret.) Sergei M. Paukov, who worked in the army's counter-intelligence, told him that there was official data from the Interior Ministry of the Ukraine, stating that every year three to four thousand people from this part of the country disappear without trace. Of these, it is estimated that about 5% of them (150-200 people) are permanently abducted by the aliens and never return to Earth.

There are many other stories about the permanent disappearance of people, the best known are those from Bermuda Triangle, but there are many other, similar places on Earth. As an example, a well-documented case is that of Frederick Valentich, aged twenty, who was flying alone on October 21, 1978, over the Tasman Sea in a small plane. At one point, Frederick radioed his destination airport that he was being followed by a cigarette-shaped object without wings, it had four very powerful green lights, and it was "orbiting" above the

---

[35] Hopkins, 1988, Jacobs, 1993, and Jacobs, 1999.

little plane. The aircraft engine has begun malfunctioning and Valentich signalled his position and confirmed the presence of the object, then there was a sharp metallic sound followed by silence. In spite of prolonged searches, no trace of the plane, the pilot, or any wreckage was ever found.

If there are permanent abductions where would the victims be transferred to? Several people, especially from the former Soviet Union, said they had encountered UFOs and their occupants who invited them to take a trip. When they accepted, they arrived on strange worlds where they met people like those on Earth. It was explained to them that these places were "reserves" for human beings set up on other planets, or perhaps on space stations, or perhaps even in another reality. Without entering into details, here are three Russian examples. The first is Anatolii Malishev's famous case, who said that he was abducted on July 21st, 1975, from Solnechnogorsk area, near Moscow, by a beautiful blue-eyed woman and two other people. They had come to a strange planet, but the landscape was like earth. He arrived in a building that moved about in all directions, and he saw a small ball of bright light metamorphosed into a man, then back to a bright ball. He also met giants and dwarves and also with some acquaintances who he knew were dead. Soon, the same ship returned him to Earth. After he told of his adventure, Malishev was examined by some experts, including a sociologist, a psychologist and a psychiatrist and he also passed rigorous medical examinations. He was also subjected to a hypnotic regression and no inconsistencies could be found in his account.

Another case happened on the night of 30/31 August 1978, with a youngster from Moscow called M. Markov, who was on holiday at Planerskoe in the Crimea. He suddenly felt the urge to bathe in the Black Sea and shortly after entering the water he saw a strange light. Without warning he found himself in an enclosure, he later called it "a robot UFO", and it had the ability to converse with him, he did not see anyone else on board. He was asked if he wanted to go to another planet with a much higher level of civilization where many earth people already lived. He hesitated, but then said he agreed provided that, after a while, he could return home. He was told that this is not possible, because if he returned he would die.

The third example is that of Viaceslav Gorbunov who reported that, in August 1989, he was living in an isolated cottage in the Vologda region. At one point a strange entity invited him to go on a trip in a round silvery ship; there was already a woman inside it. They arrived at what appeared to be another planet where he saw peaceful scenes of children playing, meadows, gushing fountains etc. but Gorbunov insisted on returning home and he was brought back to his cottage. After this incident his personality changed, and he gave up his lonely life and decided that his mission in this world was to help his fellows. He began to paint spectacular, surrealistic scenes, apparently depicting landscapes from other planets; the paintings were exhibited at several places in Russia.

Speculation about places where human specimens and possibly animals might have been taken also come from America. Psychiatrist Dr. Edith Fiore recalled that her patient, Diane Tai ,was abducted by a UFO[36] and, on this occasion, she saw herself in the middle of a group of people of all races. One of her abductors explained that they had followed human evolution for thousands and thousands of years and about 40,000 years ago, they have taken many earthlings to their planet, possibly to develop new human species. In other abductions the witnesses were told that earthly civilization would self-destruct (or be victim to some cataclysm) therefore aliens had decided to transfer a number of specimens to remote and safe locations in the cosmos.

Courtney Brown, Ph.D. (b. 1952) is an associate professor in the political science department at Emory University, Atlanta (Georgia), and a practitioner of remote viewing

---

[36] Fiore, 1990,

techniques. He wrote in one of his books[37] that, using such techniques, in March 1994, he "travelled" to a planet, where he saw people who had brought there at the end of the twentieth century. The ambience was pleasant, but people seemed confused and frightened. The masters of this place, some "greys", told Brown that the people he saw had been taken there by them, because the Earth was threatened by a catastrophe and one solution was the rescue human specimens and relocate them on other planets. Not only would human beings be transferred there, but also various earthly animals and plants, etc. People brought here would be educated in a spiritual manner to develop more harmonious ties between the physical body and the immortal soul.

Aliens perform genetic manipulation on earthlings for the same purpose. The manipulation is intended, among other things, to diminish our aggressive and destructive, tendencies, which are specific to human species and are, in large part, responsible for the catastrophic ecological and climatic changes on Earth.

If we accept that behind all these stories there is also a kernel of truth, it means that a "higher consciousnesses" that monitors us – perhaps from *hyper-civilizations* – have established some "*subsidiary reserves*", using earthly fauna, most likely in places beyond our present understanding. They permanently transfer people to these places, along with other creatures, as in a new, multiple, Noah's ark awaiting the catastrophic events of the future.

It was accept this scenario, we might speculate further that in these "subsidiary reserves", many thousands of years ago, new human races with a larger brain, superior intelligence, and other skills, might have been produced. Possibly they were specialised races, adapted for certain special tasks using genetic material from Earth. Some ufologists have wondered if perhaps certain aliens (greys and, Nordics, etc.) described in the alleged abductions, are in fact artificial or even "biorobot" human races, derived from the human species, and grown somewhere outside the Earth and sent back to us with precise tasks on short missions.

Species are extremely malleable. One only has to consider that from wolves, 10-15,000 years ago, people created, without any genetic engineering a surprising variety of breeds of domestic dogs, which have achieved various dimensions and appearance. The same principle holds true of cattle. As another example and also through selection, agricultural scientists have produced new varieties of wheat from traditional strains. But sometimes – it is known – the "perfect" variety of wheat can become vulnerable to new diseases or encounter some other issues. In these cases, the specialists will return to the genetic strains of the primitive wheat species and, through cross-breeding with them, create the new "perfect" variety.

In abduction cases similar operations might be performed, for example, some abductees reported that aliens told them that the genetic experiments are necessary because "their own species has lost its reproductive capacity" and they need to create hybrids of them and us. Would our species be like a "gene bank", corresponding to the "wild" variety of grain, and used periodically to improve any defects in hybrid races that exist in other realms? In this case, the issue of genetic compatibility between the visitors and us would also disappear. This issue, to which I will return, also occurs in other contexts.

But if the visitors have been here, not for tens of thousands, but for tens of millions of years, (which is not impossible), they could have 'subsidiary reserves', not only humans, but also of animals that have long since disappeared from Earth; for example some species of dinosaurs. This speculative hypothesis, if true, would provide an explanation for the reports about intelligent reptilian creatures that are sometimes mentioned. Staying on this hypothesis, we could find also explanations for the impossible sightings of animals that no longer exist on Earth (including Chupacabras) or perhaps even cattle mutilation.

---

[37] Brown, 1996, chapter 12.

In a 2014 interview for *Ovnis-Direct.com*, Jacques Vallée spoke about, "A series of reports of crypto-zoological phenomena that were co-located with well-documented observations of UFOs. Witnesses of these events were ranchers, industrial workers and policemen (including the tribal police). In general, those reports are not published."

What would be the purpose of hybridisation at this moment? Of the many variants proposed the most plausible seem to be, at least for me, the creation of super-intelligent or super-performing varieties of humans. This might be designed to create a much gentler and less aggressive kind of human being and if all the above is true, it follows that the "aliens" described by those who experience close encounters are, in fact, just intermediaries. In this case we can ask the rhetorical question: Who created them, what do they look like and where do they come from?

Looking for an explanation

In spite of the thousands of thoroughly investigated cases, (of which only a few have been mentioned here), we are still not able to accept the reality of the abduction phenomenon. We are again experiencing the same cultural blindness we talked about in the case of UFOs and hyper-civilizations. The phenomenon will be rejected, not only by the followers of mainstream science, but also by others, using the same old argument that extra-terrestrial abductions do not exist because, according to out current knowledge, "they cannot happen". Another reaction could be that that these abductions cannot be taken seriously because they have not been reported to the police as kidnappings.

The abductions cannot be proven experimentally as science requires, because a sceptic cannot observe the act of abduction, nor can it be brought into a laboratory to be studied. As for testimonies – that continue to multiply – debunkers say that witnesses are not proof, because human memory can be untrustworthy. Such stories – say the sceptics – are probably due to dreams, or the affects of powerful electromagnetic fields, pathological conditions, media contamination, or collective hysteria and so forth. And this does not include the possibility that the accounts are nothing more than the inventions of ufologists producing increasingly sensational stories.

For example – sceptics say –alien abduction is in fact due to false memories created by incompetent therapists conducting hypnotic regression sessions and asking inappropriate or leading questions. Psychotherapist John Carpenter responded to this accusation by saying that a quarter of the abduction details (others said even more) are consciously recalled. And many of the details recalled consciously are the same as those recovered through hypnosis. Carpenter tried to suggest various alternative and more credible scenarios to witnesses under hypnosis, but he encountered resistance as the people in question stuck to their version of events. British investigator Jenny Randles has asked several (non-abducted) people to imagine they had been abducted by a UFO and to describe in detail, including using drawings, what happened to them. Their descriptions were completely different from the reports of "real" abductions. Thomas Bullard stressed that a competent hypnotist does not essentially influence the abduction record. David Jacobs added that his hypnotic regressions were not used until all conscious the memories had been obtained and hypnosis was only used to obtain details about the chronology of the events. Jacobs also underlined that properly conducted hypnosis cannot generate "additional fantasies".

An explanation often used for abductions is that the subject may feel paralysed and may have dreams between wakefulness and sleeping, which they perceive as reality while in 'hypnagogic' and 'hypnopompic' states. These states occur naturally while an individual is either falling asleep or awakening. Although this possibility cannot be excluded, in most cases the abductions begin and continue while in the waking state. David Jacobs wrote that, of the 669 abductions he had personally examined, only 277 people were asleep when the abduction began, while the remaining nearly sixty percent were driving, walking or watching TV and so on. Budd Hopkins said: "In the first twenty years, all major UFO abduction took place outside the house, while the victims were in the car, on the tractor, or were walking, fishing, etc." and nobody had been paralysed in the bedroom. He also showed that many of the abductions involved two, three, six or even more witnesses, who later gave similar descriptions. Sometimes during abductions UFOs were seen, photographed, or filmed, by somebody else. In other examples people were seen to have disappeared from where they had been when the abduction took place. Other physical traces, such as marks left on the ground by a landed UFO, have also been observed.

John Mack commented that abduction is often perceived as a dream, but that does not mean that all abductions are dreams. He pointed out that sometimes abductions take place in an awakened state, but psychologically the victim will feel "more comfortable" to believe that everything was just a dream. Of course, on the other hand not every dream about abduction, or about non-human beings, conceals a genuine case of abduction.

As I have already pointed out, abductions often leave physical traces of aggression on the victim's body: strange pigments, bruises, wounds, nasal bleeding, scars that did not exist the previous day and unexplained gynaecological phenomena, etc. The idea that all of these events could be signs of sleepwalking, or stigmatic marks resembling the wounds of the crucified Christ, believed to appear on the bodies of certain individuals and induced by autosuggestion – cannot be accepted.

It has also been said that the stories about aliens encountered in childhood could be "screen memories" meant to mask sexual and/or physical abuse suffered in childhood. Budd Hopkins and David Jacobs rejected this explanation, pointing out that, among other things, children are usually taken to investigators by parents who are concerned about the stories they tell.

Many psychotherapists may have come close to explaining the phenomenon of abductions by suggesting that they mask 'psychic suffering', such as a dissociated personality. It is true that a small percentage of those who say they have been abducted are mentally ill and the abductions are part of their delirium. They say they are in contact with beings on other planets and that aliens scan their minds, but the stories they tell are inconsistent and incoherent. These persons are removed from the lists of cases. The "true" abductees report the same details and the same scenario, but they do not confuse fantasies with everyday reality. Numerous psychological tests (Rorschach, Wechsler, etc.), conducted on witnesses of alleged abductions did not reveal any kind of insanity. They people involved were not schizoid, paranoid or emotionally immature people. Instead, these witnesses desperately wanted to find someone to give them a confidential explanation for their experiences.

Hallucinations are also unlikely, because they usually consist of images previously seen by the patient mixed with geometric and other elements, etc Another argument against hallucinations is that many abductions have two or more witnesses, who independently report the same story. Hysterical contagion, where people can share a delusion, is also suggested as a possible explanation, but is unsatisfactory. John Mack, who examined and tested over a hundred cases, also rejected other explanations such as: lies, fantasy prone personality, hypnotisability, dissociated personality and so on.

Paul Devereaux and Michael Persinger, both professors of psychology, were convinced that the phenomenon is caused by hallucinatory states, induced in the temporal lobe of brains of some people, by the proximity of high voltage lines and radio or TV transmitters, or by electromagnetic fields generated by the tectonic stress in the Earth's crust. But not all victims were in the vicinity of these sources. Similarly, some specialists have blamed abductions on temporal lobe epilepsy, but investigation of a significant number of abductees showed that they were not suffering from this condition. In addition, this hypothesis cannot explain the similarity of many of the details reported.

Equally unconvincing as a solution to all abductions, are the explanations suggesting secret military experiments such as mind control projects, implants, hallucinogens, or similar techniques, these explanations were suggested by Helmut Lammer, a doctor of geophysics, employed by the Institute of Space Research in Graz (Austria). He believes that in addition to genuine UFO abductions (in whose reality he believes), there are also UFO abductions staged for various purposes by certain military groups. These are sometimes called 'MILABS' or Military Abductions

John Mack underlined that "A theory that would begin to explain the abduction phenomena will have to account for five basic dimensions. These are: (1) The high degree of consistency of detailed abduction accounts reported with emotion appropriate to actual experiences told by apparently reliable observers. (2) The absence of psychiatric illnesses or other apparent psychological or emotional factors that could account for what is being reported. (3) The physical changes and lesions affecting the bodies of the experiencers, which follow no evident psychodynamic pattern. (4) The association with UFOs witnessed independently by others while abductions are taking place (which the abductee may not see). (5) The reports of abductions by children as young as two or three years of age... Clearly, no explanation that addresses all of these elements is apparent at the present time."[38]

Mack said also that "I cannot discourage those who try to discover conventional explanations for the abduction phenomenon. I would only point out that, as a clinician, I have spent countless hours trying to find alternate explanations that would not require the major shift in my world-view that I have had to face. But... no familiar theory or explanation has come even close to accounting for the basic features of the abduction phenomenon."[39]

The distinguished professor asserted that the necessity to find alternative, natural explanations for this phenomenon comes either from those who do not understand the complexity of the abduction phenomenon. Or from people so stuck in their narrow vision of reality that they cannot accept anything else. For example people incapable of accepting the possibility that we are being investigated by unearthly intelligences. Mack found it interesting that there are individuals who "find unacceptable the idea that such experiences might actually be occurring. These individuals might believe in the existence of a personal God or a supreme being, yet not find possible that cosmic entities such as these might enter our physical and mental world."[40]

CONCLUSIONS

Further evidence of the presence of hyper-civilizations around us could be alien abductions. They happen all over the world and are based on the same scenario and are composed of the same stages with the same details. Thousands of cases have been thoroughly examined by academics without finding an acceptable explanation.

The abductions are carried out with discretion and those who control them try to erase the memory of the incident's from the victim's mind. The collected testimonies outline two possible objectives of this process: a hybridisation program, mainly for the improvement of the human species and the other of indoctrination, to make us more aware of our environment and of the future of mankind, both of these objectives are pursued without altering our cultural norms.

---

[38] Mack, 1995, pp.28-29
[39] idem p.398
[40] idem p.431

Aliens that come into direct contact with the abducted might be bio-robots, or members of new human races or even some new species derived from our ancestors. Could it be possible that their creators, who seem to stay behind the scenes, are the representatives of hyper-civilizations?

TRADITIONS

They could be here long ago

A *hyper-civilization* might have had the ability for hundreds of millions of years to move freely throughout the Universe. If we accept this, it is almost certain that they explored and inventoried our Galaxy down to the smallest detail. It's impossible for them not to have noticed the very special conditions that existed on our planet. Therefore, it is likely that the Earth and its creatures have been under their protection ever since.

Therefore, representatives of *hyper-civilizations* could have discreetly installed for the watchers of the reserve, maybe in underground cavities or at the bottom of the ocean or in other hidden places. Some "out-of-place artefacts" (*Ooparts*) could be signs of their past activity. But these observation posts could also be placed in other areas of the Solar System, or even in parallel dimensions (if such things exist) that are inaccessible to us, but which could be convenient for them.

The permanent presence of these hyper-civilizations around us and the more or less random encounters with some of their representatives could be recorded in the collective memory of our ancestors in the form of fairy tales, myths, religious texts and so on. The stories about "wheels of fire", or "heavenly chariots" in which non-earthly or Divine creatures travel, or fight, are found in almost all the traditions and beliefs of mankind. There are also stories about human heroes, for example the mythical King Etana of Mesopotamia, who, according to what is written on clay tablets, rose up in space with the help of a "magic eagle", to a place where the Earth was no longer visible (the description of the journey is surprisingly realistic). According to Chinese legends a flying chariot carried Emperor Huang Di (the "golden dragon"). Four kinds of heavenly vehicles – called "vimana" – are described, with a remarkable abundance of technical details, in the Rigveda and the Ramayana, or Mahabharata – all of which are Sanskrit texts older than the Bible.

Many old writings that have survived to this day relate to unexplainable aerial events. A good account of these can be found in the volume, *Wonders in the Sky: Unexplained Aerial Objects from Antiquity to Modern Times*, by Jacques Vallée and Chris Aubeck[41], which contains five hundred selected cases, from 1500 BC, until 1900 AD. Among them, it is written that in 1460 BC Thutmosis III defeated his enemies in Asia, aided by a fantastic celestial event. In 1347 BC, Pharaoh Akhenaton saw a "shining disk" descending from the sky and heard a voice demanding instructions. According to a fourth-century book by Julius Obsequens, in 464 BC in Rome, a burning object appeared in the sky accompanied by shapes and strange figures, which frightening the witnesses. In 404 BC, the Athenian general Thrasybulus, preparing for war against the Spartans, was guided by a glowing pillar in the sky. In 218 BC, in Amiterno, Italy, "A phantom navy was seen shining in the sky... beings in human shape and clothed in white were seen at a distance, but no one came close to them". In 216 BC, at Arpi, "shields had been seen in the sky". In 122 BC in Arminium, Italy, "A huge luminous body lit up the sky and three moons rose together". In 76 BC, in Rome, a spark fell from a star, became as big as the Moon and went up again. In 12 BC, in the clear sunny sky, a red-whitish, 30-metre-long object hovered for several hours and threw off fiery sparks. All over the world many other similar cases followed in the next centuries. It is interesting to note that in Rome in 1513 even Michelangelo saw a "triangular sign" on a calm night. It was bright with three tails, one silvery, the second red and the third flaming and bifurcated. Michelangelo was so impressed that he made a painting of it, which unfortunately hasn't

---

[41] Vallée, 2009.

84

survived. In the same century there were two similar reports from Romania. All these cases prove, once again, that the UFO phenomenon is not specific to one time period but has been accompanying mankind throughout our existence.

Fairies, dwarfs and the control system

in the sixties Jacques Vallée was probably the first to notice that UFO encounters, and abductions, are only modern forms of incidents that have been present throughout history and have entered into our collective memory in the form of fairy tales complete with dwarfs, fairies, elves, trolls and gnomes, etc. These tales were not bedtime stories invented for children, but a distorted and embellished memory of real events from the past.

Vallée recalls a fragment from the writings of Saint Agobard (779-840), archbishop of Lyon, in which he denounces those who believe that there is a region called *Magonia*, "Out of which ships come out and sail upon the clouds; these ships transport to that same region the fruits that have fallen because of the hail and have been destroyed by the storm". Agobard stressed that he was present when "three men and a woman said to have fallen from these ships". After a few days of captivity they were brought to the crowd to be stoned. Agobard's intervention, which convinced the people that such a trip was impossible, saved the lives of the four.[42]

Vallée notes that *Magonia* (the land of magicians, from Latin "*magus*" meaning magician) also appears in various other stories. It is sometimes a distant country, an invisible island or even a part of heaven, but also a kind of parallel universe which coexists with ours. In this latter form, it only becomes visible and tangible to chosen people and the means of passage from one world to the next are known only to goblins and those people who have been instructed by them. Vallée also quotes the writings of the Reverend Robert Kirk of Aberfoyle (Scotland), in 1691, and also the documents written by medieval and Renaissance scholars such as Facius Cardan and Paracelsus. They tried to explain the popular contemporary beliefs concerning airborne beings that apparently interfere with human activities. Among other things, they thought that miraculous creatures such as fairies, goblins, etc. form a special category along with three others: angels, the devil (with his demons) and the souls of the dead. Aside from human abductions, the people of those times believed that beings from the air were essentially benevolent, sincere and capable of helping the needy.

Vallée also analysed works by modern folklorists, for example the anthropologist Walter Evans-Wentz and his work: *The Fairy-Faith in Celtic Countries* (1911) where he spoke of beings living in underground castles, where they are forever young, and sometimes abducted young, intelligent people, and if an abducted person ate their food, they could never return home. Stories about such places, which resemble those regarding permanent UFO abductions, can be found in the folklore of many peoples, including that of Romania.

Based on these examples, Jacques Vallée concluded that the UFO phenomenon is intrinsic and has long been linked to our Earth. "The UFO occupants, like the elves of the old, are not extra-terrestrials. They are denizens of another reality... The same power attributed to the saucer people was once the exclusive property of the fairies."[43] For Jacques Vallée, the UFO phenomenon, and everything associated with it, is proof of the existence of other dimensions beyond space and time, "What we see here is not an alien invasion, it is a spiritual system that acts on humans and uses humans... UFOs could come from Earth without necessarily being human inventions, or they could come from another galaxy without necessarily being spacecraft."[44] "I propose that there is a spiritual control system for human

---

[42] Vallée, 1969.
[43] Vallée, 1989, p. 96, 134.
[44] Vallée, 1989, p.253

85

consciousness and that paranormal phenomena like UFOs are one of its manifestations. I cannot tell whether this control is natural and spontaneous; whether it is explainable in terms of genetics, of social psychology, or of ordinary phenomena – or if it is artificial in nature, under the power of some superhuman will. It may be entirely determined by laws that we have not yet discovered."[45] Vallée added that, of course, for those who care about their peace of mind, the simplest way is to deny the reality of all these facts.

J. Allen Hynek gradually adopted a similar opinion, declaring, for example, in 1976: "I have come to support less and less the idea that UFOs are 'nuts and bolts' spacecrafts from other worlds."[46] Also important are the opinions of Thomas Ed. Bullard Ph.D., a folklorist, and a participant in the 1992 abduction Conference at M.I.T., who obtained his doctorate at Indiana State University with a thesis on UFOs and their correlation with folklore themes. He published his thesis in 1988 under the title: *UFO Abductions: The Measure of a Mystery*. In his works he emphasises that folklore is full of beings from distant worlds; fairies or dwarfs are a constant in popular beliefs everywhere. In many traditions the fairies abduct people and lead them to subterranean kingdoms in which time flows at a different speed than on Earth. In many popular traditions, beings that come from another land steal or replace children and/or have sexual intercourse with human beings. All these features are reminiscent of modern UFO abductions. Other common historical aspects concerning encounters with fabulous beings and UFO abductions, also involve beings of small size, "missing time" and even stopping vehicles.

And we can see such myths everywhere, not only with the Australian aborigines, pygmies and Eskimos, but also in the folklore of many European nations. The similarity of all these traditions with the UFO phenomenon is striking and cannot be solely attributed to fantasy or coincidence.

Even today

In Romanian folk traditions there are "*wheels of fire*" that emerge from the night sky and rotate at an amazing speed and when they touch the earth they can turn into human-looking beings. Then there are the "*flyers*", male beings who descend from the heavens and then return and who come at night to the houses of young women and have sex with them. There are also children who appear from nowhere as playmates and then disappear without trace, etc. It was said that the Romanian forests have always been inhabited by female beings called "*Iele*", that abduct young people or children. These traditions were studied and described in detail by Romanian scholars such as Dimitrie Cantemir, a member of the Royal Academy of Berlin, in *Descriptio Moldaviae* (1716), and also Mircea Eliade (1907-1986) who talks about them throughout his works.

A Romanian specialist in mythology, Victor Kernbach, wrote that according to folk traditions, the Iele "live in the air, in forests, or in caves in the mountains, on cliffs, or on the shores of waters, in the weeds, or at crossroads; they often bathe in pure springs; and are believed to appear mainly at night by moonlight, they rotate in dance in remote locations and their where they dance remains burnt as if by fire, the grass can no longer grow at this place and the tree limbs nearby are also scorched". They can fly "without wings and can move at fabulous speeds, covering 'nine seas and nine countries' in just one night"; "all those who have managed to learn to sing the songs of the fairies are abducted and disappear without a trace"[47]. The ethnologist Nicolae Densuşianu (1846-1911) wrote that the Iele are "spirits with

---

[45] idem, p.243
[46] Vallée, 1992, p. 290.
[47] Kernbach, 1995

female faces, walking at night, playing and dancing". At the place where they walk, "the grass no longer grows", "a red horseshoe shape remains in the grass", or "the grass becomes a black circle". The Iele "bring musicians with them who "play the bagpipes". They "light candles" and play and dance in a circle in amongst the trees. They carry the people they meet "through the air, leaving them 'stupid' for the rest of their lives".

The above bears striking similarities to the UFO phenomenon and could not be attributed to coincidence: the nocturnal appearances, the airborne origin, the rotation of light, the attraction to the water sources, the residue left behind, the damage to the surrounding trees, the noise of a bagpipe, the fantastic speed of travel, the abduction of some people, as well as the sexual component.

In ancient times the reported events involving fairies, dwarfs and other, similar creatures, were considered normal and were treated seriously. It was only in the last four centuries following the European culture of rationalism, that such things were declared impossible and the old stories were considered as just simple metaphors, or "fairy-tales" intended for the amusement of children. But in many places, even today, these "folkloric" beings are still mentioned. In Romania for example, there are areas where even now people say they encountered "wheels of fire", "flying" or "Iele". I shall only talk about one case that I personally examined.

D.B. was born in 1968, in the north of Romania not far from the city of Sighetu Marmației. He told me that at the age of six he met and spent a time with a group of miraculous children of his age, they were supervised by a beautiful woman with white and shiny hair, about 2.5 meters high or perhaps slightly more. She was the famous "*Maid of the Woods*", a (sometimes wicked) fairy (like the "Iele"), which is known to the natives of the entire Maramureş region of Romania, which crossing Ukraine up to Slovakia. Many even said that they have met her or heard her singing. The locals are afraid of her, because there is a belief that she stole or killed the children she encountered, she sometimes also attracted young people who become non-human after encountering her. D.B. said he has seen her several times.

The "Maid of the Woods" was once seen in the context of a close encounter (possibly an abduction) with a UFO, from which she descended and then returned. I obtained a description of this encounter from two witnesses (D.B. and his mother), who gave two separate versions of the event.[48]

I am convinced that similar fairy-stories exist in many other parts of Europe and elsewhere, especially in those places where the taboo of the "such a thing cannot exist, does not exist and you are stupid if you talk about that" has not yet taken control. The additional feature of a childhood encounter with other children appearing from nowhere appears in many cases documented in ufological or paranormal literature. Among others, the famous medium Edgar Cayce, in a letter written 1933, explains that in his childhood, from the age of two, he occasionally had some strange playmates of his own age who came from an unknown place and could instantly disappear. Cayce's "readings" make many references to fairies and other spirits of nature, such as elves, gnomes, nymphs, angels and so on.

Crop circles

According to popular belief, after the dance of fairies a ring remains burned in the grass. This draws our attention to another phenomenon: *crop circles*. At harvest time in the wheat, barley or rye fields and sometimes also in the meadows there are bizarre circles, often multiple, in which the stalks are laid on the ground. Recently, complicated geometric figures of surprising beauty and forming strange pictograms have emerged. Every year, between a thousand and two

---

[48]   A more detailed description is in: Farcas, 2016, along with other such cases.

thousand formations appear, particularly in England, the United States, Canada, Japan, Australia, New Zealand, but also in many European countries. In Romania the first crop circles that appeared were in wheat and were reported in 1994 and also in 1996, they also appeared sporadically later.

Although most of the complex crop circles, sometimes called "*agrogliphs*", are unquestionably hoaxes, there are also others of unknown origin. In these, the stalks are bent but unbroken at 90^0, apparently the result of microwaves. In the most affected areas night time wake-up campaigns were organised using appropriate equipment, these detected small flying fireballs plus lights and sounds etc. Sometimes they were also filmed, but these recordings have not been authenticated.

The phenomenon is not only produced in cereal crops and in January 1966 in Queensland, Australia, mysterious circles were found in the reeds of a marsh that was inaccessible to people because of the presence of extremely venomous snakes. Similar circles have also been found in ice fields, at the bottom of the gullies, and in virgin forests, etc. In addition, most cereal crop circles have no trace of any humans passing through the cultivated field. It has also been said that the crop circles could be the result of special weather conditions, or of the action of mushrooms or of other natural factors, which is highly unlikely.

The crop circle phenomenon is old and the first document about circles in cereal crops dates from 815 and was written in Lyon in France. An English woodcut, published in 1678, depicts the so-called "Mowing-Devil", a creature with a scythe, apparently mowing (cutting) two concentric circles in a field of oats.

References to mysterious circles that appear in grain fields or in grass are also found in the book "Russian Folk Tales" by I. P. Sacharov, published in 1885 at St. Petersburg, as well as in other, earlier Russian folk tales. It was also said that between 1940 and 1943, in the UK, MI5 investigated a number of these formations in the British crop fields, suspecting that they might be signals for German pilots.

Shaping the human species?

Journalist Zecharia Sitchin (1920-2010) speculated about a Sumerian text that was at least a thousand years older than the oldest biblical writings. He interpreted it as evidence that the beings called the *Anunnaki* ("those who came from Heaven to Earth" in Sumerian) could have created the human species 445,000 years ago, through genetic engineering, including *in-vitro* fertilisation techniques, carried out on some hominids. Their intent may have been to use them as slaves in gold mines. This scenario is highly dubious, as it would be much easier to use robots on some other lifeless, gold-bearing planet as there are many in Universe. However, the supposition makes many of us wonder if the hypothetical *hyper-civilizations* could have played a role in creating and/or improving the human species?

Countless traditions say that the first humans were created by heavenly or supernatural creatures. But in many cultures, there are also allusions to the fact that, after this primordial act, there has been a continuous activity of *improving* the human species. The heroes of ancient Greece were considered to be hybrids born of earthly mothers and fathers descended from Olympus. Starting with the Sumerian deities (or demons) Lilu and Lilitu and continuing with the *incubus* and *succubus* of Roman mythology, many folk traditions mention fabulous beings from other realms that visit women and men during the night to have sex with them. The Roman historian Suetonius said that Emperor Augustus was the result of a relationship between his mother and an "incubus"; this was also said of: Plato, Alexander the Great, Caesar, the legendary sorcerer Merlin and many others. Beings of this type are present in the myths and legends of many peoples, among which are the Romanian legends of the "flyer".

A medieval theologian named Sinistrari, left us a work showing that in his era the clerics were as puzzled by the multitude of reports concerning the incubus and succubus, as modern UFO researchers are about the apparent genetic experiments that occur during abductions. Sinistrari was intrigued that the beings (in effect demons) that were involved in these encounters did not submit to exorcism (as anything Satanic did) and did not fear sacred relics or other holy objects. Consequently, he concluded that these demons did not fall into the same category as the devils that manifested during cases of possession.

If the reader does not believe these arguments to convincing enough, let me make an analogy between the activity of these "demons" and the UFO abductions where genetic interference is involved. Jacques Vallée discovered that in a French calendar from the 15th century, there are images in which "demons are depicted piercing their victims' abdomen with long needles", which is very similar to the accounts of witnesses to UFO abductions. Stories about the inhabitants of magical worlds abducting or changing children are other examples of the similarity between the genetic experiments that appear to take place in UFO abductions and those that have, for centuries, appeared in folklore.

Shamans and the star people

John Mack has noticed that in traditional societies that do not put a barrier between the material and the spiritual world, the UFO phenomenon, as well as encounters with humanoids descending from the sky, are considered to be something that is almost normal, or at least events that don't need to be reported. My colleagues and I have had the opportunity to observe the same attitude present in the population of some isolated, rural communities in Romania.

In the same way Mack thought that "today's UFO abductees are continuing an amply documented tradition of ascent and extra-terrestrial communication." [49] He quotes Mircea Eliade, who wrote that archaic myths worldwide speak of an extremely close relationship that originally existed between Heaven and Earth. "In *illo tempore*, the gods came down to Earth and mingled with men and men, for their part, could go up to Heaven" [50]. At some point, the connection with the sky was lost and mankind entered into its present state, where only a small number of special members of each culture, such as shamans, could continue to move between heaven and earth, between the people and the world of spirits.

Thomas Bullard and the Romanian historian Ioan P. Culianu, have revealed impressive similarities between UFO abductions and shamanic initiation: in both cases there are times when the subject does not know what happened, there are also out of the body experiences and transportation into a different world. There is also uniform lighting without any visible source, and they are often subjected to a frightening examination. It is normal for them to experience a complete transformation of how they think and act after these encounters . Bullard said the resemblances are too close to ignore.

In his book *Passport to the Cosmos*[51], Mack examined three examples in detail. One is Vusamazulu Credo Mutwa (b. 1921), who is a leading 'sangoma', a well-known, top-level traditional healer from the South African Zulu population. He told Professor Mack that, in 1958, while looking for herbal remedies in a desert he was suddenly enveloped by a bluish fog; everything around him became silent and then he saw himself in a room with curved metallic walls. He was stretched, naked and paralysed, on a table surrounded by at least six creatures that looked like dolls. The smell was, "electric, mixed with chemicals". He was subjected to humiliating experiences including sexual ones, similar to those reported in other

---

[49]   Mack, 1995, p.439
[50]   Eliade, 1957, p.59
[51]   Mack, 1999.

abduction reports. When he got out and found his way home, he learned that he had been absent for three days.

The Zulu population have known of such incidents "for thousands of years" and call the abductors "mantindane". According to Credo Mutwa, these creatures "Share Earth with us. They need us. They use us. They harvest things from us." Mutwa believes that a great intelligence, "Something which covers several galaxies", created the Earth, but he regards this intelligence as something material or "machinelike" rather than a God.[52]

The second example is from northern Brazil, where there are frequent accounts of unidentified flying objects that can either be silent or emit a very sharp sound and sometimes they appear as bright globes floating above water. The shamans sometimes speak about entities coming from the heavens and about strange women abducting men and leading them to places where unearthly grasses grow. The one who told John Mack about these things was Bernardo Peixoto (1933-2011), who became a shaman in his Brazilian jungle tribe, but with the help of a missionary, had the opportunity to study anthropology and obtain a doctorate through which he was able to work at the Smithsonian Institute in Washington.

While being trained to become a shaman, he was subjected to extremely harsh initiatory rites. Alone in the jungle he encountered so-called "ikuyas", who do not manifest to just anyone. Sometimes they come in the form of little men, and sometimes like bright globes or disguised in animals, but for millennia they have cared for the local tribes. They sometimes mate with the earthly women who give birth to hybrid babies. When Peixoto asked them where they came from, the creatures said, "We come from nowhere" meaning that "they are everywhere". They are messengers from the "Great Spirit" and are sent to us because we "are not capable of facing that huge energy" directly.[53]

John Mack was also contacted by healers and leaders of various indigenous populations in the United States. They told Mack that what we call "UFO abductions" have been familiar to them from ancient times and they consider them to be part of the natural order of things. When Mack asked why these beliefs were unknown to scientists and ufologists, he was told that the subject was sacred to them and could not be discussed with anyone. Especially that the beliefs of the Native Americans regarding beings coming from beyond our world are not taken seriously by white men and are simply labelled as folklore and they are not willing to accept that. Mack cites Wallace Black Elk (1921-2004), a healer from the Lakota tribe in the U.S., who said: "The scientists call them UFOs... because they are not trained; they lost contact with the wisdom, knowledge, power and gift. So, they have to see everything first with their naked eye... because they lost contact with those star-nation people."[54]

CONCLUSIONS

The traditions of peoples from all around the world, the myths and folkloric characters, which in many places are still considered to be present, seem to demonstrate the perennial presence of a high, non-earthly power over the human race. Phenomena like UFO encounters, abductions, or genetic experiments on humans, seem to have taken place since ancient times, taking the form and moment of appearance best suited to the local culture. They continue to appear nowadays in a technical form that is appropriate to our stage of development.

The antiquity of some reports and the variety of appearances make the most prominent ufologists agree that the UFO phenomenon and its associated phenomena cannot be simply visits of an extra-terrestrial civilization (and much less the preparation for an invasion), but something that is much more complex, something similar to a *control system*. All these

---

[52] Idem, p. 193, 191.
[53] Idem, p. 162.
[54] Mack, 1999, p. 10.

arguments once more support the hypothesis that we are and for a very long time have been monitored by representatives of hyper-civilizations.

RELIGIONS

Holy miracles and UFOs

Religious miracles could also be interpreted as manifestations of the activity of *hyper-civilizations* on Earth. This assumption will be challenged from the very beginning by two extremely long-lasting cultural preconceptions. Science denies the existence of religious miracles ("they are impossible, so they don't exist"). The appearance of holy characters, also called *theophanies*, are more frequently documented than is commonly believed. According to a book by Jean Sider, a French author and investigator of the UFO phenomenon, Lucien Blaise of Lyon had identified 29654 religious' manifestations (Mary, Jesus, saints, angels, etc.) that had been recorded up to 1991, these had occurred in 1272 locations in sixty nine countries. Of these, over three quarters were of the Virgin Mary and those of Jesus considerably less.[55]

Could these occurrences be related to *hyper-civilizations* and their alleged manifestations discussed in previous chapters? Jacques Vallée has analysed a number of apparitions of the Virgin: in Guadalupe (near Tenochtitlan, today in Mexico City) in 1531, in Fatima in 1917, in Medugorje in 1981, in Lourdes in 1858 and near La Salette in 1846. He emphasised that in all these cases the witnesses observed the same unusual details that are also reported in the case of UFO encounters: a dazzling light, possibly seen through the fog, a "sun dance", a bright globe, or a disc rotating very quickly, a column of light that descends from above where the witness can ascend from the earth, "yarns" or "petals" falling from the sky and melting, garments that remain dry despite rain, a cloud from which a non-earthly being emerges, low temperature, unusual silence, loss of sense of time, trance, exhaustion after contact and so on[56]. In addition, in the years when the number of theophanies increased, the "waves" of UFO observations also intensified. Reverend B.W. Palmer of Haines City (Florida), examined several hundred "holy apparitions", and found one hundred and eighteen reports of "sun dance", and other phenomena that frequently occurred in UFO reports.

I have also found these parallels in Romania. For example, on June 15, 1935, around 16.00-17.00 hours, in the village of Maglavit, not far from the Danube, a 28-year-old shepherd named Petrache Lupu saw an old man with white beard who appeared in a white cloud that was floating above the earth. After delivering a religious message, the 'old man' disappeared into a "square cloud". Because the shepherd was shy he did not report the message, so the old man reappeared a week later. Believing that the old man was God, thousands of pilgrims visited the location. Over a year later on the anniversary of the miracle, they witnessed a frightening "sun dance".

On August 29, 1935, a similar miracle occurred in the village of Parepa-Rusani (50 km north of Bucharest), when twelve years old Maria Petre saw a bright, blue-eyed man with a white beard descend through a tunnel of white clouds.

During the 20th century there were almost ten such encounters in Romania and in all of them there are details usually reported in UFO encounters. Some UFO abductions also have traits that are similar to holy apparitions. For example, Jacques Vallée considers that the abduction experience is real, traumatic and extremely complex and it can be subsumed into a mystical-religious ecstasy, disguised in the technical language specific to our century.

A notorious case is that of Betty Andreasson-Luca, investigated by Raymond Fowler. She has repeatedly encountered sacred characters during several UFO abductions. When she

---

[55] Sider, 1995.
[56] Vallée, 1989, p.192-195.

was 13 years old, she was told that she would enter something called, the 'Great Door' and see the glory of "the One." Under hypnosis she was asked to give more details, but she could only say that, "I cannot take you past this door... I just cannot tell you about it... Words cannot explain this. I understand that everything is one..."[57]

On another occasion during an abduction, Betty encountered tall, white-robed entities called Elders; they said to her that they were ambassadors of "Oh", who is "the external, internal, eternal presence. What we know as omnipotence, omnipresence". Betty asked: "Do you know who Jesus is? Do you know Jesus Christ?" And the tall one said, "Yes, he is the hypostasis". Betty answered, "He is my saviour." And he said "Yes, I know" In Christian theology a hypostasis is one of the three persons comprising the Trinity, but Betty said she didn't know this word.[58]

At first Raymond Fowler, who investigated the case, hesitated to publish these details, considering that the mixture of UFO experience and mystic ecstasy would be considered in bad taste if not actually a blasphemy by most people with a traditional western education. But then he thought that by putting aside what we regard as embarrassing "contamination" and keeping only what we declare "essential", we risk seriously deforming the objectivity of the research.

The above case is not singular. I had occasion to present similar cases from Romania. Miss S from Brașov, who was not religious or interested in the UFO phenomenon, had several strange encounters including out of the body experiences. In one instance she arrived in a round room with computer-like devices, here she met several people, who were, "Tall, with long hair, some were bearded, dressed in white clothes". She identified these people as the apostles Peter, Simon and Paul (a little later in other, similar encounters, she also met the same beings). Then she saw herself in front of a "great door" at the end of a rectangular corridor. When the door opened she said she was overwhelmed by a dazzling white light from which a superhuman being appeared and its face was covered. She was told that if she saw his face she would die[59]. The scene reminds us of the biblical verse: "You cannot see my face, for no one may see me and live" (Exodus, 33; 20).

In the same book, similar Romanian cases are described. A jurist, M.G. reported a classic UFO abduction, in which she was shown historical and biblical scenes, especially the crucifixion of Jesus and the decapitation of St. John the Baptist. She said she even saw the Holy Trinity. A foreman, C.B. has reported a complex encounter with "an energetic being who, the human mind, no matter how much it strives, cannot imagine, it was a power that he could not describe in words". An engineer, G.M., who had several possible UFO abductions, met an old man with a white beard several times; he understood that this was God the father.

I could add that in Romania my colleagues and I found that, especially in the countryside, people considered that UFO sightings, although unusual, are part of the natural order of things. On several occasions when we asked the witnesses what they thought these apparitions might be, we received the answer: "What else could they be than signs of God?"

The above examples above that the UFO phenomenon and religious belief seem to be more closely linked than it might appear at first glance. This connection has also contributed to the birth of the phenomenon of *contactees*. In the 1950s George Adamski, Truman Bethurum, Daniel Fry, Howard Menger, Orpheus Angelucci, John McCoy, George Hunt Williamson, Ray and Rex Stanford and some others declared that they were in constant contact with the aliens who visit our planet in UFOs. Some even said they were accredited as the representatives of aliens here on Earth. This connection has also led to the creation of religious sects that worship extra-terrestrials, such as the Church of Scientology (founded by L. Ron Hubbard), the Raelians (Claude Vorilhon, who changed his name to Rael), the

---

[57] Fowler, 1991, p. 144
[58] Fowler, 1995, p.193
[59] Farcaș, 2016

Aetherius Society (George King), and the tragic Heaven's Gate group (Marshall Applewhite), thirty eight members of which committed mass suicide in 1997. However, the actual number of sects that continue to worship aliens is much higher.

In ancient writings

The connection between the UFO phenomenon and holy apparitions is not a mere anomaly that is a characteristic of our time. In all the traditions that underlie the old religions, Divinity descends to Earth from Heaven and then climbs back again, usually in vehicles surrounded by a fantastic light show involving clouds or fog. Sometimes a "chosen" individual is abducted, meets 'holy' characters then returns, carrying a message intended to improve things on Earth.

In the following, I will give examples the above using quotes from the Bible, a book that helps define our culture.[60] However, I do not regard the Bible as definitive proof, or something which cannot be challenged. But my conviction is that this holy book keeps, albeit in a distorted form, the memory of important events that our ancestors witnessed and that impressed them so powerfully that they felt the need to record them for posterity

Among these biblical events are many that resemble current UFO reports. Thus, as the Jews are led out of Egypt, "the Lord went ahead of them in a pillar of cloud to guide them on their way and by night in a pillar of fire to give them light, so that they could travel by day or night" (Exodus, 13; 21). When "the angel of the Lord appeared to him, in flames, from within a bush, Moses saw that though the bush was on fire, it did not burn up" (Exodus, 3; 2). The "flames" do not seem to be of a fire because they do not burn the bush, but rather they are the dazzling light of a vehicle from which God and his angels appear. The same is true for the mountain "ablaze with fire" (Deuteronomy, 5; 23). But whoever recorded what happened, did not have the appropriate word for a dazzling light that stayed on the ground and was visible at night, except for "fire".

There are many other strange flying vehicles in the Bible that exhibit UFO-like behaviour.[61] At the birth of Jesus, "The star they had seen when it rose went ahead of them until it stopped over the place where the child was" (Matthew, 2; 9). This star moves and stops, so it is not an astronomical phenomenon. Other episodes that can be interpreted as UFO encounters are the bright apparition in the context of Transfiguration of Jesus, or the conversion of Saul (Paul) through an apparition of Jesus on the road of Damascus. In the latter case we have another common feature of UFO encounter, namely the different perception of the same event by different witnesses.

Jesus when resurrected "Was taken up before their very eyes and a cloud hid him from their sight. They were looking intently up into the sky as he was going, when suddenly two men dressed in white stood beside them. 'Men of Galilee', they said, 'why do you stand here looking into the sky? This same Jesus, who has been taken from you into heaven, will come back in the same way that you have seen him go into heaven'". (Acts, 1; 9-11). What better word than "cloud" could the writer of this text, given his limited vocabulary, use to describe a miraculous vehicle floating in mid-air, then ascending into heaven? In order to help us understand that for the ancients, "cloud" could also mean a UFO, Pastor Barry H. Downing, who carefully examined the similarities between the above cases and the UFO phenomenon, gives a comparison with the term "flying saucer", that has been used since the forties and has the same meaning.

The "two men dressed in white" mentioned in the context of The Ascension, are obviously angels. In the Bible, angels are Divine messengers and servants and it is not mentioned

---

[60] For quotations I used mainly the New International Version of the Bible.
[61] Many other examples are in Cooke, 2005

anywhere when and how they were created. Angels travel between Heaven and Earth and convey the will of the Lord to the human race and take any appropriate action. In contrast to their traditional image, nowhere in the Old Testament are angels described as having wings, harps or an aura around their heads (the cherubim, seraphim, or ophanim are something else, not angels). But the angels do compare very well with the "Nordic" aliens of UFO abduction reports.

Angels or other "aerial races" are also present in Buddhist and Hindu religions and can be also be seen in Sumerian, Assyrian and Egyptian bas-reliefs and paintings. We should also remember that the djinn of the Islam, or the daemon of ancient Greeks, are sometimes interpreted as beings that mediate between angels and humans but are not necessarily evil or malicious.

According to the Bible, the first character abducted into heaven was Enoch, the seventh Patriarch after Adam. Canonical texts only say that "Enoch walked faithfully with God; then he was no more, because God took him away". (Genesis, 5; 24), or "By faith Enoch was taken from his life, so that he did not experience death: He could not be found, because God had taken him away." (Hebrews 11; 5).

Enoch's heavenly journeys are described in more detail in three other documents, among which the most important is *Book of Enoch*, which is written at the first person. Being considered as "apocryphal", this old text did not find a place in the canonical Bible. However, the book was accepted and preserved by the Christian church of Ethiopia and Eritrea and in the past two centuries it has been translated into many languages. In Eastern European Orthodoxy, another Slavonic version was also preserved, it is called the 'Book of Secrets of Enoch', it is more fragmentary but richer in detail. Finally, references to Enoch are also found in the Book of Jubilees and also in some Dead Sea scrolls.

In the Book of Enoch the beginning of the "abduction" is briefly described, yet the similarities with some details of modern reports of a UFO abduction are striking: "From this moment I have not seen myself in the midst of the children of men, but have been seated between two spirits... Then my spirit... took the flight to heavens" (69, 3; and 70, 1). The Slavonic book of Enoch's Secrets is more explicit. Enoch woke up when his name was called by two men who were as tall as he has ever seen on Earth. "And their faces shone like the sun and their eyes were like torches and their faces burst out" (the similarity with the two men seen at the Ascension of Jesus is striking). "Afterwards, they took me on their wings and put me on a cloud. And here's the wonder! The clouds began to move. And again, exalting me above, I saw the air and above I saw the ether; and they brought me into the first heaven".

This "flanking" by two (or three) emissaries is common in many UFO abductions. Enoch also writes: "I saw myself surrounded by clouds and thick fog... favourable winds were lifting my wings and hurried my way. I was so going up to Heaven and soon came to a wall built of crystal stones" (Of course, neither angels nor Enoch had material wings). Then, according to Enoch, in the "seventh heaven" he met God.

Enoch is not the only figure mentioned in the Bible who experienced events that resemble UFO abductions. "When the Lord was about to take Elijah up to heaven in a whirlwind... suddenly a chariot of fire and horses of fire appeared and separated the two of them and Elijah went up to heaven in a whirlwind." (2 Kings,2; 1, 11). What else can produce a "whirlwind" and at the same time a "chariot of fire", other than a UFO? But how else would a witness two thousand and a half years ago describe a luminous, spinning, vehicle, which could swiftly ascend into the sky carrying a human being?

Even more interesting is Ezekiel's close encounter: "I saw a windstorm coming out of the north – an immense cloud with flashing lightning and surrounded by brilliant light. The centre of the fire looked like glowing metal and in the fire was what looked like four living creatures... Wherever the spirit would go, they would go, without turning as they went. The appearance of the living creatures was like burning coals of fire or like torches. Fire moved back and forth among the creatures; it was bright, and lightning flashed out of it. The creatures sped back and forth like flashes of lightning. As I looked at the living creatures, I saw a wheel on the ground beside each creature with its four faces... Each appeared to be made like a wheel intersecting a wheel. As they moved, they would go in any one of the four directions the creatures faced; the wheels did not change direction as the creatures went. Their rims were high and awesome, and all four rims were full of eyes all around... When the creatures moved, they also moved; when the creatures stood still, they also stood still; and when the creatures rose from the ground, the wheels rose along with them, because the spirit of the living creatures was in the wheels. Spread out above the heads of the living creatures was what looked something like, a vault, sparkling like crystal and awesome... Above the vault over their heads was what looked like a throne of lapis lazuli and high above on the throne was a figure like that of a man. I saw that from what appeared to be his waist up he looked like glowing metal, as if full of fire and that from there down he looked like fire; and brilliant light surrounded him. Like the appearance of a rainbow in the clouds on a rainy day, so was the radiance around him." (Ezekiel, 1; 4-27).

From this text, one can feel the narrator's difficulty, given his limited vocabulary aligned to the ancient Middle East, in describing an obviously technical vehicle that was capable of flying thanks to the "spirit of the living creatures" which today we would probably call its "propulsion mechanism". And, most likely, the scribe had no other term than "living creatures", for some mechanisms that were moving alone.

It seems that the prophet Isaiah also had space flights. However, they were removed from the canonical Bible and were preserved only in Slavonic in the apocryphal: "The Vision of Isaiah". As in Enoch, history begins one night when the prophet is visited by two tall men sent to take him to Heaven. Here he is shown a number of sacred mysteries, after which he is brought home.

In the Islamic tradition, one night accompanied by the archangel Gabriel (Jibril), the Prophet Muhammad was transported into the sky by a fabulous animal. The Prophet then visited eight heavens.

Genetic engineering?

The parallel between the UFO phenomenon and religious traditions preserved in the Bible, also includes moments that can be interpreted as either interventions for the creation of the human race, or improvements to the genetic quality of human beings. According to the Old Testament, "God [Elohim] created mankind in his own image, in the image of God he created them; male and female he created them. God blessed them and said to them, 'Be fruitful and increase in number; fill the Earth and subdue it. Rule over the fish in the sea and the birds in the sky and over every living creature that moves on the ground.'" (Genesis, 1; 27,28). If we accept, even metaphorically, the description of this event as well as the hypothesis of hyper-civilizations, we can speculate that when Elohim (originally a plural God) "created mankind in his own image", he did not necessarily consider a physical identity, but, rather, an intellectual and moral one as mankind was to become a future *hyper-civilization*, responsible, among others, for the well-being of the Earth's biosphere.

An interesting reference to genetic engineering is found in the note: "Lord God caused the man to fall into a deep sleep; and while he was sleeping, he took one of the man's ribs and then closed up the place with flesh. Then the Lord God made a woman from the rib..." (Genesis 2, 21, 22). Even if we consider this text as a metaphor, one cannot fail to notice that using genetic engineering a woman can be cloned from a man's cell (not necessarily a whole rib), by removing the Y chromosome, while a possible reverse operation would have been much more complicated and required the procurement of an additional Y chromosome from another source.

But the interventions with the genetic structure of mankind do not stop here, it is only the beginning. It is written in the Bible that "the sons of God saw that the daughters of humans were beautiful, and they married any of them they chose... and had children by them. They were the heroes of old, men of renown." (Genesis 6; 2, 4). The Book of Enoch (Chapters XVII-XI) is much more explicit. It says there were two hundred "children of the heavens", no doubt angels, and their chief was Semyaza, who, from the outset, warned his subordinates that they what they did was wrong, and they would be punished for it. However, he did not have the authority to oppose them, so they continued.

If we take this statement as true we can ask: were the angels (who had children with the earthly women) male, and did they belong to the human race? This is normally the only way they could have viable offspring, or did they conduct genetic experiments on the women? Anyway, according to the Book of Enoch it was these interventions that displeased God and these angels were severely punished and their offspring, the giants (or Nephilim), were destroyed by the Flood.

The Book of Enoch also reveals another scenario for the cause of the Flood. Enoch wrote: "my son Methuselah took a wife for his son Lamech and she became pregnant by him and bore a son. And his body was white as snow and red as the blooming of a rose and the hair of his head and his long locks were white as wool and his eyes beautiful. And when he opened his eyes, he lighted up the whole house like the sun and the whole house was very bright... And his father Lamech was afraid of him and fled and came to his father Methuselah. And he said unto him: 'I have begotten a strange son, diverse from and unlike man and resembling the sons of the God of heaven; and his nature is different, and he is not like us... it seems to me that he is not sprung from me but from the angels... And now, my father, I am here to petition thee and implore thee that thou mayest go to Enoch, our father and learn from him the truth, for his dwelling-place is amongst the angels.'"

Interestingly, Lamech's first suspicion is that at that time the child was procreated by an angel. That allows us to assume that interventions by angels in the creation of human beings with special properties must have been perceived as something quite normal.

Methuselah went to Enoch and told him of the miracle. Enoch answered and said unto him: "The Lord will do a new thing on the Earth and this I have already seen in a vision and make known to thee that in the generation of my father Jared some of the angels of heaven transgressed the word of the Lord... and have united themselves with women and commit sin with them and have married some of them and have begot children by them. And they shall produce on the earth giants not according to the spirit, but according to the flesh and there shall be a great punishment on the earth and the earth shall be cleansed from all impurity. Yea, there shall come a great destruction over the whole earth and there shall be a deluge and a great destruction for one year. And this son who has been born unto you shall be left on the earth and his three children shall be saved with him: when all mankind that are on the earth shall die. And now make known to thy son Lamech that he who has been born is in truth his son and call his name Noah; for he shall be left to you and he and his sons shall be saved from the destruction... for He, the Lord, has showed me and informed me." (Chapter CVI; 1-20)

Using the logic of these accounts, we can wonder if Noah was white and blond (or perhaps an albino) and was the appropriate hybrid required by God to continue the human species, while the rest of humanity was destroyed (at least using the logic of the Bible). We can also wonder what his parents and ancestors have looked like if the appearance of the new-born worried them so much. Also, according to this text we see that God himself (and not just the rebel angels) was involved in experiments to improve the human species.

If we accept the biblical text, we see that after Noah, God also intervened on other occasions to create beings that were better than the human species. This seems to include not only also the conception of Jesus, but also other miraculous births (Isaac, John the Baptist). The fact that on the day of the conception an angel appeared – in the case of Jesus or John the archangel Gabriel (Luke, 1, 26, etc.) – seemed to be quite normal.

In ancient writings there are many other stories about alleged sexual relationships, "After the Flood", between angels and earthly women. Jacques Vallée notes that "The most remarkable cases of sexual contact with non-humans are not found in spicy saucer books, nor in fairy legends; they rest, safely stored away, in the archives of the Catholic Church"[62]. He points out (according to the writings of Anatole France) that he refers to Latin authors such as: Justin, Flavius Josephus, Athenagoras, Lactantius, Tertullian, Marcus Ephesian, Eusebius of Caesarea, St. Ambrose, St. Augustine and others. Also, from them we find that women have to cover their heads before entering a church to pray, for the bizarre reason that they should not 'tempt the angels', a practise that, to this day, still occurs in many places. It is also a sign of the virulent misogyny that existed in the Catholic Church, where women were feared and mistrusted.

Temptations of the Devil?

A person of faith who reads the above will inevitably wonder if everything that relates to the UFO phenomenon, and particularly to abductions and other strange manifestations, are ultimately the "work of Satan"? A supporter of this view is the Reverend Bob Larson, an exorcist and an expert on cults. He is convinced of the reality of both UFOs and the abduction phenomenon, but he says that the interpretation of biblical texts in the ufological sense is a result of the activity of Satan and of his demons[63]. Analysing the activity of the UFO cults, he concludes that a sinister force deliberately builds a new religious system in the preparation for the spiritual domination of the world by transforming a miracle of faith into a simple technical operation.

In addition, Larson says that there are no aliens in the Universe because they are not mentioned in the Bible, and the human race is the result of a unique act of grace from God. If there are more worlds – he wonders rhetorically – have they all fallen into original sin? And was Christ crucified in each of them to save the people from this sin?

The above arguments, which are also supported by other authors – including, from my experience, the Romanian Orthodox Church – can raise serious issues for a fundamentalist Christian, but it would be viewed with reserve, by, say, a Hindu, Buddhist, Taoist and even a Muslim, or Jew, etc? All of these very, very ancient religions, many of them with hundreds of millions of adherents, claim that they are also honourable paths to the Divine.

Perhaps some clarifications are needed for Christian believers. Most of the abductees describe the visitors as beings full of love and goodwill, who (beyond genetic experiments) try to protect us and suggest positive actions and do not want to interfere with our free will. No abductee has reported any anti-religious or anti-humanist message or that any desire for destruction had been given to them. On the contrary, in many cases those abducted have been entrusted with messages calling for the prevention of possible disasters, be they nuclear or ecological etc. Neither have they been promised special powers or advantages in exchange for a commitment to negative actions or behaviour.

After the abduction experience many go through a process of spiritual transformation and become concerned with pacifist or ecological problems and frequently feel more and more connected to every creature that lives in the Universe. Many of the abducted speak of a connection with the Divinity, the Source, the Creator, or more generally something described

---

[62] Vallée, 1989, p.125
[63] Larson, 1997

as a 'Great Love'. This, plus the appearance of the visitors coming 'down from the skies', have made many researchers believe that the visitor may be angelic in nature.

Church pays attention

Surprisingly, the most interesting comments on the possible links between the UFO phenomenon, extra-terrestrial visitors and religion, come from the Catholic Church. For example, in 1999, when Pope John Paul II was asked by a child if there are extra-terrestrials, he replied: "Remember always: They are the children of God, just as we are." In 2014, Pope Francis said he is ready to baptise aliens, adding: "Who are we to close doors?"

Monsignor Corrado Balducci (1923-2008) was official Exorcist for Rome, former diplomat in the Papal Nunciature in Washington, DC, past member of the Vatican's Curia of the Holy See and personal friend of Pope John Paul II. He has gone on Italian public television several times to proclaim that extra-terrestrial contact is a real phenomenon. Monsignor Balducci emphasised on many occasions that encounters with the Star Visitors: "1) are NOT demonic, 2) they are NOT due to psychological impairment, 3) they are NOT a case of entity attachment, but 4) these encounters deserve to be studied carefully."[64] Richard Boylan commented that "since Monsignor Balducci is a demonology expert and consultant to the Vatican and since the Catholic Church has historically demonised many new phenomena that were poorly understood, his stating that the Church does not censure these encounters is all the more remarkable." Boylan commented also that "This Vatican insider's declarations on Italian national television represent technically the first declaration by a tacit representative of a major power government, even if 'speaking as an individual', that Star Visitors contact is real and happening and deserves serious study."

In 2006, Jesuit Brother Guy Consolmagno, Ph.D., an astronomer at the Vatican Observatory on Mount Graham, Arizona, wrote for the Harper's Magazine "There are, unquestionably, nonhuman intelligent beings in the Bible", quoting the saying of Jesus: "I have other sheep that do not belong to this fold". (John 10:16) as an allusion to the existence of other inhabited worlds.

There are more such comments from Vatican insiders. It has also speculated in the media that the Vatican would have received from priests through 'Apostolic Nunciatures', many reports of encounters with extraterrestrial visitors, that it was forced to accept the reality of the phenomenon and prepare for a "revelation" of alien presence on Earth.

It is worth mentioning also the complementary view of the Dalai Lama, the highest authority of Tibetan Buddhism. Regarding visitors coming with UFOs, he told Prof. John Mack, whom he met twice: "The devastation of the planet's ecology was destroying not only the habitat of plants and animals but the realms in which the spirits reside as well. Perhaps this has left them no choice but to manifests in our world, to appear to us".[65]

CONCLUSIONS

The manifestations of 'holy entities' among humans are much more usual than we think. The effects accompanying these apparitions have many features in common with UFO encounters: impressive lights, levitation and much more. In addition to these, in the earliest religious writings particularly in the Bible, there are accounts of other common features: abductions in heavenly realms, where the witness meets 'heavenly beings', various forms of genetic experiments, and requests to preserve the health of the Earth.

---

[64]   e.g. in Boylan, 2006
[65]   Mack, 1994, p.416.

All this shows that there is a link between religious phenomena and the UFO phenomenon. This proves, once again, that above us could be higher powers and consciousness that have controlled the evolution of humankind for thousands of years. The magic accompanying their actions is another argument which strengthens the hypothesis of the presence of hyper-civilizations around us.

AKASHA

The super-memory

American medium Edgar Cayce (1877-1945) had a special quality: if requested by people that were in need of assistance (mainly for health issues) when he was in a state of trance, he answered their questions in an effective way that far exceeded his eight-grade school education. Al Layne, a hypnotherapist with whom he had collaborated at the beginning, characterised the state in which Cayce entered on these occasions as "an auto-imposed hypnotic trance that induces remote viewing". The medium, however, preferred to use the simpler and straightforward term 'readings'. These were usually recorded by his wife Gertrude or his son Hugh Lynn. The Virginia Beach Foundation archives, which bear his name, hold the records of 12,250 such "readings"; Of these, about 9400 are medical diagnoses and the others are related to other subjects: medicine, psychology, history, natural and human sciences, etc, as well as prophecies (which have not generally been fulfilled).[66]

His "readings" are written in the first-person plural as if he dictated them with other persons sitting next to him. They contain quotes such as: "we can see the body...", "we find it is...", "we suggest to..." etc. In addition, in these "readings", Cayce did not speak of persons, but of "entities" and instead of "God" – although he was a religious person and sometimes preached – he used alternatives such as "Creative Forces" or "Universal Forces".

The medical diagnostics contained in the "readings" were of great precision and were accompanied by prescriptions for effective treatments and used medical terms that Cayce should not have been aware of and when awakened from the trance and told what he had said he was amazed. At one point Cayce was charged with the illegal practice of medicine but was absolved in court thanks to the testimonies of several important friends who testified that he had never pursued or obtained any material benefits, and the individuals who were given the readings, did so on a voluntary basis. Among the people who supported Cayce were U.S. President Woodrow Wilson, the inventor Thomas Edison, and the composers Irving Berlin and George Gershwin.

Cayce said that in a state of trance he was reaching a huge archive or library with his mind. It was as if a hand took a book and opened it to the right page for him to read. Cayce called this archive *Akasha*, and said that it was the Universal memory, where "upon time and space is written the thoughts, the deeds, the activities of an entity – as in relationships to its environs, its hereditary influence; as directed – or judgement drawn by or according to what the entity's ideal is. Hence, as it has been oft called, the record is God's book of remembrance."[67]

In the Sanskrit language, "akasha" means "ether" or "heaven". For Hindus, "akasha" is the basis and essence of all things in the material world: it is the fifth and finest element of the Universe besides fire, air, water and earth (plasma, gaseous, liquid and solid states of matter), being the first in the order of creation. It is eternal, ubiquitous and imperceptible. The term '*Akashic Record*' is attributed to Alfred Percy Sinnett, who in 1883 wrote about the Buddhist belief in "a permanency of records in the Akasa" and about the ability of some people to access and read these records. In 1927 Alice A. Bailey wrote that the Akashic Record is like an immense photographic film, registering all the desires and earthly experiences of our planet. Those who perceive it will see pictured thereon: The life experiences of every human being since time began, the reactions to experience of the entire animal kingdom, the aggregation of the thought-forms and so on; but only a trained occultist can distinguish between actual experience and the pictures created by the imagination. In line with this

---

[66] Koechlin, 2000
[67] Edgar Cayce, Reading 1650-1

vision, the Akashic Records are also known as "The Book of Life," which stores all the information for every individual who has ever lived on the Earth.

It has long been speculated that as a universal memory, the Akashic Records could be the source for the phenomenon of *channelling*, through which a person with special abilities allegedly receives information, insights, images, inspiration and revelations etc. Like Cayce, many healers, religious people, artists said they had access to a huge repository of knowledge that they sometimes said was placed at a so called "*astral level*". This idea occurs in different forms throughout history in most of the Earth's cultures. It was said that this was the source from which the prehistoric shamans, biblical prophets and famous oracles, such as the one at Delphi, obtained their information. Even the ancient poets began their poems with an invocation to the Muses, who were goddesses through whom they believed they received their verses, which were in turn extracted from a vast library of knowledge. Several religions and sects possess holy books which their traditions state were revealed or dictated in antiquity by a non-earthly intelligence using the same kind of store of wisdom.

An example of channelling could be *automatic writing,* when the hand of a medium or channel seems to write by itself as it puts information on paper, this can include text, music and works of art. The 'medium' is sure that what is on the paper did not come from them, but are messages dictated by someone else but using their hand. There have been dozens of books written in this way; for example, a Brazilian medium, Chico Xavier (1910-2002), is credited with four hundred and ninety six books that were mostly written in this way. His books sold fifty million copies, and the profits were used for charitable purposes. The phenomenon of automatic writing has been known about for a considerable time and many studies have been devoted to it, but no satisfactory explanation has ever been found.

I have personally had the opportunity to examine some texts made through automatic writing, particularly those of Mrs. M.C., of Bucharest. She received messages from several entities that, according to her, "Do not give you peace until you write". The messages filled a stack of notebooks which were full of small, neat writing and also drawings and symbols, which she has subsequently tried to explain.[68]

Another, related, phenomenon is *xenoglossy*, the state in which someone starts talking in a language they do not know. They do not understand the message, which sometimes also appears in written form in an unknown alphabet. A well-known example is that of a young schoolteacher from Blackpool, England, named Ivy Carter Beaumont, also known as "Rosemary". One evening in December 1927, in a friend's house – Dr. Frederic Herbert Wood – her hand began to draw some strange symbols resembling hieroglyphs on paper. She explained that "her hand is guided by an unknown and strange will" and the phenomenon was repeated several times. Wood, intrigued, showed the drawings to an amateur Egyptologist Alfred J. Howard Hulme, who found that they were indeed meaningful texts written in Egyptian hieroglyphics.

On August 8, 1931, Rosemary suddenly began to utter strange and incomprehensible words. The Egyptologist Alfred Hulme was again consulted and was convinced that she was speaking in an ancient Egyptian dialect. Nobody was fully conversant with the ancient Egyptian spoken language (it was highly unlikely that Rosemary would know it). The ancient Egyptian texts that are available only contain consonants, not the vowels and at first Hulme did not understand anything that Rosemary had said, but, after removing the vowels from what she had said, he obtained some meaningful sentences. Then he drew up a list of questions based on the language Rosemary's had used and on December 5, 1931, in the presence of Dr. Wood, Hulme and other experts, Rosemary gave twenty-eight answers, again in old Egyptian. From these answers, Hulme deduced that the messages had come from a Babylonian princess named 'Telika', who lived 1400 years before Christ and had come to

[68] Farcaş, 2016

Egypt at be at the court of Pharaoh Amenophis III and might even have been the victim of a harem conspiracy. In 1936, the phrases pronounced by Rosemary were also recorded on a disc. There are many similar examples of xenoglossy and even if they are not quite as spectacular, they are equally unexplainable.

Extrasensory perception

Although many documents about the U.S. Army's remote viewing projects have been declassified and published since 1995, the general public still does not know too much about them. In 1972, the CIA provided modest funding for extrasensory perception experiments at "Stanford Research Institute" in Menlo Park (California), then renamed *SRI International*, it was a private institute under the leadership of two specialists in lasers: engineer Harold E. Puthoff Ph.D. and physicist Russel Targ Ph.D. During these experiments they used two people with incredible natural talents: one was Pat Price, a former policeman and the other was Ingo Swann, an artist and author. During these experiments, which took place between 1972 and 1974, Uri Geller was also occasionally involved

At SRI, Ingo Swann (1933-2013) while participating in a project called .SCANATE', set up a technique called, *Controlled Remote Viewing* (CRV), through which, after a suitable training in six stages lasting about two years, any person could became a remote viewer. In other words to transmit their consciousness to any point on the planet (and elsewhere), seeing and describing in detail buildings, installations, rooms, persons, etc. at that location.

The CRV technique involved transcendental meditation exercises, and "hemispherical synchronisation" of the EEG frequencies of the brain – using something called a "Hemisync Device", created by Robert A. Monroe (1915-1995)[69]. Teams of two people were trained: an operator, or *medium* (who had passed through the first two phases) and his *monitor*, who had also received complementary training. The information received by the medium's unconscious mind was transmitted and recorded in a well-defined way. The medium was requested to eliminate, as much as possible the interventions from the conscious mind (words, rationalisations, imagination etc.). The only person allowed to interpret what the medium said was the monitor. He was also the one who noted everything reported by the medium using a special sign language.

Through the SCANATE project, Swann trained over a dozen people, also called "psi spies". In 1976, the Central Intelligence Agency (CIA) transferred the remote viewing project to a secret intelligence unit of the Defense Intelligence Agency (DIA) at Fort Meade in Maryland. After 1984, CRV military training was completely taken over by the army, and the projects were given various names: *Grill Flame*, *Centre Lane*, *Sun Streak*, and *Stargate*.

One of those who participated directly in these activities for seventeen 17 years, and was one of the best remote viewers, was Lyn Buchanan. He trained more than three hundred people in using these techniques. According to Buchannan, between 1986 and the spring of 1995, the remote viewing team received more than two hundred specific tasks from military bodies. They were requests to obtain information not accessible in other ways from various places. Among these were monitoring Russian nuclear submarines and missile launchers plus chemical weapons storage facilities, as well as finding hostages, spying on political, military, and economic plans, locating people and solving crimes and so on. Subsequently, using complementary methods of espionage, it turned out that the information obtained had been remarkably accurate. The accuracy of the CRV techniques was not perfect (as any remote viewing can be), but in 1982 the creators of the method already knew that – using specific training techniques – success rates could reach 65-95%.[70] Since 1995, when these projects

---

[69] Monroe, 1971
[70] Buchanan, 2003

were discontinued, several of the former military remote viewers set up civilian organisations, which continue to use the techniques they learned for the commercial purposes and also for the general public.

Of course, remote viewing using extrasensory perception is not just about the military projects mentioned above and is not confined to the USA. For instance, I know of a few examples in Romania; here are three of them: Valentina Gârlea from Iaşi, a blind woman, who has had no specialist training, who can see "with the third eye" the state of the internal organs of a human body, as well as the aura, and can contribute to the diagnosis of some diseases. Dowser Vasile Rudan who was able to detect ancient underwater water supply networks, ancient walls, and underground cavities, etc. and the engineer Marian Constantin Borş, who obtains information about the human body using only a small metallic rod and is able to assist physicians. But examples of this type can be found in all countries and cultures.

The three minds

So remote "extrasensory perception" works, at least sometimes, although it cannot be explained using current scientific knowledge. Russell Targ, one of the SRI executives, has emphasised that for the time being it is only known that the precision of extrasensory perception does not decrease with increasing distance between medium and target. And it is also known that it is unlikely that an electromagnetic field is involved.[71]

To understand the remote viewing phenomenon, CRV creators have advanced an explanation that might initially seem surprising. Simplifying things a bit to make it easier to understand, they took into account the three main components of the human mind: the conscious mind, the unconscious mind and the collective unconscious. The first two components are in our brain and are scientifically accepted, while the third component would have an extracorporeal location and would be common to all humanity. This third part is only a hypothesis which provides a possible explanation but cannot be scientifically examined. But it is assumed that this unique collective unconscious is shared among all human beings, in other words it is connected to minds as well as some other mechanism. Consequently, the collective unconscious "knows" everything that exists everywhere on Earth.

If we accept this idea there is a practical issue. How does the conscious mind of an individual access the wealth of information that is in this collective unconscious? The CRV specialists have emphasised that the two main conditions needed for this purpose are: the unambiguous identification of the target through an "address" and establishment of communication between the conscious mind and the unconscious mind of the medium. The whole process of CRV training was geared towards acquiring these two mechanisms, because an untrained mind does not usually have them.

The "Address" can be any element by which the target is uniquely identified. For military remote viewers, the address of a place was defined using specific geographic coordinates. If the target was a person, the identifier would be an accurate portrait. However, communication between the conscious mind and the unconscious mind of a person poses more problems. The most important two are: the lack of a common language for communication and the activity of the conscious mind, which can cover and distort the signals coming from the unconscious.

The conscious and the unconscious mind "do not speak the same language", so in order to establish communication, CRV creators have developed an artificial language of gestures with very simple grammar and found that the best "interpreter" is the body itself. Acquiring communication techniques between two minds involves long, boring, but ultimately effective training.

---

[71] Targ, 2004

No less difficult is the "jamming" problem. The signals coming from the unconscious mind can be compared to pale phosphorescence, which cannot be seen in the dazzling light of the sun, but which becomes visible in the dark. In order for the conscious mind to receive the signals, "brightness" of consciousness must be diminished as much as possible, but not completely. A word, a surprising detail, an unexpected emotion, or even too much information on the "target", can "awaken" the consciousness and block communication.

The "altered state of consciousness", also called the "non-conceptual state of mind", which is necessary for extrasensory perception, can be achieved through CRV techniques, but has also been achieved by shamans, biblical prophets, or ancient oracles. They achieve this state using psychotropic drugs such as Ayahuasca in the Amazon, or the underground gasses found in Delphi and also through asceticism or extreme fatigue. Other methods include those used by the whirling dervishes and the use of drumming by ritual dancers. A lesser diminishing of the conscious mind can even occur in discos through the obsessive, endless rhythmic repetition of simple sounds. Of course, to access the collective unconscious some other conditions are also required.

Initially, when establishing a connection with the target, the CRV operators had the impression that their consciousness was being transported to the location indicated by the coordinates they had been given, or by the instructions they had received. However, as they researched the mechanisms involved, they realised that, in fact, when a medium accesses a target, the image (or copy) of this object already exists in the collective unconscious, thus, implicitly, also in the medium's mind as a kind of "miniature virtual reality". Therefore, the medium does not access the physical reality itself through his unconscious, but only a duplicate of it which is *already in his extended mind*. The operator (or medium) does not go to the real target, but only needs to look for the copy of the target in his own mind.[72] An important outcome which we should not lose sight of, is that between physical reality and its virtual copy there may be differences caused by various mechanisms, including filters, models or taboos, etc. that exist in the operator's mind and, above all, as a set of cultural archetypes in the collective unconscious.

An interesting fact is that military remote viewers can be sent to see not just what is in a certain place, but also what *was* there in the past. This proves that what we named the "collective unconscious" not only accesses, but also records the events. And those events recorded remain there in a "virtual reality" type storage – perhaps we can call it a "*super-memory*" – which contains everyone's entire life plus the entire history of the world we live in.

The idea of the existence of a collective unconscious which somehow connects all humanity and is full of "cultural archetypes", was proposed in 1916 by the Swiss psychiatrist and psychoanalyst Carl Gustav Jung (1875-1961). Jung accepted the existence of a "collective memory" in which elements of a cultural nature taken from the people of previous generations have been stored and that our minds are connected to this "memory" – exchanging data in both directions – without the intervention of the conscious mind.

In another context, Alfred Rupert Sheldrake (b. 1942), former biochemist at the University of Cambridge, also thought about a collective memory. In 1981, he came to the conclusion that "natural systems, such as termite colonies, or groups of pigeons, and also orchids, or insulin molecules inherit a collective memory of all the previous experiences of their species".[73] He called this process "*morphic resonance*". By making a comparison, Sheldrake said that when it remembers something, the human brain works more like a "TV receiver" that connects to a remote station (that is, to his own part of the collective mind) and not as a "video recorder". In other words, he suggested that memory, if not of thought, exists

---

[72] Buchanan, 2003
[73] Sheldrake, 2009

to a certain extent, elsewhere, but not in the brain. Sheldrake was also convinced that inherited genetic information is not completely encoded in genes or other epigenetic material, claiming that much of it would come through "resonance" with data recorded somewhere else by previous members of the species. He was convinced that the same resonance helps a cat, or a dog know that their master is coming home long before they can be seen, and the same type of information tells homing pigeons how to get back to their coop. Some also wonder if the collective unconscious can explain telepathic communication or other forms of extrasensory contact.

There are other researches that seem to argue for the existence of a mysterious external data base linked to our minds. For example, Malcolm Gladwell published in 2008 in *The New Yorker* an article showing that since 1922, 148 major scientific discoveries have been made by different people from different locations around the world, practically simultaneously. He based his conclusion on the fact that "we all go to a common information bank, when we try to think of something specific"[74].

But the fact that our recollections and our whole life seem to be written in a "super-memory" raises countless other issues and I will return to this later..

Remote influence

Ingo Swann was not only a remarkable remote viewer, but also had the ability to remotely *influence* certain objects or phenomena. For example, in experiments conducted in 1971-72, at City College in New York, from a distance of eight metres he managed to modify the temperature of a thermistor (a temperature sensitive resistor) sealed inside a vacuum flask. Though generally disputed by official science, accounts of such effects of the mind on inanimate objects, actions called *psychokinesis*, or *telekinesis*, are still documented.

As an example, we can quote a well-studied case, that of Nina S. Kulagina (1926-1990), also known as Nelia Mihailova. For twenty years she has undergone experiments, first with Professor Leonid L. Vasiliev (1891-1966) from the Leningrad (Skt. Petersburg) University, then with other Russian researchers, including two Nobel award winners. Many of these experiments, which were filmed, are now accessible to the general public. Only using thought Kulagina moved glasses, slices of bread, cigarettes and so on, without touching them. Light objects were placed under a bell jar or a glass plate to keep them away from air movements. From a bunch of match sticks she could extract only one that had been marked, while she was surrounded by a metal cage to shield any electromagnetic waves. In another experiment she used her abilities to speed up, reduce and then stop the beating of a frog's heart that was floating in a solution. That suggests the possibly sinister, damaging and harming potential uses of psychokinesis something that was probably trialled by the security services of the USA, Russia and elsewhere.

In a famous filmed experiment at the Uhtomski Institute in Leningrad (today St. Petersburg), from a distance of two-metres, Kulagina separated the yolk and the white of an egg, which were floating in the salt water of an aquarium, sending them into two different corners of the tank. The task was completed within thirty minutes and monitoring devices showed that her pulse reached two hundred and forty (four beats per second), in conjunction with a brain wave frequency of 4 Hz. The ratio of frontal and occipital potentials, normally between three and four, was fifty, and in addition, her body emanated a magnetic field equal to the tenth part of the Earth's magnetic field. At the end of the experiment the woman was completely exhausted, the amount of glucose in her blood had grown alarmingly and she had become almost blind, her senses of taste and pain were altered, and she was dizzy and had

---

[74] Wilcock, 2011, p. 92 to 94

lost one kilogram of body weight. There is also evidence that since at least 1965, there have been official U.S. psychokinesis projects orchestrated by the USAF and NASA,.[75]

Psychokinesis is also related to *levitation*, when the "object" moved under the influence of the mind was, in this case, the body of the subject. Examples of levitation are mentioned in the writings of Apolonius of Tyana, Porphyrios, Iamblicus, and Maximus of Tyre, and also in the New Testament, which accredits this ability to Simon Magus (Acts, 8). But in the Bible and other religious writings, there are many individuals who levitate, among which are angels, Enoch and others.

It is claimed that more than a hundred Christian saints levitated; among them were: Toma d'Aquino, Tereza d'Avila, and Maria Magdalena de Pazzi. The best known case is probably the Franciscan monk St. Joseph of Cupertino (1603-1660), who is said to have begun to float during religious services. His levitations were seen by Pope Urban VIII, Prince Johann Friedrich von Brunswick, and a Spanish ambassador. More recent cases include the noted mediums Daniel Dunglas Home and Collin Evans. To the examples of influence mentioned above, remote healing, mind control, or affecting a person's health can be added. Experiments of this kind, conducted in 1993 by Dr. William Braud and Marylin Schlitz, included animals and biological cultures, these experiments were independently repeated.[76] But there are many other similar cases, including some which I have personally examined in Romania.

Unfortunately, all above exposed remote influences are officially challenged, saying that current science cannot explain them, and illusionists can also simulate that they levitate, move objects and so on.

Out of the Body experience

Another phenomenon that has been often mentioned, even if science cannot explain or accept it, is *extracorporeality,* through which the spirit is apparently detached from the body without losing consciousness and is aware of what is happening around it. I personally encountered cases like this in my own family. A known case in Romania is that of former police commissioner Ilie Cioară (1916-2004). After 1945 the Communist authorities sentenced him for political reasons, to five years and six months imprisonment. Sitting in inhuman conditions with another sixty detainees in the same room, he learned to leave his body at will. He wrote: "First I went out through one hand, then through the other. Then through my legs and, above, I reconstituted myself back... I was able to go far away in this form. I often visited my wife in Braşov, then my brother and my sister-in-law. I saw everything they were doing. Each time I looked around took note of a detail and then told them". At first, Ilie Cioară was surprised that none of them saw him. He tried to speak but he was not heard. He could not interact with the objects either. "I tried to pull a bottle that was on the table. But my hand passed through it as if there was nothing there". He also stated that during some of his extra-corporeal trips, he met the souls of some deceased people, and he obtained certain information from them.[77]

The interested reader can find descriptions of countless such stories. In 1943, G. N. M. Tyrrell suggested '*Out of the Body Experience* (OBE)', as the term for them, and this was adopted by other researchers, including Celia Green (1968) and Robert Monroe (1971), as an alternative to the terminology used up until then, such as "astral projection", or "soul travel".

Interestingly, there are also – albeit few – parallel voluntary OBE experiences, when two people are simultaneously able to have an OBE. Upon return, the events perceived are independently confirmed by each participant.[78]

---

[75] Fowler, 1991, p.187
[76] Targ, 2004, pp.158-160
[77] Cioară, 2001
[78] Targ, 2004, p. 192

The modern approach to voluntary extracorporeal experiments began in 1964 with the research of the psychology professor Charles Tart. One of his subjects was Robert A. Monroe, who, in 1958, discovered that he could dissociate himself from his physical body. Later, Monroe conducted experiments on his own.[79] To explore the phenomenon more comprehensively, in the early seventies Monroe set up and became executive director of the Monroe Institute in Afton (Virginia). Ingo Swann was one of those who was involved in his OBE projects.

Although not recognised scientifically, extra-corporeality has always been known. Ancient traditions, including those of Egypt and Greece considered that human beings possess (at least) three bodies: the physical mortal one, the energetic body, which doubles with the physical body and ensures its integrity, and a spiritual body that under certain conditions can detach from the first two through OBE. Many traditions consider that such separation also occurs in dreams while asleep.

Ancient authors wrote about OBE journeys, include Plutarch, Plato, Aristotle, St. Augustine and some others who said they had experienced these events themselves. An expert in this field is Ioan Petru Culianu, who talks about Hermotimus of Clazomenae, who was a seer versed in out-of-body travel. While his body was lying in a cataleptic state, his soul visited various places he was able to describe precisely after awakening. He died while in this state, because, thinking he was dead, his wife gave his body to his enemies who burned it so that his soul would have no place to return. Other psychics from ancient Greece, who were said to be capable of inducing an OBE, were: Aristeas, Epimenides, Empedocles and others. The last of these even wrote a work on this subject, entitled *"Peri ten apnoum"* (about the state at the edge of death)[80].

The Christian Church mentions that many saints, including Saint Francis of Assisi, Saint Anthony of Padua, Saint Teresa of Avila and others, including some from the last century, had this ability. In European culture, among the writers who evoked or even experienced OBE, were Goethe, Musset, Maupassant, Poe, Baudelaire, and, more recently, Aldous Huxley, Arthur Koestler and Ernest Hemingway.

In 1978, Dean Sheils of the University of Wisconsin, conducted a study on seventy non-Western cultures. He was surprised to discover that 89% of them had a tradition of travelling outside the body. The shamans say that in this way they were in touch with the spiritual worlds and they could attain this state by consuming substances like ayahuasca.

There are many reports (including some I examined in Romania) in which the "abduction" of the witness was done not in the physical body, but "out of the body" in a spiritual form or "double" and in some cases it's hard to tell in which way the abduction took place and in many reports the aliens themselves appear in a spiritual form. The antiquity of this dilemma, as well as the difficulty in describing what occurred during an abduction is appears in a note from the Apostle Paul: "I know a man in Christ who, fourteen years ago, was caught up to the third heaven. Whether it was in the body or out of the body I do not know – God knows. And I know that this man – whether in the body or apart from the body I do not know, but God knows – was caught up to paradise and heard inexpressible things, things that no one is permitted to tell." (2 Cor, 12; 2-4).

OBE is not the same thing as remote viewing and the relationship between them and the collective unconscious still has to be clarified. A number of other issues also remain, including whether OBE is an attribute of human beings that emerges naturally at a certain moment in the evolution of our species, or is an attribute resulting from that "control system" exercised over us by a superior power.

---

[79] Monroe, 1971
[80] Culianu, 1991

Near death experiences

OBE's have also been reported by people who have returned from clinical death, that is by those who have gone through a *near-death experience* (abbreviated to NDE).

As an example I will mention two cases from Romania. Professor George Litarczek (b. 1925), a member of the Academy of Medical Sciences, reported that following an internal haemorrhage he entered a coma and had to be operated on urgently in an operating theatre where he had never been until that incident. During surgery, he saw himself floating over his body and could later provide details he perceived while in a state in which he was unconscious. A second case concerns a woman who was injured following an accidental fall down a lift shaft. She saw a tunnel, like a long, truncated tube with the narrowest end nearest to her. At the opposite end she arrived at a place with a very pleasant light and a landscape of grass, flowers and birds that sang. "I was very happy there, until a voice told me several times: What are you doing here? Back! Your time has not arrived yet." After making her way back she returned to the hospital room where she had been admitted.[81].

Kenneth Ring Ph.D., from the University of Storrs, Connecticut, has gathered twenty one cases of people who were blind from birth who, during an NDE, were able to see. There is also a case where a doctor, who was attending to a comatose patient lost his pen and could not find it anywhere. The patient, who had been watching the scene during an NDE, after he recovered was able indicate the location of the missing pen, the pen was then recovered.[82]

Researches on the near-death experience were brought to the attention of the general public by Raymond Moody (b.1944), through two famous books: "Life after Life" (1976) and "Reflections on Life after Life" (1977). In 2008 in ten Dutch hospitals the Dutch cardiologist Dr. Pim van Lommel organised, a study of three hundred and forty four survivors of cardiac arrest. Of these, sixty two patients (18%) returned with memories; 50% of them said that although they knew they were about to die, they had positive emotions, 30% reported travelling through a tunnel and seeing a non-earthly landscape or had an encounter with deceased relatives. Approximately 25% had an OBE experience and communicated with a "being of light", 35% saw a brief review of their life and 8% met a boundary beyond which they were not allowed to pass.[83] Other statistics found that between twenty six and fifty percent of people who had an NDE experience said they had an OBE as well. In many accounts, those recovering from clinical death had the feeling that the bright realm, sometimes called "Astral", was in fact their "true home".[84]

It may be surprising at first glance, but the NDE experience has many features in common with UFO abductions. Jenny Randles describes "a near-death experience caused by a reaction to a drug administrated by a dentist. The patient underwent the typical OBE and tunnel experience. However, instead of entering a world of light, he entered a UFO! Aliens warned him that the Earth was in trouble..."[85] And this was not an isolated case.

In 1990, Kenneth Ring Ph.D., together with Christopher J. Rosing, created a project called "Omega", to highlight the potential similarities between UFO abductions and NDE. The results of the project were published in 1992. Among other things, Ring (and other researchers) pointed out that those who had had a "near-death experience", often say that, in common with some UFO abductees, they also met "Nordic" type visitors, they were beings like 'angels'.

At the end of the project Ring wondered: "Could it be that the world of the NDE and that of UFO abductions, for all their difference, are not after all universes apart, but a part of the

---

[81] Dulcan, 2008, pp.151-153.
[82] Dulcan, 2013, p.119.
[83] Wilcock, 2011, pp. 103-105.
[84] Mack, 1999, p. 224
[85] Fowler, 1995, p.279

same universe? Could it be that the NDErs and UFO experiencers have more in common with one another than we have previously suspected?"[86]

Dr. John B. Alexander, who studied the science of death, thought that despite differences in reported factors, the two phenomena could even have a common cause. Jean Sider wrote in one of his books that the source of the ghosts of dead people could be the same source that generates UFOs and aliens.

The many common features between UFO abductions and the accounts from people who recover from clinical death were noted by Ufologist Raymond Fowler. In both cases the person concerned had the impression that they left their body and headed for a light. They experienced a sense of unity and bright beings, sometimes wearing long robes. Those having the experience felt that they were also made of light and communicated telepathically. They felt they had returned to their true home ad did not want to return to Earth and understood that the most important thing is *love*.

Based on the above, Fowler even said that: "It is my opinion that NDEs and UFO abductions are controlled by the same intelligences" and "whoever controls the UFO phenomenon is intimately connected with the afterlife of human beings."[87]

Afterlife and reincarnation

The examples and arguments mentioned here seem to prove the existence of a "spiritual double" of the physical body, a double that can travel long distances and, in certain situations, can contact deceased relatives or sacred beings. On the other hand, in ancient times this kind of spiritual body was not only accepted by virtually all existing cultures and traditions, including monotheistic religions, but these cultures were convinced that this spiritual double survived, in one form or another, after the death of the physical body.

Can we accept this belief? At first sight the reality of the NDE phenomenon seems to be proof of the survival of the soul after death. However sceptics doubt this, saying that all the accounts come from people who had come back to life, so they have not really dead.

An interesting story about this issue comes from Lyn Buchanan, one of the best military remote viewers. He said that during his training, for months he was only given people who were dying due to illness, accidents, explosions and wounds, etc as targets. He estimated that in total he tracked abound sixty-seven individuals. His monitor directed him to track the target until they dies than follow them beyond this point. Buchanan classified the situations he encountered in these exercises into four categories, which he called "heaven", "hell", "forgetting" and "reincarnation". Heaven was something like our world, but in a perfect form and in many cases the soul was greeted by the spirits of others who had died. Hell, which he never saw for more than a fraction of a second, was like "a brilliant darkness" with an orange light on the horizon that was blocked by "something" that looked like a person who was to waiting for the newcomer. In "forgetting", the person he was tracking suddenly "disappeared" and could no longer be found. In the fourth instance, the one he called "reincarnation", when Buchanan was trying to contact the deceased he saw someone else in their place, it was not a new born baby, but someone around twelve or thirteen years of age.[88]

But even Buchanan warned that such claims must be treated with caution for two reasons. First, a basic rule is the "calibration" or verification of the information received from the remote viewers using a "feed-back" process, which is confirming the data by comparing it to reality; this phase was missing here. In addition, we must not forget that between reality and its virtual copy, is what the remote viewer actually accesses in the "collective

---

[86]   Ring, 1992, p.110
[87]   Fowler, 1995, pp. 277, 279, 309
[88]   Buchanan, 2003

unconscious", and there are differences here caused by many mechanisms, including cultural filters, models and taboos, etc.

A popular argument for the survival of spirit could be the many accounts of ghosts. In a paper posted in 2010 on an Internet site dedicated to NDE, Dr. Kenneth Ring cited cases of people who were clinically dead (but were restored to life) who appeared to close friends as a ghost. Subsequently, both of the people involved in these strange encounters were able to independently verify the details. It is likely that the reader will have come across many stories concerning persons who, at their time of death appeared in the form of ghosts, mainly in front of loved ones. In this regard, the astronomer and famous writer Camille Flammarion (1842-1925) gathered dozens of these cases.[89]

Another, even more intriguing argument for the survival of the spirit is the alleged phenomenon of reincarnation. For example, from time to time a story appears in the media concerning a child who remembers that, in another life, they were someone else and describes events, usually significant, complete with the names of people, places and other details which they could not know by normal means. Surprisingly and inexplicably, in many cases when the information was checked it was found to be accurate.

These are not just urban myths or traditional beliefs but are a phenomenon that has been systematically studied by qualified researchers. Ian P. Stevenson (1918-2007), a professor of psychiatry at the University of Virginia, according to some sources in the early 1960s he identified about three thousand cases of alleged reincarnation. He selected twenty of them which he personally investigated, and in 1966 published the results. Seven of these cases came from India, three from Sri Lanka and two from Brazil, seven from Alaska and one from Lebanon. Stevenson found that those concerned remembered traumas and specific events, apparently from another life. He pointed out that these cases did not prove the existence of reincarnation, but undoubtedly showed the existence of a phenomenon that could not be explained by coincidence, exaggerated interpretations or deceit.

Investigations of the same type were conducted by other researchers, including Phyllis M. H. Atwater, Jim B. Tucker, Sandra Anne Taylor and others, who have added to the list of cases and possible interpretations. If the "reincarnation" was of a recently deceased person, they verified the places, people, names, buildings and objects described by the alleged "reincarnated" individual and it turned out that they mostly corresponded, despite the fact that they had no way of knowing about them.

We could also include the story described in a previous chapter, concerning Miss Rosemary from Blackpool, who, while in trance, remembered fragments from the life of an ancient Egyptian princess in the list of cases of supposed reincarnations. In Romania, I am also aware of several cases where people recalled past lives.

The idea that the human spirit survives physical death and returns to Earth, then reincarnates and starts a new life in a new body and after that body dies, reincarnates in a third, is found in many secular and religious traditions. This process, also called *metempsychosis*, is not only accepted as real by Hindu's, but also by the Taoists, Confucians, Zoroastrians and some of the Native American and Australian peoples. The Celtic druids, Pythagoreans and Orphics in ancient Greece, Mithraics, Manicheans and also the ancient Egyptians, believed in reincarnation [90]. Thinkers such as Giordano Bruno, Campanella, Leibniz, Hume, Goethe, Benjamin Franklin, Lev Tolstoy and others were also believers in reincarnation. The Christian religion does not formally accept the existence of reincarnation but does not explicitly deny it.

---

[89]   Flammarion, 1923
[90]   Kernbach, 1995

In the strict sense reincarnation poses some problems. One is of a logical nature: admitting that mankind is descended from a primordial couple, conventionally called "Adam and Eve" (a hypothesis agreed on by religions and some geneticists), if there were only two people there were only two spirits and currently there are over 7.5 billion. So how do we explain where all these spirits came from? Also, today, here on Earth the number of births is higher than the number of deaths, so, to make reincarnation work we have to assume that human spirits are being created for the first time and are not the result of the reincarnation of other people; but this is never mentioned. If we assume that the spirits of the people here on Earth are only a fraction of the enormous populations of spirits from the whole Universe and that they might also transmigrate into animals or even plants, we might wonder if all these spirits existed at the time of the "Big Bang", when the Universe was born...

There are also some well-documented facts which require us to adopt a broader view of alleged reincarnations. One such case, which was intensively studied and publicised, is that of David Paladin (1926-1984) who was the son of a Navajo mother and a white missionary father. David was an alcoholic at eleven years of age and left his reservation and got a job as merchant seaman. He enlisted as soldier in the US Army during the Second World War and was sent to spy on the Germans; but he was captured. He was tortured and eventually left for dead in a prison camp. It was almost two and a half years before he regained consciousness and during this time he was sometimes heard muttering words in Russian. When he recovered, he was asked about his identity and promptly replied: "I am a painter, my name is Vasili Kandinski". Vasili Kandinski, was a Russian who became a naturalised German, then adopted French citizenship and became one of the greatest painters of the 20th century, and was perhaps one the first to introduce the concept of abstract art.

Paladin tried to prove his identity by revealing several facts and little-known details of Kandinski's life and through the Red Cross he requested and received the brushes, paints and other requirements necessary for painting. He produced a number of works that were appreciated by the artistic community, and their style resembled the artwork produced by Kandinski.

David had no prior knowledge of painting and it is unlikely that had heard about Kandinsky. Gradually regaining his identity, Paladin continued to paint in the same style, and also in the Navajo tradition and began teaching painting in a college. He dedicated the last twenty years of his life, until he died in 1984, to painting and community-based activities. While painting, he no longer seemed possessed by Kandinsky's spirit, but it seemed as if he was in some sort of trance, as if the artistic inspiration came from elsewhere.

Initially we might regard this as an example of reincarnation, but Vasili Kandinski died in France on December 13, 1944 while David was 18 years old, therefore this is not reincarnation in the usual sense of the word. Dr. H. N. Banerjee of Rajasthan University in Jaipur who had studied several cases of reincarnation, said that maybe Kandinsky's spirit entered Paladin's body by taking advantage of his weakness and the fact that his spirit was absent. There are several examples of this type of case.

In the light of what we have seen here, a hypothesis that might explain this is that Paladin's unconscious mind, taking advantage of the weakness of his conscious mind, had contacted (some might say "resonated") with "Kandinsky's copy" in the Akashic Records, which he temporarily assumed as his own identity.

Such a mechanism might also explain other recollections of "previous lives" without resorting to the mechanism of reincarnation. Thus, the objections to reincarnation, exposed at the beginning of this subchapter, would disappear without affecting the related assumptions about the survival of the spirit as it is accepted by the Christian church.

But why did this involve Kandinsky? Another hypothesis could be that Kandinsky's spirit, recorded in "Akasha", could have had the ability to take the initiative and in this case wanted to find a way to continue his work on Earth using another body.

The theory whereby a person's spirit can leave a damaged body and be replaced by another spirit that possesses the body was examined by Ruth Montgomery (1912-2001), who was a well-known journalist accredited to the White House under Six Presidents, before she became interested in spiritual matters. She called it the *"walk in"* process, where a spirit enters a body and uses it for a period of time.[91] Montgomery claimed that much of the information she received, using automatic writing, was from spirit guides. Other authors, including Scott Mandelker and Brad Steiger, have made similar claims in their books.

Virtual worlds

Therefore, reliving details of a deceased person's life, and regarding them as your own, is not a final proof of reincarnation or of "past lives". Rupert Sheldrake also suggested that "If we admit the existence of a kind of eternal collective memory on which we all may draw, the same as what we call collective unconscious, or Akasha, one might tune in to particular people in the past who are now dead and, through morphic resonance, pick up memories of past lives." He says that this doesn't prove "that you were that person".[92]

In a previous chapter I have tried to outline some of the developments that will mark the future of mankind, and I have shown that we are about to create virtual world on our computers, in which we could store copies of someone's entre life. A *hyper-civilization* that arrived on Earth millions of years ago, could have created a kind of virtual world as a part of its "control system" and could have stored everything about our world in it.

Based on what kind of hardware? They would not have needed a supercomputer similar to one of ours. They may have had much subtler means to store their data base, perhaps using the fifth state of matter normally inaccessible to us that the old ones called "akasha", or perhaps some other exotic means, such as the dark matter or dark energy that has been theorised by physicists. Their hardware could even be placed in a parallel dimension, but most likely behind the presumed virtual reality built by a *hyper-civilization*. Because here lies a science and technology that by far exceeds anything we can imagine.

By monitoring the progresses of earthly civilization, the representatives of *hyper-civilizations* could systematically record – in a virtual reality form – the facts, images and thoughts that are of value to them. Remarkable achievements in science, art, crafts and so on, in other words the history of mankind and all the spiritual values that have ever mattered.

I previously mentioned that, in an extremely distant future, we may wish to give those who are in the virtual worlds a fragment of autonomous will, some initiative and perhaps even a spark of consciousness. This could be the ability to know who they were and have the awareness that they are beyond the boundary of physical death and possibly that they still have something to accomplish on Earth. For *hyper-civilizations*, millions of years more advanced than we are, it would have been easy to accomplish all this.

If we accept that every human beings mind is connected to the "collective unconscious", it means that an "avatar" of a person, that is their virtual copy recorded in this "super-memory", begins to accumulate data from their birth until after their physical death, everything is recorded. Therefore, this "avatar" possesses everything that the person did in their life, and it can be seen by anyone who comes into contact with this "super-memory". And if we admit that the avatar might have a degree of consciousness, then it might also be able to manifest on its own initiative. We might speculate that such a process could explain

---

[91]   Montgomery, 1986
[92]   Sheldrake, 1992, apud Mack, 1995, 418

the appearance of "ghosts" in places that an individual was attached to, or that people in the virtual world might try to continue their existence by channelling, or even by taking possession of individuals in the material world.

The idea that there is a place where we can record people's lives or perhaps only those who have special value is not new. Comments about the Akashic Records, or the Book of Life, can be found in folklore and myths throughout the Old and New Testament. It is traceable at least as far back as the Semitic peoples and this includes the Arabs, the Assyrians, the Phoenicians, the Babylonians and the Hebrews. Each of these peoples had the belief that there is some kind of celestial tablet which contains the history of the human race, as well as some essential spiritual information. In ancient Egypt, to remove a name from of a record was the equivalent to destroying the fact that the person had ever even existed.[93]

For example, we read in the Bible that: "Whoever has sinned against me I will blot out of my book" said The Lord to Moses (Exodus, 32; 33); those redeemed by Christ are contained within the Book of Life (Philippians 4;3); those not found in the Book of Life will not enter the Kingdom of Heaven: "Another book was opened, which is the book of life. The dead were judged according to what they had done as recorded in the books" (Revelation, 20;12).

References to the fact that in Heaven all the things on Earth are recorded including injustices and all people's thoughts, as well as the fact that the names of sinners will be wiped out of the holy books, also exist in the apocryphal Book of Enoch.

A very different realm

Of course, the supposition that our memories and our entire life are written in a "super-memory" raises countless other problems. Is this super-memory a natural property of the human race or of all living creatures? Or is it installed by some non-earthly intelligence by using the natural properties of matter? If so, is it completely artificial? How does it work? Does it also contain a part of the conscious mind and in that case a person cannot even be conscious without the need for this super-memory and so on. No human being has the final answer to these questions, but we can at least speculate.

For example, we can speculate that the fact that a thought or a memory can simultaneously be in both our brain and "beyond" it in the super-memory, using the concept of "*quantum entanglement*", which is a fundamental property of quantum physics.

The nature of virtual reality stored in the "collective unconscious" also raises some issues. A person who apparently suffered a UFO abduction told Professor John Mack that the "spiritual entities" he encountered said to him: "We don't consist of physical data... we are not in space/time. We don't have any form",[94] or "The past, present and future are one", or that, in their world, "Everything is always present".[95] Raymond Fowler also wrote that an entity told to abductee Betty Andreasson-Luca, that their time is not like our time, although they know perfectly well what our time is, adding that they can reverse the passage of time.

Similar information was obtained by Dr. Raymond Moody, Prof. Dr. Dumitru Constantin-Dulcan from Bucharest and by others, from patients who returned from an NDE. They stated that they had arrived at a place where there is no linear time, but a continuous present, including the three forms of time – past, present and future.[96]

These seemingly paradoxical statements become perfectly understandable, on the assumption that those entities exist inside a kind of sophisticated memory. As a rather simplistic comparison, at any given moment a DVD contains the entire sequence of events in a movie. The past, the present and the future of any episode are simultaneously on that disc. If we return to the

---

[93]   Todeschi, 1998
[94]   Mack, 1995, p.243
[95]   Mack, 1999, pp. 55-56
[96]   Dulcan, 2013, p. 103

beginning of the film we can follow what occurs during the film, or by reversing the DVD, the time and so on.

In a similar way, using the "super-memory", some people could *travel in the past*, and relive the events as though it were reality. I recall the fact that the American military remote viewers were trained for such "trips", accessing not just any point in space, but also any moment in the past. But this 'time-travel' is not accomplished in physical reality (as supposed in some SF stories) but in its copy, in the virtual reality stored in that super-memory. The "time-travelers" might even be involved in some incidents. In doing so they will not disturb the events as they happened (an act which would lead to serious paradoxes), but, at most, affect the virtual "copy" of them that will return to the original form for the next visitors.

Obviously, the question arises regarding whether travel like this can also be made *into the future*. It is astonishing how many people are convinced that the future already exists and that if you have the adequate tools: oracles, divination, playing cards, coffee, cryptic texts (Nostradamus type), etc. you can see what it is.

Undoubtedly, certain future events are predictable: when will the sun rise tomorrow, when will the winter solstice and eclipses occur over the next hundred years, when will some comets appear and so on. But these predictions have limits. The vast majority of thinkers accept that reality, especially that which is influenced by human beings, are subjected, not only to mechanical causality, but also to *free will*. Therefore, to a certain extent the future depends on countless unpredictable human decisions, which can, in time, have important consequences.

But we can assume that in the super-memory we are talking about, *forecast scenarios* are also stored. These include future events with a high probability of occurrence to the extent that they are predictable. The scenarios would be accessible to some "travelers in the future", in a way similar to someone travelling in the past.

Over the years many people have said that they received information about future events through channeling or during UFO abductions. The predictions of ancient prophets and our forebears often contain *catastrophic warnings*. A famous example from antiquity is the Book of Revelation of St. John of Patmos, in which the end of the world is foretold. But, surprisingly, the same kind of warning was received by many people during UFO abductions. They said that they have been shown– on screens or by other means – a future with destroyed cities, where mankind had been exterminated and so on. I have found many similar reports, including some from Romania. Their large number and similarity suggests that their source could be in the same super-memory where scenarios of a possible future, some of them apocalyptic, are stored and that a number of people have obtained access – in one way or another – to these scenarios. Of course it does not mean that the scenarios will definitely materialise, but they could be warnings that events like these are likely to occur.

If we accept all of this, the next question is who created these scenarios and who included them in the super-memory? Are they the result of a natural process? For example, emanations of collective fear or of an often-threatening future? Or are we confronted with "magic" that could be attributed to the presence of a *hyper-civilization*? If so, why were they put there? Are they part of some "cosmic plan" with an unknown stage director", that Carl Gustav Jung spoke about?

But with regard to the spiritual beings existing in "Akasha" or perhaps some other similar areas of reality, there are even more surprising hypotheses A clue comes from Dr. Courtney Brown, professor at Emory University in Atlanta (Georgia). In 1991 he learned the techniques of remote viewing in the "Stargate" project and also attended courses at the Monroe Institute. In 1995, Brown established and became the director of "The Farsight Institute" in Atlanta, Georgia, where he developed the *Scientific Remote Viewing* (SRV) method, an improved version of CRV.

In his books[97] Brown states, among other things, that – using some of the techniques involved with remote viewing – he contacted a place that he has been told was "The Headquarters of the Galactic Federation". Typically, a remote viewer or a person having an OBE journey, sees the objects and people in the target area, but he cannot physically interact with them and the remote viewer is not seen because of their incorporeal nature. The beings Brown found also all had a 'spiritual consistency', and saw him immediately and welcomed him, saying that they were glad that, "Finally, we also have arrived". They said that this spiritual form is the only way we can contact them. The entities confirmed that they have been on the Earth for a long time, but they will not officially come into contact with us until we mature. They also confirmed the reality of human abductions, genetic experiments and other kinds of intervention.

Brown said that he was led to someone who seemed important, the being had an impressive stature rather like Buddha. This being told him that for the time being, as long as earthlings are brutal and undisciplined; they will have to undergo important transformations before they can begin their cosmic journey come into direct contact with representatives of other civilizations. Human beings are evolving very slowly, but the evolved civilizations are waiting patiently, because, in the galactic sense, because in the future they depend on our contribution. At first, to Brown this claim seemed unlikely given the huge gap between our levels of development. However, a similar message also came from others who had experienced encounters with aliens.

Another interesting communication, which Courtney Brown says he received, is from the so-called "Galactic Federation", which represents an invisible, astral and transcendent world. He was told that that physical beings would not be able to contact the Galaxy. Although the physical world is real and one of collective progress and major achievements, it is temporary, and spirits can only spend a limited time there before returning to the realms of the astral spheres.[98]

Of course, this "vision" must be viewed with care, because remote viewers do not access reality, but only a copy of it which is full of archetypes, and information obtained in this way is never 100% accurate. Perhaps *hyper-civilizations* have found a way to leave the material world– the one that does not allow us to travel faster than the speed of light – and are now everywhere in the Cosmos in a non-physical form and use an Akasha-type structure, not only to record their combined consciousness, but thanks to their knowledge and advanced technologies, to interact with the material world.

Once again the evidence we have examined in this chapter suggests the probability that there are powers around us that possess "magical" means through which they can be any where at any time, and are able to control, directly or through "material intermediaries", things that happen on Earth and probably in other corners of the Universe as well. Could these powers be the *hyper-civilizations*?

CONCLUSIONS

Military projects involving remote viewing seem to have been achieved using a form of the collective unconscious, which is connected to everyone's minds and along with other information are continuously recorded. These records seem to be organized in a virtual reality super-memory. A medium can sometimes access the information from this super-memory through phenomena like channelling, automatic writing, xenoglossy and dowsing etc.

Out of the Body Experience (OBE) and Near-Death Experience (NDE), suggest that a person has a spiritual body as well as a physical one. The spiritual body could be related to the

---

[97]   Brown, 1996 and Brown, 1999.
[98]   Brown, 1996

person's life recording in the super-memory, a record that stays there after the physical body disappears. Some clues suggest that this "spiritual double" could preserve some rudiments of consciousness. The resonance of a human with such a record could explain the alleged cases of reincarnation, or 'walk-ins', and perhaps even the appearance of ghosts. Perhaps it could also manifest as a form of time-travel.

The above shows that the super-memory or collective unconscious overlap the "Akashic Records" and the "Book of Life". This raises a question: Is the collective unconscious, or Akasha, a natural process in our evolution and/or an entity controlled (and perhaps even created) by a hyper-civilization? Some arguments, including the often apocalyptic messages received by mediums etc, tilt the balance toward the second option.

WHAT CAN WE HOPE FOR?

An unimaginably complex reality

Hopefully the arguments presented in the previous chapters were convincing enough to allow the *hyper-civilization* hypothesis to help answer Fermi's paradox. Many of the unexplained phenomena that happen on Earth may be the "magic" produced by *hyper-civilizations* that discreetly remains with us for long periods of time. Of course, this is only a hypothesis that fits what we know, but it is not necessarily the only answer. In particular, the hypothesis of the "Akasha" super-memory is just one possible explanation, but it is one that seems to me the most plausible and explains that phenomena we have addressed in the previous chapters. The explanations we have suggested do not fully explain all the 'miracles' that surround us, but let's not allow that to narrow our vision just because, at present, we cannot answer all the questions. The discoveries that will surely occur in the centuries and millennia that follow will undoubtedly open other gates and reveal explanations that at present seem impossible.

Sceptics may contest the evidence offered in the previous chapters supporting the presence of hyper-civilizations around us, saying that we have to rely on mainstream science and that cannot explain phenomena like this. In this case more convincing evidence would be required. However, before answering I think a digression would be useful. On the one hand I would like to present some arguments that we could use to argue against this type of scepticism and on the other hand I would like to discuss the issue of the limits of knowledge.

I fully agree with a famous statement made in 1927 by the geneticist J.B.S. Haldane: "I have no doubt that in reality the future will be vastly more surprising than anything I can imagine. Now my own suspicion is that the Universe is not only queerer than we suppose, but queerer than we can suppose". A simplified version of this idea has also been attributed to the astrophysicist Arthur Stanley Eddington: "The Universe is not only stranger than we imagine, it is stranger than we can imagine".

Indeed, reality is much stranger than science books tell us and more than we can believe. Thousands of testimonies have been gathered about the fact that rarely, in some very special situations and only for a short time, the laws of physics as we know them do not seem to have been be respected. In the previous chapters I have mentioned some examples from those that may relate to the phenomenon we are discussing.

It was reported that – after a tornado – wooden objects have been found buried in metal structures or embedded in wooden objects, or a cane was thrust into a brick wall.[99] In some UFO abductions, the witnesses said their physical body passed through a wall, or a closed window. It was reported also that, allegedly, the aliens explained to some abductees that, in some special conditions, that for a fraction of a second the state of solid bodies could change, after which they returned to their original form. It was also said that, when asked, the ET's explained that this was achieved by "synchronising vibrations".

There are thousands of reports about UFOs that mention alien ships, giant globes, and formations of lights that are seen in the sky. They can remain motionless as if they are weightless, or fly in zigzags and at sharp angles, but when they are on the ground they leave traces as if they weighed many tons. Sometimes they fly into space and on other occasions they become invisible in an instant. In some UFO abductions the victim is levitated, and other entities levitate next to them and it often happens that a light beam comes from the craft and this lifts a human, an animal or even a car into the craft.

---

[99] Wilcock, 2011, but also Watson, 1974, Fort, 1919, and many others.

It was also reported that in Chile, on April 25, 1977 at around 04:15, Sergeant Armando Valdes disappeared during a patrol in front of five of his men, this occurred when two 'bright lights' approached them. He reappeared after fifteen minutes, but his beard showed five days of growth and the calendar on his watch showed that he might have been missing for five days. When debriefed the sergeant did not remember anything, but he did not think he had been abducted. Chinese researcher, Shi Bo, reported a similar case that occurred to a soldier, Wang Qin Hua, who vanished and was found a few hours later, but his hair and beard showed several days of growth[100]. On the other hand, in 1975, in Arizona, Travis Walton was abducted in full view of six people and was not found for nearly a week. When he reappeared, he did not seem to have changed and he spoke as if only a few hours had passed.

In 1989, Linda Napolitano, whose case was investigated by Budd Hopkins, recalled under hypnosis that during her childhood she was abducted from a crowded swimming pool, while surrounded by her parents and relatives. As she was lifted from the ground time seemed to stop everything around her froze, even the water droplets hung motionless in the air. After spending several hours with her abductors she was returned to the same place. The moment she touched the earth everything returned to normal and nobody had noticed anything unusual.[101] The case was similar to that of M.G., which was investigated by me. When he was eleven his consciousness was 'abducted and he remembered this happening. He saw that his body, which remained on a balcony, was frozen in time. When returned he saw his home and his body had remained "frozen". Now he noticed that "people and cars on the street were frozen too".[102] These anomalies do not seem to be a recent phenomenon. There are similar stories in fairy tales as well as in the writings of some religions and they could all be genuine memories of past events.

The cases mentioned above, as well as others of the same kind, make us to suspect that there is an intelligence around us that has mastered, not only advanced technologies, but can also modify space and time as it desires and in a way that we cannot understand.

For over a century, physicists have been struggling to bring all the laws of space, time and matter under a single umbrella, to achieve a *"theory of everything"*. At present the best candidate for this is the so-called *"M-theory"*. According to this theory all elementary particles and all forms of energy in the Universe are hypothetical "strings" with a single dimension (length) and is placed on a two-dimensional membrane. However, in order for this model to function the strings and membranes must be part of a Universe possessing eleven dimensions. So, the fact that we only see three spatial dimensions (length, width, height) plus another one of time would be just a local situation, suggesting that our world is only a small part of a much more complex structure. In that "complete" Universe there would another seven dimensions. Where are they? Why do we not see them? Physicists have proposed explanations, but they cannot be verified using practical experiments. But it is good to remember that all these theories are only *mathematical models*, made to closely match reality; in other words they are only constructions of the human mind. Even our most elaborate laws and theories are not reality but only images of it; they are close enough, but not perfect.

Where is the Akasha super-memory, which we discussed about in the previous chapters located? As I said, it is unlikely that there is a huge supercomputer hidden somewhere to host it. A hyper-civilization must have found a simpler and more sophisticated solution. Could it be something like the alleged "memory" of water? Research in that direction was made at the Madeleine Ennis of Queens University in Belfast by the French immunologist Jacques Benveniste, and also by the Japanese researcher Masaru Emoto. The apparent success of homeopathy is a compelling argument that such a memory exists, although all this evidence

---

[100] ˀ Bo, 1993, p.208-215
[101] Hopkins, 1996, p.206
[102] Farcas, 2016, p.211

currently remains inexplicable (and therefore contested) by mainstream science. There are also stories suggesting that not only water, but many other materials could have a natural "memory". For example haunted places and houses that have kept the remembrance of some horrors that happened long ago in their walls. This is a variant on the very similar 'stone tape' theory, which suggest that solid matter may have a memory

Regarding about the memory of matter, we can ask – what matter? The usual one or perhaps "cold dark matter"? The so-called *Lambda-cold-dark matter model* – another trendy physical theory – suggests that matter in the Universe would comprise three kinds: the usual one that we see and feel (only 5% of the total), the "cold dark matter" (23%) and "dark energy" (about 72%). The latter two have not been found by any researcher or instrument, they are only a theory. In fact, we only see a tenth part of the 5% of *ordinary* matter. In 1998, the astrophysicist Rudolf Schild suggested that "*vacuum energy fluctuations*" could be used by an advanced civilization to travel faster than light. Therefore, we can ask what other properties are hidden along with these invisible, "dark", components of reality (or if even they exist?) and also if they are the cause of many phenomena that are presently considered inexplicable? In addition, no one can guarantee that the future will not shed light on other unpredictable forms of what we call matter and energy.

Another facet of the complexity of reality is illustrated by *quantum physics*. At the beginning of the last century, physicists, starting with Max Planck, showed that energy, matter, and perhaps also space and time are not continuous, but are constructed of very small "quantum" packages. Their study gave rise to quantum mechanics, revealing at the elementary level of matter new properties that were increasingly strange and less intuitive. For example, in 1982 at the University of Paris, a team led by physicist Alain Aspect discovered that, under certain circumstances, some elementary particles, such as electrons, instantly "know about each other" no matter how far away they are. The phenomenon has been called "*quantum entanglement*". Does this "instantaneous data exchange" not somehow transcend the limitations of speed of light? Might this property be used in the future to communicate and perhaps even to teleport objects over cosmic distances?

However, we should agree with Jacques Vallée who said in a 2014 interview for *Ovnis-Direct*, that "It seems to me that, in their enthusiasm, some researchers use quantum physics a little bit too much: and since these mechanisms remain mysterious, they can be stretched to explain a lot of phenomena in an exaggerated way".

But if we enter into speculation there are some really interesting theories. In 1993 David Barclay, a UK ufologist, suggested the hypothesis that paranormal phenomena are happening in a virtual reality that we are in contact with. He added: "Everything we consider real could be a hologram – even you who are reading this page". A similar assumption is the "Matrix hypothesis", which says that the entire Universe, including the human race and everything on the Earth, could be kind of a game, simulated on the "computers" of some higher consciousness, just like in "*The Matrix*" movie and its sequels. In the same way some Oriental mystics claim that reality is a "maya", an illusion that turns our perceptions into physical objects but only after it passes through our senses. In Tibet and India, there is also a belief that the human mind can materialise thoughts in the form of an entity called a "tulpa".

Evolutionism and creationism

Beyond the scientific theories through which we try to understand reality, and beyond the speculations about the fabric of reality, there is a fundamental question that had preoccupied mankind from its beginnings: was the world the result of a natural evolution or it was created by an act of will? If the latter is true who was the Creator? And what were – more specifically – the steps in both creating and improving the human race?

There are two possible main approaches. The first is the *"creationist*, top-*down"* theory that assumes from the beginning there was an omnipotent and omniscient Divinity, a conscience that, being all knowing, created everything that exists, from the most advanced forms to the smallest elements of reality. The second approach is the *"evolutionist, bottom-up"*, theory of physical matter, that gradually evolved in an unimaginably large number of small random steps, from the simplest forms to the complexity of the current world, from inert to conscious, even creating forms that have far outstripped our earthly technological civilization and which we have called *hyper-civilizations.*

Since Darwin science opts for this second approach, the evolutionist one. Scientists say that God, being almighty and capable of creating the Universe in one gesture, would not have needed the four billion years of continuous struggle, to create the first life forms to the present technological civilization, which for most of the time only consisted of microorganisms.

My personal conviction remains that the inability of some of us to accept evolution is largely because of the inability of our minds to contain the many random events, mutations, extinctions and victories have happened to the absolutely *countless* creatures born on the *entire* surface of the Earth, throughout *each day and hour* of these past four billion years. Many times in discussions I have found, that – for many – there is not a great deal of difference between four million years and four billion years, both of them being "lots", possibly something not much greater in our minds than four thousand years. It is not a problem; it is just the acknowledgement of the limits inherent of the human mind, limits that we should take into account.

But creationism has also its arguments. Such an argument is the so-called *anthropic principle* (from the Greek *"anthropikos"*, that means "human"). The equations by which we describe how the cosmos operates, contain a number of so-called "universal constants" (the speed of light, gravitational constant and at least ten others); their magnitude has been determined by careful measurement. Physicists have noticed that these constants have exactly the right values that allow us to exist for both earthly civilization and the whole Universe. If one or two of the universal constants were only a few percent greater or smaller, the stars would not have been stars, planets and life would never have been born, not to mention technological civilizations or hyper-civilizations. Therefore, from the point of view of the anthropic principle, the Universe seems especially created so that we humans, the observers of that Universe, can exist.

One of the evolutionists' responses was that – just as there are many stars in the Universe, but only a very few of them host intelligence around them – there may also be in a supposed *Multiverse*, a huge number of all kinds of universes, with various universal constants, the vast majority of them "less successful" from our point of view, universes which have no intelligence to observe them "from within". Our universe is among the very few privileged ones.

It has also been said that there could also be other forms of intelligence, and not necessarily based on carbon chains or on DNA. Perhaps they exist in other dimensions, in other states of aggregation of matter and in other planes of reality, for example in "etheric" or "sub-quantum" and "spiritual" worlds, or in forms we cannot even imagine. Just as an example, Leon Lederman, the Nobel Prize laureate for physics, in 2000 speculated that extraordinary form of life or intelligence might exist in neutron stars, the extremely dense cores of former stars, in which processes are happening millions of times faster than in the biological world.

The opposers of the creationist explanation still have an argument: It is true that the *"Deus ex machina"* solution – that is, the acceptance of a Divinity that created everything (through a "Big Bang") – is at first sight simpler, or so it seems using *"Occam's razor"*, that this explanation could be simplistic and is only a pretext to stop us from making further judgments, when we get tired of thinking. If the Divinity has created everything – the evolutionists ask – did it emerge "*ex nihilo*", i.e. from nothing? Who and what gathered all the wisdom and science necessary to create the Universe with everything it contains along with the universal constants? If we accept the hypothesis that "Divinity has always been" the same hypothesis can be applied even more credibly to the laws that have led to evolution, starting with the Big Bang and the other variants.

But, to be fair, we have to accept that none of the arguments, creationism and evolutionism is strong enough to allow us to reject either of them. Therefore, I think the wisest way is to be modest enough to recognise that our minds have limits when they try to answer such questions. In addition, we should have the courage and the realism to accept, among other things, that within the limits of rationality, the human mind cannot at present distinguish between the "magic" of *hyper-civilizations* and what we know as sacred, holy, or Divine. There is no sufficiently convincing evidence to tilt the balance to one side or the other.

Limits of human perception

As has been said, the Universe is stranger and more complex than we *can* imagine. In order to even partially understand it, on the one hand humans rely on their biologically limited senses, using culturally and technically limited instruments and on the other hand, their mind, which is far from perfect and which uses mostly words, mathematical and logical operations, or theories, all of which are culturally limited.

Sceptics do not accept evidence based on testimonies (particularly those of the "magic" mentioned in previous chapters). We have to admit that they are partially right. Usually we all have the impression that we perceive reality "as it is" and in good faith it is sufficient to tell what we have perceive. Unfortunately it's not always like that. From what we perceive, the information passes through a number of important "*filters*", which can radically change the transmitted message.

The first "filter" is perception itself. It uses a mechanism that gradually builds from the first day of life using "bricks", which we continue to use to identify all the complex objects that we will encounter throughout our lives. We have talked in a previous chapter about "cultural hypnosis" and also about the phenomenon of *imprinting*, which makes us relate everything we perceive to a limited number of elements acquired during our education and other activities, experienced in the early years of life and which can actually produce a "mental blindness" toward certain aspects of reality. Because of this we may actually observe things, but we cannot see them because we have no reference point against which to relate them.

So, we do not simply look (or hear, or feel), above all we *recognise*. And we recognise what we already have in mind based on past experience and training. Simplifying this a little, it's as if we have a number of boxes in our mind and what we see must fall into one box or another. For example, if a religious person sees the luminous human form floating in the air, they will classify it in the "box" labelled "angel", and once the perceived thing falls into this box it will automatically receive all the appropriate attributes. So, our person will also see the angel's wings. Once the word "wing" (with the corresponding box) is perceived, the process will be repeated, and the witness will also see feathers. If the same event was classified as a "devil", the subject would also automatically see horns, and so on. And if they had a "box" for "alien humanoid" in their mind, the witness would known that such a thing does not exist, so they would reject this "recognition".

All of these aspects make us realise that our perception only works properly when we are in a familiar environment, and it can lead us to the wrong outcome if it is confronted with a reality which we have not previously encountered.

But perception also has other "filters" and traps. As we have shown in the chapter on UFO abductions, those who investigated this phenomenon have underlined the importance of so-called "*screen memories*", by which the memory of a traumatic event is replaced by an "improved" version that is acceptable to the conscious mind. The perception has many unconscious steps, so we should not surprised to learn that some analysts have suggested that these "disguises" were "borrowed" from the collective unconscious, which the witness's mind was connected to. In this regard it is particularly interesting that holy apparitions from areas of Catholic faith in Western Europe or Latin America, people almost always meet the Virgin Mary, while in around ten cases that I know of in the predominantly Orthodox region of Romania, the witnesses have always met with God the Father, or with Jesus, or with some of the apostles, but practically never with Virgin Mary. Probably for the same reason the followers of each religion meet their own Holy Being and the explanation is deeply buried in the collective unconscious mind. Investigative journalist Jérôme Bourgine observed that, in similar situations, "some met Jesus Christ, Muhammad, or even Vishnu, according to their cultural archetypes"[103] Dr. Dumitru Constantin-Dulcan also wrote that during the Near Death Experience, those who met a "Being of Light" perceived it as "the Supreme Being, God, sometimes as Jesus but, depending on the religious affiliation, it was also described as Buddha, or Allah."[104]

Neither are UFO encounters exempt from this bias. Carl G. Jung himself tentatively suggested that: "UFOs are real material phenomena of an unknown nature... [on which] unconscious contents have projected themselves and given them a significance they in no way deserve"[105]

Another "filter" is the fact that we often see what we want to see and not what we actually see. Psychologists call this "*wishful thinking*", or "*self-delusion*". And, conversely, we may not see what we don't like to see or don't want to see. In the case of the phenomena listed in the previous chapters, the main reason for not to see an alien "magic" could be the fear of an encounter with a higher civilization. The personal happiness of most people is, to a great extent, the state in which they have an answer to every major question. Such an encounter could break the image the person has about the world, leading – as John Mack said – to an "ontological shock" that produces extreme fear and disorientation.

At the same time, confrontations, confirmations and invalidations with perceptions obtained through other senses as well as other possible effects, are made. All the above alterations most often happen in the unconscious mind, so the subject becomes convinced that what they perceived was not modified in any way.

When the perceived things arrive into the rational consciousness of the witness, other "filters" await them. Here, they should respect certain taboos, beliefs, fears and social conventions, etc. which are deeply rooted in the mind of the subject. Those perceived will be improved if they have distressing details and sometimes will be even changed to reflect a desired reality. They will be also checked in respect of preconceptions, accepted doctrines, and scientific theories, etc. They also they have to comply with another list of conditions so that they fit "head and tail". Some gaps will have to be filled and some statements verified, so they do not to contradict one other.

If inconsistencies that cannot be rectified are encountered in this process, the entire perception will be rejected; this is like the famous anecdote concerning a peasant who sees a

---

103   Bourgine, 1993, p.134.
104   Dulcan, 2013, p. 94
105   Jung, 1969, pp.117-118

giraffe for the first time in their life and exclaims: "Such an animal does not exist". Not being able to accept what they saw, the witness preferred to say that perhaps what they had seen was an illusion, which they would try to forget as soon as possible in order to regain the safety of their own world-view. If the perceived phenomenon is accepted, it will still have to pass a final "filter", the one of time that unconsciously changes memories. However, finally the witness will be convinced that he says is the truth.

If we accept the above what can we accept based all the accounts of various "miracles" etc as "evidence? A sceptic might say that as a result of what we have seen here, it would be acceptable to reject any testimony and throw everything into the trash. But if we do so, we will lose the last "Ariadne's thread" which could lead us to the source of the mysterious phenomena. The best attitude adopted by those who report incredible phenomena, is to obtain eyewitness accounts, consider them as "facts" of a special kind and, when examining them, keep in mind all possible deviations from was perceived. By comparing tens or hundreds of such "facts" about similar situations, a skilled analyst will be able to select the cases with common relevant details and will be able to remove the particular cultural influences that affect each witness. On cases with common details statistical methods may be applied to determine the likelihood that a certain assumption about the reality perceived is true. This will create the opportunity to get a better picture of the truth that lies behind them.

Powers and limits of science

If we have a collection of related "facts" from a certain realm of reality, the next step suggested by a rational approach, will be to try to build a *scientific theory* to explain them. The purpose of this theory is to allow us to make *predictions* in unprecedented situations. That's how science works. But can we construct a scientific theory based on the phenomena listed in the previous chapters: UFO, OBE, NDE, Akasha etc.? The answer is rather negative. Here's why:

The incontestable successes of science are due to its rigorous method. This method requires that the "facts" it takes into account have to be repeatedly *observable* or be *experimented* on in a laboratory and possibly also be measurable. A scientific theory must have the ability to anticipate the existence of new facts that emerge, which can then be confirmed or denied when confronted with reality. To this end, its truths are not allowed to change over time and an extra advantage is obtained if the theory is a "formal system" built around some clearly defined concepts and axioms.

Unfortunately, few of the "facts" mentioned in the previous chapters meet the above required conditions. We cannot bring a UFO or an alien into a museum, where every sceptic is to be able to see them. We cannot reproduce a UFO abduction in a laboratory. We cannot measure or even record one's perceptions in the state of NDE or OBE. In other words, because of its self-imposed rigors, science *cannot approach* a number of areas of reality, such as very rare phenomena, those inaccessible to experimentation or observation and those that do not occur at the command of the experimenter (such as UFO close encounters). Science cannot approach the inner feelings of people (remote viewing, channeling, OBE, NDE and others), nor the mechanisms of free will, intuition, consciousness and creativity, as well as the unpredictable strategies of life, art, politics and sport, etc. For example, science seeks repeatable phenomena to build theories on and to make predictions based on them, while genuine creators are those who produce unrepeatable works and surprise us with their unpredictable creations. Therefore, it is clear that a "science of the creation process" is impossible by definition.

But remaining outside the fundamental scientific approach are "gnoseological" issues (the question of whether the process of human knowledge is infinite or not), or "ontological" issues (for example, do we live in a "virtual reality", or does God exist). For the last problem, for about three or four centuries, science has found a slightly embarrassing solution, by placing the Divinity into a "transcendent" world. The subjective and spiritual issues were left to religion, while the material, objective field was entrusted to science, though the same thinkers admitted that Divinity sometimes intervenes in the real world (as in miracles). This is at best contradictory. Even if the solution was acceptable in those times, in the 21st century there are more and more people who doubt it and are convinced that there is only one reality that contains both matter and spirit.

I will give just one notorious example of a situation that goes beyond the skills of science, but there are many others that are similar. Kary B. Mullis, was awarded the 1993 Nobel Prize in chemistry, wrote that on a summer evening in 1985, he was alone near his cabin, in the mountains, when he met a "glowing raccoon" who said, "Good evening, doctor". He answered and the next thing he remembered was that he was walking in the early morning along a road near the cabin. He had no signs of injury or bruising. In one of his books Mullis concluded: "I wouldn't try to publish a scientific paper about these things, because I can't do any experiments. I can't make glowing raccoons appear. I can't buy them from a scientific supply house to study. I can't cause myself to be lost again for several hours. But I don't deny what happened. It's what science calls anecdotal, because it only happened in a way that you can't reproduce. But it happened."[106]

Despite what I have mentioned above, official science insists that it is the *only way* for a valid study of *all reality*. When it encounters facts from a category that it cannot approach using its methodology and therefore cannot explain, instead of saying: "I apologise, but I do not the skills to study this", or even "I hope I will understand this sometime in the future", science often prefers to leave the impression that those facts (rare events, channelling, holy appearances, etc.) did not happen and they must be simple illusions, hallucinations or misunderstandings and so on.

This "arrogance" refers, among other things, to the UFO phenomenon. In 2012 Lord Rees, said: "Only kooks see UFOs". More open-minded scientists – as Jacques Vallée noticed – don't question the actual existence of UFO phenomenon, but "the ability of modern science to deal with it. In private conversations with Professor Condon, in 1967, I heard him express a similar view"[107] We recall that Professor Condon led the investigation that caused the Air Force's Blue Book project to close. It seems that the professor had told others that the UFO issue resembled that of God's existence, that is, "An area in which science has nothing to say".

In recent centuries the arrogance of the "truth holders" existed in Europe .When in, 1801, the astronomer Piazzi discovered the first asteroid – Ceres – the philosopher Friedrich Hegel "demonstrated" that this was not possible. Some time before this in the French Academy, the chemist, Antoine Lavoisier, also claimed that meteorites cannot exist, saying: "Stones cannot fall from the sky, because there are no stones in the sky". Even Galileo Galilei invited cardinals, who were preparing to condemn him, to look through his telescope and show them that, for example, Jupiter had satellites. The Cardinals "knew very well" what the reality was, and they were not willing to be duped by a charlatan. We may also recall the examples I have mentioned in the subchapter on temporal provincialism.

Unfortunately, even today, just as the ufologist and physicist Stanton Friedman summed up, UFO observations and other paranormal phenomena are systematically met with expressions such as: "Do not bother me with the facts, my mind is made up". For example, the sceptics are convinced that everything about UFOs is supported only by "kooks", but they

---

[106]   Mullis, 1998, p. 136
[107]   Vallée, 1992, pp. 290-291

don't give any references to said kooks, or any data to back up their opinion, because they don't know of any such data, and refuse to read any of the evidence.

Professor Hynek wrote somewhere that one day, at a lunch; Carl Sagan told him that UFOs are a non-sense. Hynek asked him if he formed this opinion by studying a large number of cases and the answer was: "I know nothing about this subject". Then Hynek said: "Carl, you know that we, scientists, do not comment on any subject unless we studied it well enough". He replied: "Yes, I know, but I do not have time for that".

In all such cases it has been forgotten that any scientific theory has limits. Based on scientific laws – those of Newton, Maxwell, Einstein and many others – very precise and useful predictions have been made and much of our current knowledge is based on these predictions. But any scientific law is created by people and may encounter situations where it is no longer valid, being "falsifiable", as said Karl Popper (1902-1994) one of the 20th century's greatest philosophers of science who underlined that fact that the law is not scientific. As an example, much was written about the fact that in 1846 the French astronomer Le Verrier discovered planet Neptune purely through calculation, that is, he predicted its position in the sky using only mathematics and scientific laws concerning the theory of celestial mechanics. But the fact that he calculated the position of another planet, which he called Vulcan and would have had an orbit closer to the Sun than Mercury is ignored. This planet has never been found because, despite the correct calculations, it does not exist. This time the theory of celestial mechanics had failed.

In school, we were told about the "laws of nature". The above examples point to the fact that no one knows everything about these laws. We only know about the laws of Newton and Einstein and so on, which do a good job of approximating the "laws of nature", but do not necessarily agree with them. Scientific theories, no matter how accurately they describe reality, are not reality itself, nor its basis, but are abstract human constructs that are well suited to the reality for which they were created, but they have inherent limits; so confusing them with reality is a fundamental mistake.

It is understandable that we need to examine any extraordinary proof very closely and ask whether it corresponds to what we consider possible, in accordance with the laws known to science. It is absolutely normal that we should automatically reject incoherent statements, or those that clearly contradict unanimously established facts. For example, we will not accept assertions such as: "The Sun is rotating around the Earth", "The Earth is flat", or "There is a hole in Antarctica through which airships can travel to the Hollow Earth".

But we have to avoid falling into the other extreme. We hear sometimes that: "Science has shown that X cannot exist" or that "It has been mathematically demonstrated that Y must exist". These statements are logically incorrect. According to the "falsifiability" criterion mentioned above, no scientific law can say with 100% accuracy something about a phenomenon in the real world that has not yet been identified. Therefore, we cannot reject evidence by only relying on theories. At most we can say that a reported story contradicts currently known laws, but not that it is impossible.

The claim that science is the only path to knowledge brings with it a well-known anecdote, the one with the drunk who, in the middle of the night, was looking for his door keys under a street lamp although he did not know where he had lost them, because the light was much better there. Today's materialist science does not only claim that any research should be done under its "street lamp", but insists that there is nothing outside the lighted area, though some "keys" that might be extremely important for humanity, could be somewhere else.

Sceptics and debunkers

Not only sceptics, but also many ordinary people ignore the limits of the scientific approach outlined above. Under the "cultural hypnosis" of the contemporary Western vision of the world, they tend to consider all the facts presented in the pages of this book: UFOs, abductions, remote viewing, channelling, OBE, NDE and the others, as nonsense, mainly because of rumours, pranks, exaggerations, illusions, hallucinations, psychological illnesses, secret military experiments, erroneous interpretation of little known natural phenomena and so on. They will usually say that "extraordinary claims require extraordinary evidence" and insist they will not accept them until they can see and touch the proof.

Conversely, it is significant that, often, sceptics who use this argument have no problem believing (without any evidence) in the existence of a God who created us in his likeness, or anything else their holy books say. This demonstrates the bizarre double standards and irrationality of our minds.

The situation is explained – Professor John Mack said – not just by the great confidence in the efficiency of science, but also by the fact that our vision of the world is fundamental to our psychic balance. It gives us security to know that we are the masters of our existence. Asking or attacking our conception of the world produces terror.

Ufologist Budd Hopkins made a comparison between a genuine sceptic and a debunker. A debunker – for example a critic of the UFO abduction phenomenon – believes in the existence of Ultimate Truths, which he accepts. Hopkins considered that a true sceptic may accept a case as possibly authentic or reject it as a deception or as a misunderstanding, or whatever, while the debunker only has one fixed opinion, he/she knows that the incident, whatever it may be, cannot involve a genuine UFO encounter. This rigid position is related to a kind of quasi-religious fundamentalism.

To accept the point of view of those who only accept what is observable, experimental or measurable – considered Mack – would mean the *a priori* exclusion of a large amount of data, only because they contradict a certain perception of the world. This is an irrational and even dangerous approach in knowledge. To exclude data just because it does not match a certain vision of reality can ultimately stop the progress of science and keep us in ignorance.

Manifesto for a Post-Materialist Science

As a reaction to stubborn scepticism, as well as to the narrow vision of official science, more and more scientists are beginning to ask for a paradigm shift. In July 2014, several internationally known scientists in biology, neuroscience, psychology, medicine and psychiatry, including Mario Beauregard PhD, Gary E. Schwartz PhD, Lisa Miller PhD, Larry Dossey MD, Alexander Moreira-Almeida PhD, Marilyn Schlitz PhD, Rupert Sheldrake PhD and Charles Tart PhD, signed and published a document called "*Manifesto for a Post-Materialist Science*", originally developed at the University of Arizona[108]. Over 300 other scientists, philosophers, MDs and leading thinkers have also signed this manifesto to show their support for it. I have included the very important conclusions of this document below. The reader will find it includes many of the topics addressed in this book.

1. The modern scientific worldview is predominantly predicated on assumptions that are closely associated with classical physics. Materialism—the idea that matter is the only reality—is one of these assumptions. A related assumption is reductionism, the notion that complex things can be understood by reducing them to the interactions of their parts or to simpler or more fundamental things such as tiny material particles.

2. During the 19th century, these assumptions narrowed, turned into dogmas and coalesced into an ideological belief system that came to be known as "scientific

---

[108] Manifesto, 2014

materialism." This belief system implies that the mind is nothing but the physical activity of the brain and that our thoughts cannot have any effect upon our brains and bodies, our actions and the physical world.

3. The ideology of scientific materialism became dominant in academia during the 20th century. So dominant that a majority of scientists started to believe that it was based on established empirical evidence and represented the only rational view of the world.

4. Scientific methods based upon materialistic philosophy have been highly successful in not only increasing our understanding of nature but also in bringing greater control and freedom through advances in technology.

5. However, the nearly absolute dominance of materialism in the academic world has seriously constricted the sciences and hampered the development of the scientific study of mind and spirituality. Faith in this ideology, as an exclusive explanatory framework for reality, has compelled scientists to neglect the subjective dimension of human experience. This has led to a severely distorted and impoverished understanding of ourselves and our place in nature.

6. Science is first and foremost a non-dogmatic, open-minded method of acquiring knowledge about nature through the observation, experimental investigation and theoretical explanation of phenomena. Its methodology is not synonymous with materialism and should not be committed to any particular beliefs, dogmas, or ideologies.

7. At the end of the 19th century, physicists discovered empirical phenomena that could not be explained by classical physics. This led to the development, during the 1920s and early 1930s, of a revolutionary new branch of physics called quantum mechanics (QM). QM has questioned the material foundations of the world by showing that atoms and subatomic particles are not really solid objects – they do not exist with certainty at definite spatial locations and definite times. Most importantly, QM explicitly introduced the mind into its basic conceptual structure since it was found that particles being observed and the observer – the physicist and the method used for observation – are linked. According to one interpretation of QM, this phenomenon implies that the consciousness of the observer is vital to the existence of the physical events being observed and that mental events can affect the physical world. The results of recent experiments support this interpretation. These results suggest that the physical world is no longer the primary or sole component of reality and that it cannot be fully understood without making reference to the mind.

8. Psychological studies have shown that conscious mental activity can causally influence behaviour and that the explanatory and predictive value of agentic factors (e.g., beliefs, goals, desires and expectations) is very high. Moreover, research in psychoneuroimmunology indicates that our thoughts and emotions can markedly affect the activity of the physiological systems (e.g., immune, endocrine and cardiovascular) connected to the brain. In other respects, neuroimaging studies of emotional self-regulation, psychotherapy and the placebo effect demonstrate that mental events significantly influence the activity of the brain.

9. Studies of the so-called "psi phenomena" indicate that we can sometimes receive meaningful information without the use of ordinary senses and in ways that transcend the habitual space and time constraints. Furthermore, psi research demonstrates that we can mentally influence – at a distance – physical devices and living organisms (including other human beings). Psi research also shows that distant minds may behave in ways that are nonlocally correlated, i.e., the correlations between distant minds are hypothesised to be unmediated (they are not linked to any known energetic signal), unmitigated (they do not degrade with increasing distance) and immediate (they appear to be simultaneous). These events are so common that they cannot be viewed as anomalous or as exceptions to natural laws, but as indications of the need for a broader explanatory framework that cannot be predicated exclusively on materialism.

10. Conscious mental activity can be experienced in clinical death during a cardiac arrest [this is what has been called a "near-death experience" (NDE)]. Some near-death experiencers (NDErs) have reported veridical out-of-body perceptions (i.e., perceptions that can be proven to coincide with reality) that occurred during cardiac arrest. NDErs also report profound spiritual experiences during NDEs triggered by cardiac arrest. It is noteworthy that the electrical activity of the brain ceases within a few seconds following a cardiac arrest.

11. Controlled laboratory experiments have documented that skilled research mediums (people who claim that they can communicate with the minds of people who have physically died) can sometimes obtain highly accurate information about deceased individuals. This further supports the conclusion that mind can exist separate from the brain.

12. Some materialistically inclined scientists and philosophers refuse to acknowledge these phenomena because they are not consistent with their exclusive conception of the world. Rejection of post-materialist investigation of nature or refusal to publish strong science findings supporting a post-materialist framework are antithetical to the true spirit of scientific inquiry, which is that empirical data must always be adequately dealt with. Data which do not fit favoured theories and beliefs cannot be dismissed a priori. Such dismissal is the realm of ideology, not science.

13. It is important to realise that psi phenomena, NDEs in cardiac arrest and replicable evidence from credible research mediums, appear anomalous only when seen through the lens of materialism.

14. Moreover, materialist theories fail to elucidate how brain could generate the mind and they are unable to account for the empirical evidence alluded to in this manifesto. This failure tells us that it is now time to free ourselves from the shackles and blinders of the old materialist ideology, to enlarge our concept of the natural world and to embrace a post-materialist paradigm.

15. According to the post-materialist paradigm:

a. Mind represents an aspect of reality as primordial as the physical world. Mind is fundamental in the universe, i.e., it cannot be derived from matter and reduced to anything more basic.

b. There is a deep interconnectedness between mind and the physical world.

c. Mind (will/intention) can influence the state of the physical world and operate in a nonlocal (or extended) fashion, i.e., it is not confined to specific points in space, such as brains and bodies, or to specific points in time, such as the present. Since the mind may nonlocally influence the physical world, the intentions, emotions and desires of an experimenter may not be completely isolated from experimental outcomes, even in controlled and blinded experimental designs.

d. Minds are apparently unbounded and may unite in ways suggesting a unitary One Mind that includes all individual, single minds.

e. NDEs in cardiac arrest suggest that the brain acts as a transceiver of mental activity, i.e., the mind can work through the brain but is not produced by it. NDEs occurring in cardiac arrest, coupled with evidence from research mediums, further suggest the survival of consciousness, following bodily death and the existence of other levels of reality that are non-physical.

f. Scientists should not be afraid to investigate spirituality and spiritual experiences since they represent a central aspect of human existence.

16. Post-materialist science does not reject the empirical observations and great value of scientific achievements realised up until now. It seeks to expand the human capacity to better

understand the wonders of nature and, in the process, rediscover the importance of mind and spirit as being part of the core fabric of the universe. Post-materialism is inclusive of matter, which is seen as a basic constituent of the universe.

17. The post-materialist paradigm has far-reaching implications. It fundamentally alters the vision we have of ourselves, giving us back our dignity and power, as humans and as scientists. This paradigm fosters positive values such as compassion, respect and peace. By emphasising a deep connection between ourselves and nature at large, the post-materialist paradigm also promotes environmental awareness and the preservation of our biosphere. In addition, it is not new, but only forgotten for 400 years, that a lived transmaterial understanding may be the cornerstone of health and wellness, as it has been held and preserved in ancient mind–body–spirit practices, religious traditions and contemplative approaches.

18. The shift from materialist science to post-materialist science may be of vital importance to the evolution of the human civilization. It may be even more pivotal than the transition from geocentrism to heliocentrism.

Steps for paradigm change

John Mack said that his work of exploring the abduction phenomenon "Has led me to challenge the prevailing worldview or consensus reality which I had grown up believing"[109] Also, in a 2014 interview for "*Ovnis-Direct*", Jacques Vallée summed up the UFO issue in the following way: "(1) The UFO phenomenon does exist and (2) Knowing that, we just have to renegotiate what we mean by reality"

The "manifesto" above – with which I agree almost 100% – asks for a similar change in the accepted world-view for rethinking what we consider as reality. In this respect, the first issue raised by all the "magic" we are confronted with should be to accept that there is *only one reality*, both material and spiritual.

The second issue raised is to change our *way of thinking*. In a PBS/NOVA interview, John Mack said that the difficulty for our society and mentality is that we have "a kind of either/or mentality". "It's either, literally physical; or it's in the spiritual other realm, the unseen realm. What we seem to have no place for – or we have lost the place for – are phenomena that can begin in the unseen realm and cross over and manifest and show up in our literal physical world. So, the simple answer would be: Yes, it's both. It's both literally, physically happening to a degree; and it's also some kind of psychological, spiritual experience occurring and originating perhaps in another dimension".

John Mack was a family friend of Thomas Kuhn (1922-1996), one of the most outstanding philosophers of science in the 20th century, and a former professor of science history at Berkeley, Princeton and Massachusetts Institute of Technology. As Mack wrote: "What I found most helpful was Kuhn's observation that the Western scientific paradigm had come to assume the rigidity of a theology and that this belief system was held in place by the structures, categories and polarities of language, such as real/unreal, exists/does not exist, objective/subjective, intrapsychic/external world and happened/did not happen. He suggested that I simply collect raw information, putting aside whether or not what I was learning fits in to any particular worldview."[110]

Mack said the study of abductions is just one of the areas that question the "materialist paradigm". So, we need a method of acquiring knowledge that is capable of investigating human experience by itself, as rigorously as we investigate the physical world. It would

---

[109] Mack, 1995, p.3
[110] Mack, 1995, p.8

require "a new psychology, a different science, with an epistemology not only confined to sensory, empirical knowledge", a "science of living", or a "science of the subjective".

A third important issue is that one of the mandatory openings to post-materialist science, should be the reconsideration of *witnessing* as evidence of truth. In the first part of this chapter I set out the drawbacks of testimony. There are at least three factors which we can use to increase the reliability of reporting incredible facts: (1) *credibility* of the story, which also depends on the quality of the witnesses and their mental and emotional health, their integrity and observer qualities, the absence of external influences and of the witnesses interests and preconceptions, the intensity and authenticity of their emotions and the lack of personal advantages and so on; (2) *strangeness*, which is the difficulty of explaining what was observed using accepted theories; (3) the *statistics*, the number of reports of the same phenomenon and the independence of the witnesses and especially the repetition of other details in different reports, especially those which were not communicated through the media so they could not contaminate the witnesses. When people from different countries, cultures, religions and occupations, share a similar story that has dozens of matching features, despite the fact that they knew nothing about it and did not read any literature about it, the statistics show that these are not fantasies or coincidences, they are a real phenomenon and although we may not understand it, we have no right to sweep it under the carpet.

Of course, in each case we must also take into account the possible distortions caused by the "filters" to which perception is subjected, the mechanisms which we spoke about at the beginning of this chapter. In this way we can attempt to reconstruct the perceived events; and even this process can never be perfect. But if certain details resemble those of hundreds or even thousands of other cases that we know about, it means that there is 'something' behind them, 'something' happened, and it cannot be ignored.

Therefore, there are means to reconsider the witness in how knowledge is acquired. In 1999 professor John Mack met Monsignor Corrado Balducci, who on this occasion emphasised the great importance of the testimony that underpins our daily lives. Rejecting the accounts of authentic witnesses – he said – would have disastrous consequences on society and religion. A society cannot survive for any length of time if there are those who say that the truth will not be believed. Both religious belief and UFO research are based on the testimony of witnesses. The Catholic Church takes reports of UFOs very seriously, precisely because of the large number of statements that are in agreement. Catholics have long established criteria for establishing the conditions under which testimony (for example, of a miracle) can be considered or not. Mack noted that such criteria also exist in other religions, such as Buddhism.

CONCLUSIONS

Reality is much stranger than we like to believe or are able to imagine. The arguments put forward in the preceding chapters are only a small part of this strangeness. In order to understand this very complex reality, humans can only rely on their biologically and culturally limited senses and minds.

The scientific approach requires that all evidence be observable and/or examined on demand and sometimes it also has to be measurable and explained using current knowledge. Therefore, our materialist science cannot approach facts such as UFOs, abductions, remote viewing, channelling, OBE, NDE and many others. However, sometimes sceptics state that those facts did not happen, because – according to existing theories – they are impossible. This, though it is accepted that none of today's scientific laws can predict something about an unknown phenomenon with 100% certainty.

As a reaction to stubborn scepticism, as well as to the narrow vision of official science, more and more scientists are beginning to ask for a paradigm shift, for example toward a "post-materialist science". That means, among other things, that we should accept that there is only one reality, both material and spiritual, change our "either/or" way of reasoning and under certain conditions and using the appropriate statistical tools, accept witness testimony as evidence.

WHAT WE HAVE TO DO?

A higher consciousnesses

Based on the arguments presented in the previous chapters, I suppose that we could agree that it is extremely likely that there are consciousnesses that have overseen our planet, for very long time. There are countless testimonies: religious, folkloric, mythological, ufological and paranormal etc., which can be explained in this way. These are not illusions or hallucinations, as they occur too many times in the same scenarios and with the same details.

What could the identity of these consciousnesses be? According to the hypothesis presented in this book we have called them *hyper-civilizations*, stating that, with few exceptions, their attributes lie beyond our understanding. I have tried to show that, over time, their "magical" manifestations have been interpreted in a great variety of ways specific to each epoch and culture. From the actions of characters from folklore and religion, to technologies that interest the military and even mysterious genetic manipulation.

There is very little certainty about the nature of the superior power that oversees us. Therefore, I appeal to the reader's goodwill in this chapter to allow me a bit more speculation.

Taking into account how complex the cosmos appears to be, above us there could be a series of *hyper-civilizations*, whose structure it is unlikely to be revealed to us in the foreseeable future. Those who visit us are probably just the emissaries from a lower level of this hierarchy. In their manifestations, they use the disguises provided by the cultural archetypes contained in the collective unconscious of the area they visit. Their appearance can be material, spiritual, or both, changing from one state to another in a way that is difficult for us to understand and using "laws of nature" beyond those we are aware of. Sometimes they may appear as sacred characters from different religions, or sometimes as dwarfs, fairies, and even as aliens descending from UFOs. Equally confusing and packed in cultural archetypes are the revelations and information that, from time to time, some people allegedly receive from those visitors.

The belief that, somewhere above, higher consciences are following our "material" existence here on Earth is thousands of years old. Such a long oversight naturally raises the questions: is this for a *purpose*? Do they expect something from us? Some people believe that that they created us because they needed slaves for mining, or to produce bioenergy, or to select those with a certain type of DNA and so on. They said even that humans could be nothing more than guinea pigs in some cosmic genetic or social experiment.

Several religions advance the idea that each human being is born to fulfil a *mission*. Is somebody expecting a result from us, a product, or a "harvest"? A "fruit" that need to ripen? If so, are there small individual goals such as in personal development, or boundless devotion towards a Divinity? Or perhaps a collective goal, such as general happiness and the transformation of the Earth into a paradise? Or they do expect us to carry out some other kind of work even though we do not understand why? Jean Sider believed that we would never be able to understand what the consciousness that monitors us really wanted, saying: "It's as if the bees would try to determine the nature of the beekeeper and understand the meaning of its activities around the hive."[111]

Certain traditions consider the Earth and the materiality of our existence on it as a *school*. In its simplest form, as is found reincarnation, the spirit of a deceased person returns to the body of a new-born to pass through a new series of trials that will add to its super-

---

[111] Sider, 1995

consciousness (which it only possesses in a non-material state). It will thus improve itself spiritually through new lives, advancing toward a state of perfection when the cycle of reincarnation ends, and the accumulated "super-consciousness" reaches a state of Nirvana and dissolves into the Universal Consciousness, which it enriches. Other approaches speak of spirits wandering through the cosmos until they materialise on Earth and other material worlds, until they complete their education.

These scenarios raise some issues. Beyond the paradoxical aspects of the alleged phenomenon of reincarnation presented in a previous chapter, in order to speak of a truly individual spiritual progress through reincarnation, it would be natural for every human to consciously remember previous lives. The fact that many people have, in their minds, the images of some deceased individual's life may well mean, as I have already argued, that they have had access to data about those lives, data recorded in a universal, virtual reality type, super-memory also called 'Akasha'.

The forbidden knowledge

I believe that an important suggestion regarding the possible objectives that a cosmic consciousness expects from human beings comes from a policy of non-disclosure about the knowledge they possess.

In a naive approach, at an encounter of two civilizations situated on different levels of development, if it is benevolent the superior civilization should help the other one, by passing on its science and technology. In a previous chapter I argued why, on the contrary, a *hyper-civilization* would forbid such a transfer on the basis of the principle of "minimal intervention".

In traditions and myths of many peoples there are some strange allusions to such a policy. It is written that Adam and Eve were punished because they ate the fruit of the tree of knowledge. Book of Enoch shows that a group of angels, headed by Azazyel, revealed 'mysteries that they should not have known' to human beings', regarding weapons, jewellery, sorcery, drugs, astronomy, fortune telling, mining, ways to kill, writing, abortion, etc. Fortunately – is written in The Book – "the great secrets have remained undisclosed". The angels in question were harshly punished and were eternally chained – according to same Book – into "abysses full of embers". But the same weird interdiction and punishment is also found in the myth of Prometheus, who was chained because he has conveyed the mystery of the fire to humans. Are not these histories telling in a hyperbolic and fantastic way events that actually occurred the past?

What is the explanation for such a ban? There seem to be several reasons. One is *caution*. Some people, apparently abducted by UFOs, said that the aliens told them that they fear our aggression and xenophobia that causes all our technology to become weapons. The actions of humans are primarily driven by evolved forms of animal instincts, including: the thirst for possession, power, sex and the pleasure of humiliating opponents. Since it has these tendencies if humanity had access to the technology of *hyper-civilizations*, it would become a huge threat to peaceful civilizations in the Universe.

Some say that mankind does not deserve such a rough characterisation. They argue that most people are on the side of "good" and that the animal in us is effectively held back by culture and civilization. Indeed, around us we often see manifestations of kindness toward people; but if we examine it in depth, this kindness does not seem to be completely detached from our animal instincts. Many people do good, or refrain from doing harm for fear of Gods punishment or hope for a reward in the afterlife. But fear, or a desire for reward, is a primitive motivation common in animals. Other generous gestures are only due to a strict education from childhood, or some extremely strong reflex connection that make you to act in a certain way without thinking about it, which is close to a Pavlovian reflex, something that is also found in well-trained dogs. Fortunately, there are also some exceptions to the above, but there are very few and I will return to them later.

The ban on communicating knowledge to people could also have a second explanation. If we ever get indisputable proof of the presence of a *hyper-civilization*, if this evidence could be seen by everyone, it would be a *"culture shock"* that would destroy all our social, religious, economic, political, military and cultural structures. As I said in the first chapter, religion would be forced to accept that there are ways towards Divinity and other hierarchies of intelligence in the Universe, apart from the dogmas set out in sacred books. Science would have to admit that many of the concepts and theories on which it currently relies are of no value. If we discover that there are infinitely better technologies than ours, the economy would collapse, the stock markets would shut down, and many businesses would cease trading, and the global effects would be impossible to assess. The army would face serious problems, because in a military confrontation with such an advanced civilization we would have no chance. In this situation many people would forget national affiliations and, instead, consider themselves to be "citizens of the Earth" or even "of the Cosmos". It would be a blow to nationalism and politicians, but it would also result in an increase of patients at psychiatric hospitals, because many people, who were previously confident and sure of their position in society, would become challenged and insecure.

But I assume that – apart from the reasons given above – the non-disclosure of knowledge could have another explanation. A *hyper-civilization* might be waiting patiently, for something that only we can give something that could not be achieved if they intervene. Some people stated that, after being abducted, the aliens told them that they are *waiting for something from us that only we can accomplish*, without any outside help.

Perhaps those who are waiting do not want to make the mistake we made half a millennium ago, when the conquistadors and other discoverers of new lands "shared", or perhaps 'imposed' would be a better choice, what we had the best of at that time: Christianity, European science and technology and later Cartesian rationalism with the frailer civilizations of the Inca and Aztecs. Although the action was "paved with good intentions", we actually forced our "cultural hypnosis" on them, making them "mentally blind" to some aspects of reality, in the same way as we were, though until then they had seen the world in a different way. This European zeal led to the disappearance of some alternative human ways of perceiving reality, thus narrowing the set of tools of knowledge for all mankind.

We became aware of how lucky we were only recently in view of the fact that other civilizations, such as the Chinese and Indian, had already been mature and strong enough to resist this unifying movement and today they are offering the West, art and medicine, etc. and other cultural items that we might never have attained. We can think of yoga, acupuncture, the engravings of Hokusai and countless other elements that have enriched the way that we now perceive reality. It is only today that we begin to realise that we destroyed, other, more fragile sources of culture and knowledge, such as had been those of the Incas and the Aztecs. As a result, today we try to protect diversity and cultural heritage of mankind, that belongs to everyone, including the visions of so-called "primitive" thinking.

In order not to make the same mistake, we can assume that the hypothetical *hyper-civilizations* will show us their vision of the Universe, or their science and the technology they possess, so that it does not destroy the *originality* of the solutions we will find that allow us to mature to a level that is specific to our civilisation and allow us to integrate with the *hyper-civilizations* out there in the universe. Even a single example of their advanced technology, with all its unforeseen side effects, could overwhelm and wipe out our entire culture and the desired outcome – the original vision – there would never come to fruition. Not only would our established evolutionary process be destroyed, but with it our possible future as a *hyper-civilization*.

At the end of a previous chapter I mentioned that Courtney Brown said he had learned about spiritual entities refused to contact us until we "mature", because they "Are important to the future of our contribution". If we accept this statement as valid, I believe that what they said it true, because until we mature our civilisation could collapse under the impact of encountering a *hyper-civilisation*. Meanwhile, representatives of the higher civilizations could evaluate and harvest our ideas, views and original creations, perhaps storing them in the Akasha super-memory.

Creation and human beauty

In a previous chapter, to emphasise the vast gulf in technology and evolution between *hyper-civilizations* and us, the human race was compared with ants, but the comparison is a bit exaggerated because of the possibility of our potential future as a *hyper-civilization*. The emergence of a civilization like ours must be a very rare event in the Galaxy, or even in the Universe, something that only happens once in millions of years. So, if that is the case we should be unique and worthy of interest.

Our species separated from the animal kingdom and started on the road that, with luck, will bring it to the same level as *hyper-civilizations*. Maybe the biblical statement that says, "Let us make man in our image" (Genesis, 1; 26) alludes to this fact, if we accept that this "image" is rather spiritual than physical. The fact that our species has a measure of almost god-like control over its destiny in the manner of a *creator*, in other words it has free will, is found in other biblical verses, for example in the note: "I said, you are gods; all of you are the sons of the Highest" (Psalms, 82; 6).

Sometimes it is said that an artist's inspiration comes from other worldly sources (this could be partly true, considering the ideas regarding the collective unconscious). In ancient times it was said that this inspiration came from the muses. But I still believe that "The Art of Fugue", along with his other brilliant compositions, were not "assigned" and "channelled" to Johann Sebastian Bach by a superior entity and he just transcribed them. I prefer to imagine that these Higher Spirits were pleased and surprised to learn about the beauty of "The Art of Fugue" (even if Bach did not finish it) and of everything else he composed.

If we ask what art is, the simplest answer is, "*creation of beauty*" But as the ancients noticed, beauty has many levels and forms. The simplest of these is the beauty of the inanimate world: a crystal, a mountain peak, the movement of the stars, a sunset, but there is also the beauty of mathematics, symmetry and proportion. On a higher level there is the beauty of life: a flower, the leap of a gazelle, or the perfection of the human body. This is the beauty of health, vigor, biological harmony, elegance of movements and optimal functionality.

But the splendour of the first two levels cannot be compared to those on the next level where we find *human beauty* – the beauty of specific human acts. It is obviously not about the beauty of the body of an athlete or the perfect shape of a young woman, which is physical, but the *beauty of the human spirit* and the social harmony that derives from it.

The universal drama of Oedipus or Faust, the sculptures of Praxiteles or Rodin, the paintings of Michelangelo or Rembrandt and the music of Bach or Beethoven, are nothing but the expression of the beauty of the artist's soul, namely the understanding and rendering of human beauty in contrast to human ugliness.

The concept of human beauty is a very important among the topics we are discussing here. At the same time it is a seldom used concept; which is why I ask the reader's permission to examine it more closely. This kind of beauty is not only found in art, but in everything that has true human value, such as moral acts or in gestures that initially seem to have little value. Human beauty includes everything from the skill to make bread to building a space ship, beautifying an alley with flowers or creating a symphony. In this sense human beings are beautiful if they do anonymous charitable acts or anything else that is useful, or when they appreciate, protect and cultivate any beauty they encounter, no matter who produced it and at the same time reject anything ugly. A person possesses human beauty if they enjoy the beauty of their fellow humans and do not stand aside if this beauty is threatened.

But an individual is beautiful, not only in their acts, but also through their potential. The physical, psychological, moral or professional destruction of a human being means destroying a whole range of countless beautiful human actions that comprise their life, both in the past and in the future.

Of course, a human being is only beautiful if they do this without expecting reward or recognition. As many thinkers, including Emmanuel Kant, noted, the love of beauty is very different from the motivation we have inherited from animals, because it is not associated with any selfish, personal or group interest and, in particular, with the desire to possess objects, privilege or position.

Accepting the hypothesis discussed in this book, we understand that mankind is halfway between animal and *hyper-civilization*. Every human being is close to one extreme or the other. There are some who plant and protect flowers and there are others who step on them without thought, just because the road is shorter there. There are people who rejoice if they see that their fellow humans creating beauty or become more beautiful, just as there are those who try to sabotage that creativity because of envy, or for the pleasure of showing who is stronger. There are some who celebrate the uniqueness of the individual and others who aim to enrol everybody into hierarchies where the individual becomes a standardised, interchangeable piece. There are some who understand the beauty of rebelling against convention and opening up new horizons and there are others who glorify humble and fearful obedience to some alleged ultimate truths. There are many other comparisons.

A little earlier I said that many people do good acts, or refrain from doing harm, as a reflex, or in case they are punished, or perhaps in hope of a reward. All these are primitive motivations similar to those of animals. Consequently, human beauty seems to be an indicator that those who love beauty will create it for the pleasure of those around them and are ready to defend it wherever it is threatened. They don't do this from instinct, nor reflex or fear, or because they expect reward or recognition. They act because beauty, even if it does not belong to them, is something extremely important, sometimes more important than wealth, possessions or power. And the destruction of something beautiful: a flower trodden by the boot of a passer-by, a valuable building facade destroyed to be replaced by something tasteless, or an injustice done to a human being and so on, cause them unbearable pain. These are people who do good acts without any self-interest. They will never damage the beauty of other humans, nor things of beauty created by our species.

So, we understand that specifically human motives are the *beautiful* and the *ugly*, those that reflect – emotionally, consciously– the harmony of the world, as well as that between humanity and the world. It is hard for me to understand why the concept of "human beauty" is so rarely mentioned in our culture, as it could be a focal point that unites many attributes of authentic human qualities that have the ability to clarify – as I will try to show – other essential concepts such as *good* and *evil*, or *love*. It seems plausible to me that our race will be only considered mature, by these who are waiting for it to happen, only when everyone places human beauty as their first concern. Perhaps this is one of the facets that *hyper-civilisations* expect of us.

The love and the good

In the cases and comments I have mentioned, and which are possibly connected with the activities of *hyper-civilizations*, the concept of "*love*" is constantly repeated. We can find it in religious books and Marian Visions and in the stories of UFO encounters. We also find it in near-death experiences and in encounters with a "Being of Light" and so on. As an example, John Mack wrote: "What is the vision of a possible human future that the abductees have brought back to us from their journeys? The connecting principle, the force that expands our consciousness beyond ourselves, appears to be love."[112]

I believe that, in fact, in all these cases, *love* is the natural, selfless inclination of a human being to identify, cultivate and protect human beauty. Love defined in this way stems exclusively from the human need for beauty, and it is a human one, not from the fear of hell, or the hope of some Divine reward. And it is not a reflex gesture of compassion that results from habit. We can find this aspiration towards the generalisation of love in what Pope Francis said on October 11, 2017, at a general audience in Saint Peter's Square, namely that "the Last Judgement is not to be feared, because at the end of history there is the merciful Jesus," and therefore "everything will be saved. Everything."

Love is directed to the people who possess human beauty and also the beauty they create. It is natural to love what is created by human hands; we should not to spoil it or waste it, starting with bread on the table or with a flower planted in the garden or with the dreams of a child. In a reciprocal way, somebody has as much capacity for human beauty as they have love, that is, they have the capacity to appreciate human beauty in other people and the beauty of their creations.

Obviously, the love we are talking about is not the same as physical love, sexual attachment or love of the family. Naturally, our love is more intense towards family members, friends, place of birth, language, religion, culture, country. But this love is not complete unless it is at least accompanied by an attempt to understand and love human beauty around the globe. And if I use patriotism as a pretext to exclude or even destroy the beauty of those who are not of my nation or of my religion, this gesture can no longer be called love, it is a humanised form of territoriality and herd behaviour, both inherited from our ancestors.

Love, understood in the way described above, is – in my opinion – the only truly human attribute that generates authentic *good*, both in act and as an ethical concept. This is what the ancient Greeks perceived when talking about *kalokagathia* (from *kalos* – beautiful and *agathos* – good, virtue). Also, Aristotle saw a relationship between beauty (*kalon*) and virtue, arguing, in his "Nicomachean Ethics", that "Virtue aims at the beautiful". And, through the mirror, the ugliness of the human spirit and disregard or the destruction of human beauty, allows us to give a proper definition to the concept of *evil*.

We should be very careful here, because many people, following the *Manichaean tradition*, which has left its traces in Christian religions, simplify things and transform "good" and "evil" from the qualities of some human acts into personified entities. In this way, "*the Evil*" can easily become human and sometimes you will be told that you are on the side of "*the Good*" when you kill someone from that group. All religious or nationalist wars and many other barbaric conflicts and acts were based on this logic. In fact, in all of this only the animal side of humans is manifested dressed in populism to excuse atrocities, while the concept of "human beauty" is completely ignored.

Many messages received by those who went through close encounters and abductions said that mankind must mature. Perhaps the measure this maturity will be the generalisation of authentic love based on human beauty. One clue might be the advice of Saint Paul the Apostle, who wrote: "But now we still have faith, hope, love, these three; and the greatest of these is love" (Cor I, 13,13). I find it terrifying! For the Apostle Paul, love was more important than hope (in the afterlife, the second coming of Jesus etc.) and even faith. Perhaps

[112] Mack, 1995, p. 420

one "fruit" desired by the consciousness that oversees us, is an all-encompassing love between people. Maybe this is the most desired fruit.

Confrontation or pluralism

In the previous chapter, we considered the extreme complexity of reality and the limits of our means to understand it. No human being ever obtained definitive answers to major problems through science, revelation or other methods. To solve these problems, complex intellectual constructions were developed: e.g. scientific theories, philosophical systems, religious dogmas and so on. But they only provide a provisionally satisfactory knowledge of reality.

An important effect of this situation is that, in many areas, some thinkers come to a one conclusion while others come to another one. If two scientific theories disagree, it is customary to carry out a so-called *"crucial experiment"*. In other words in a laboratory or in reality, it is attempted to reproduce the situation in which the two theories contradict each other. In this way it can be seen which theory is correct and has been conformed by experimentation. But sometimes such experiments just cannot be performed. As a result, there will always be "truths" supported by some and alternatives and even opposite truths supported by others without being able to decide who is right. If, in materialist science, such situations are relatively rare, they are much more common in the fields of religion, philosophy, ufology, the paranormal and folk lore, etc., where crucial experiments are almost impossible to carry out.

Faced with contradictory truths about a problem that concerns them, a person will usually attach the truth to the one that seems more compelling, plausible, or desirable. They will do this because every human being needs *conviction* to support their decisions. In most cases the choice will not be theirs, but will be shaped by their ancestors, parents or teachers according to the culture to which they belong. And if everyone around him has the same belief these will no longer be assertions that have an alternative but will become *certainties*.

Through such processes it is a fact that where millions of people support one "truth" and elsewhere, others millions of others support a contrary "truth", neither will accept that their truth is neither certain nor definitive. In this respect religions are a good example, as Dr. David Barett stated, "There are more than ten thousand religions in the world, of which one hundred and fifty have at least one million followers".[113] But we can easily find examples of conflicting truths, each with many adherents, in nationalist disputes, or between political parties, business people, as well as between artists, philosophers, and scientists.

Most individuals are resistant when you want to change their beliefs. Dr. Bernie S. Siegel, a surgeon at Yale University, said he has found that people are dependent on their beliefs like drug addicts; and if you try to change them, they will react like a user deprived of their narcotics.[114] I have already mentioned the fact that, to a great extent, happiness is the state in which you have an answer to any question which comes to your mind. Martyrs – of all religions – preferred (and prefer) to die rather than give up the truths of their faith. They died happy, knowing they will end up in that beautiful place that their religion has promised them. Often, their murderers (or victims) were equally well indoctrinated with exactly opposite "truths".

The attachment to one's own truth when confronted with a contrary truth, often degenerates into intolerance, fanaticism and the desire to destroy the alternative truth by force, possibly even by killing its supporters. Sometimes millions of believers in one truth face millions of believers in the opposite truth and the outcome of often bloody. Every

---

[113] Wilcock, 2011, p. 128
[114] Siegel, 1986.

individual in the conflicting camps is overwhelmed by the belief that they hold the Ultimate Truth and the others are mistaken. Each part is convinced that it is fighting on the side of "the Good" and the others are the representatives of "the Evil", who must be mercilessly destroyed.

Can we accept that shedding blood is a way to prove who is right? Unfortunately, what is happening around us clearly proves that this way of thinking has not characterised, only the past centuries, but even today many still think this way. It seems that until we understand the value of human beauty it is unlikely that we will stop killing one another. In the light of what we discussed, i.e. the truth that every human is part of this beauty, if I cannot convince someone, by *unanimously accepted facts* (not by theories or dogmas), that he is not right and, at the same time I cannot accept claims his of truth, it means I have abandoned my love for that human. And if I choose to "persuade" him through violence, I will destroy a part of the world's beauty and diversity.

By understanding this state of affairs what can we do? There are three possible solutions. The first is to *withdraw*, and reject, or avoid those who support ideas contrary to my own. The second solution is to promote *tolerance*. I accept the idea that other people may have a different opinion to mine, but that will not change my convictions. Unfortunately, both of these paths only maintain the current situation which could degenerate at any time under an outburst of fanaticism.

The real solution is the third one. It's called *pluralistic thinking*[115]. It requires us to consider that *all* the truths and theories held by people we are interested in. Let us understand that no truth is definitive and that the multitude of different points of view always contains more truth than any individual point of view. In the next step, we will examine the truths considered and will try to reject as many of them as possible (but only by obvious and generally accepted *facts*). Then, we will retain all those ideas and theories that we have not been able to discard. In this way we obtain a "plurality of truths", some of which may possibly contradict each other. In the following, we will endeavour to base our decisions on *all* this plurality of truths and theories taken *simultaneously* (perhaps with a different degree of trust for each).

Only as an example I will quote from a letter from the Italian ufologist, Eduardo Russo: "I can testify from our own (Italian) 30-years long experience, that intelligent people with diametrically opposing viewpoints may work together in ufology (in the same organisation), even if they disagree on the very essence of the UFO phenomenon. Of course it's not always an easy path, but it's worth a try. We all share an interest in the subject (even we are on different sides for different reasons) and have a rational approach and willingness to work together. We can build upon this foundation".

If I adopt such a method I will use in search of Divinity in all existing religious beliefs *simultaneously*, including atheism. In the same way I am proud of being Romanian and I will present myself in this way, but I am also be proud to be European. Moreover, I can see how a Vietnamese, a Zulu, or Quechua also feel their national pride as members of the human race and as citizens of the Earth and of the Cosmos.

At the same time, I will fight for the preservation of all forms of culture: including language, religion, philosophy, myths, folklore and traditional medicine, etc. Globalisation is only acceptable if it does not lose anything in its plurality of visions about the world.

Even though this path – of pluralistic thinking and of love of the alternative truths of others – is undoubtedly difficult and probably scandalous for many, I think it is the *only way* that can lead to extinguishing the violence generated by the existence of alternative "truths".

---

[115] Farcas, 2009

Consequently, adopting pluralistic thinking by the great majority of human beings could be a "fruit" expected by the 'higher powers' that are monitoring us.

The first step for this is to accept that *there is no unique and ultimate Truth* (in any field and no matter how much apparent authority is carries) and that the intellectual richness of mankind lies precisely in the plurality of all points of view. We will have to recognise our limits, overcome pride and cherish the opinions of others, be ready to accept that our questioner may also be right and maintain a permanent dialogue. The next step is for each of us to *internalise* this dialogue in the spirit of *pluralist thinking* and, at the same time, continue to seek the best answers together. This is the only way that can present any hope of revealing higher truths beyond our current parochial visions.

If we accept the hypothesis developed throughout this work, mankind could be like a vast orchard, planted and cared for by a higher power and consciousness and waiting for a precious harvest. But, at the same time it could be a huge "sociological" experiment to see how we resolve our different views about subjects such as religious truths, or how we change our animal behaviour using the love of human beauty.

Some contactees and abductees reported that they were told that human beings will be left to find their own solutions. They have the free will to choose whether to kill each other or not; they have the freedom to decide whether they want to develop in peace or to blow up the planet. Whatever happens; those who are watching us will continue to gather data about us in a super-memory and may intervene to save some specimens for a gene bank.

On the basis of the above I believe that we still have some time; perhaps no more than a few centuries and during that period we will either destroy ourselves through our thirst for power and possessions, or in the name of some "ultimate truth", or humanity can raise itself to the next level, that of love of human beauty and pluralistic thinking.

CONCLUSIONS

From its beginnings, mankind seems to have been supervised by a presence that uses countless disguises, that are appropriate to the place and epoch in which it appears. This presence has been describe, in various ways, in myths, fairy tales, religions and ufology. This may be evidence that for a long time we have unwittingly been in contact with hyper-civilizations.

Is this presence waiting for something from us? The fact that it apparently forbids and prevents any disclosure of its existence may be a sign that it is awaiting (and maybe even harvesting) the fruits of our original vision of reality, something that has been developed without any external aid.

Some alleged messages that have been received also suggest that this higher presence will not come into direct contact with us until we have matured sufficiently. This process may need two requirements: (1) That human beauty becomes the motivation that overcomes the negatives produced by instinct and reflex, and spontaneously generates peace, love and goodwill, and (2) we stop claiming to possess the ultimate truth and adopt a system of pluralistic thinking, and use it systematically it in our reasoning and decision making and apply it to all subjects, even if some of them contradict one other.

MAIN SOURCES

- Vladimir **Azhazha**, Evgeni Krushelnitski, *NLO vokrug nas (UFOs Around Us* – in Russian), Golos, **1992**;
- Alice A. **Bailey**, *Light of the Soul* on *The Yoga Sutras of Patanjali – Book 3 – Union achieved and its Results*, Lucis Trust, **1927**;
- David **Barclay** & Therese Marie Barclay (editors), *UFOs The Final Answer?* Blandford Press, **1993**;
- Seth D. **Baum**, Jacob D. Haqq-Misra, Shawn D. Domagal-Goldman, *would contact extraterrestrials benefit or harm humanity? A scenario analysis*, **2011**, https://arxiv.org/abs/1104.4462;
- New International Version of the **Bible**;
- Shi **Bo**, *L'Empire du Milieu troublé par les OVNIs*, Axis Mundi, **1993**;
- Jérôme **Bourgine**, *Le Voyage astral. Enquete sur les voyages hors du corps (in French)*, Editions du Rocher, **1993**;
- Richard **Boylan** Ph.D., *Vatican Monsignor Corrado Balducci's Pronouncements: "Star Visitors Are Real"*, **2006**, http://www.drboylan.com/balducci2.html;
- Courtney **Brown**, Ph.D., *Cosmic Voyage – Scientific Discovery of Extraterrestrials Visiting Earth*, Dutton, Penguin Books, **1996**;
- Courtney **Brown**, Ph.D., *Scientific Remote Viewing, Extraterrestrials and a Message for Mankind*, Dutton, Penguin Books, **1999**;
- Courtland D. B. **Bryan**, Close *Encounters of the Fourth Kind*, Penguin Books, **1995**;
- Lyn **Buchanan**, *The Seventh Sense,* Paraview Pocket Books, a Division of Simon & Schuster, **2003**;
- Ilie **Cioară**, *Realitatea supremă și condiționarea umană* (in Romanian), Ed. Herald, **2001**;
- Giuseppe **Cocconi**, Philip Morrison, *Searching for Interstellar Communications*, Nature volume 184, pages 844–846 (19 September **1959**);
- **Cometa**, **1999**, UFOs *and Defense: What must we be prepared for? (Les Ovni Et La Defense: A quoi doit-on se préparer? – in French)*, https://www.bibliotecapleyades.net/sociopolitica/sociopol_cometareport01.htm#pdf files;
- Patrick **Cooke**, *The Greatest Deception: The Bible UFO Connection*, The Oracle Research Institute, **2005**;
- Ioan Petru **Culianu**, *Out of this World: Otherworldly Journeys from Gilgamesh to Albert Einstein*, Shambhala, Boston, **1991**;
- Paul **Davies**, *Are We Alone? Philosophical Implications of the Discovery of Extraterrestriel Life*, Basic Books, **1995**;
- Richard M. **Dolan**, *UFOs and the National Security State. Cronology of a Cover-up 1941-1973*, Hampton Roads Publishing, **2002**;
- Barry H. **Downing**, *The Bible and Flying Saucers*, Berkley Books, New York, **1989**;
- Dumitru Constantin-**Dulcan**, *În căutarea sensului pierdut (in Romanian)*, Ed. Eikon, Cluj-Napoca, **2008**;
- Dumitru Constantin-**Dulcan**, *Mintea de dincolo (in Romanian)*, Ed. Eikon, Cluj-Napoca, **2013**;
- Freeman **Dyson**, *Origins of Life*, Cambridge University Press, **1999**;
- Mircea **Eliade**, *Myths, Dreams and Misteries*, Harper and Row, New York, **1957**;
- Dan D. **Farcaș**, *Labirintul cunoașterii (in Romanian)*, Ed. Paideia, București, **2009**;

- Dan D. **Farcaş**, *UFOs over Romania*, Flying Disk Press, **2016**;
- Edith **Fiore** Ph.D., *Encounters*, Ballantine Books, **1990**;
- Camille **Flammarion**, *Death and its mystery – proofs of the existence of the soul,* The Century Co. (Vol.1-3, 1921-**1923**);
- Charles **Fort**, *The Book of the Damned*, Horace Liveright Publisher, **1919**;
- Raymond E. **Fowler**, *The Watchers*, Bantam, **1991**;
- Raymond E. **Fowler**, *The Watchers II*, Wild Flower Press, **1995**;
- Curtis G. **Fuller** ed., *Proceedings of the First International UFO Congress,* New York: Warner Books, **1980**;
- Florin **Gheorghiţă**, *Fenomenul Valentina (in Romanian)*, Ed. Polirom, Iasi, **1998**;
- Guillermo **Gonzalez** and Jay W. Richards, *The Privileged Planet: How Our Place in the Cosmos Is Designed for Discovery*, Regnery Publishing, Inc., **2004**;
- Terry **Hansen**, *The Missing Times – News Media Complicity in the UFO Cover-up,* Xlibris, **2000**;
- Budd **Hopkins**, *Missing Time: A Documented Study of UFO Abductions*, Richard Marek Pubs, **1981**;
- Budd **Hopkins**, *Intruders. The Incredible Visitations at Copley Woods*, Ballantine Books, **1988**;
- Budd **Hopkins**, *Witnessed. The True Story of the Brooklyn Bridge UFO Abductions*, Pocket Books, **1996**;
- J. Allen **Hynek**. *The UFO Experience: A scientific enquiry,* Henry Regnery Company, Chicago, **1972**;
- J. Allen **Hynek** in Fuller, Curtis G. ed., *Proceedings of the First International UFO Congress*. New York: Warner Books, **1980**;
- J. Allen **Hynek**, Philip J. Imbrogno, Bob Pratt, *Night Siege – The Hudson Valley UFO Sightings*, Ballantine Books, New York, **1987**;
- David M. **Jacobs**, PhD, *Secret Life, Firsthand documented accounts of UFO abductions*, Fireside, Simon & Schuster, **1993**;
- David M. **Jacobs**, PhD, *The Threat, Revealing the secret alien agenda*, Fireside, Simon & Schuster, **1999**;
- David M. **Jacobs** (ed.), *UFOs and Abductions. Challenging the Borders of Knowledge*, University Press of Kansas, **2000**;
- Carl G. **Jung**, *Flying Saucers: A Modern Myth of Things Seen in the Skies*, Signet Books, New York, **1969**;
- Michio **Kaku**, in Coast to Coast AM https://www.coasttocoastam.com/article/transcript-excerpts-michio-kaku?mode=print, **2005**;
- Leslie **Kean**, *UFOs: Generals, Pilots and Government Officials Go on the Record*, Crown Archetype, **2010**;
- Victor **Kernbach**, *Dicţionar de mitologie generală (in Romanian)*, Ed. Albatros, Bucureşti, **1995**;
- Dorothee **Koechlin** de Bizemont, *L'Univers d' Edgar Cayce*, Ed. Robert Laffont, Paris, (Vol:1-4), 1985, 1987, 1992, **2000**;
- Bob **Larson**, *UFOs and the Alien Agenda*, Thomas Nelson Inc., **1997**;
- Joel **Levy**, *The Doomsday Book: Scenarios for the End of the World*, Vision Paperbacks, London, **2005**;
- V.M. **Lipunov**, *God Being Scientifically Discovered* (Published in Russian Journal "*Zemlya i Vselennaya*", N1, p.37, **1995**), http://www.pereplet.ru/nauka/super_ratio.shtml;

- John **Mack** M.D., *Abduction, Human encounters with aliens*, Ballantine Books, New York, **1995**;
- John E. **Mack**, M.D., *Passport to the Cosmos*, Crown Publishers, **1999**;
- *Manifesto for a Post-Materialist Science*, http://opensciences.org/about/manifesto-for-a-post-materialist-science, **2014**;
- Chuck **Missler**, Mark Eastman, *Alien Encounters*, Koinonia House, **1997**;
- Robert **Monroe**, *Journeys out of the body*, Doubleday, **1971**;
- Ruth **Montgomery**, *Aliens Among Us*, Fawcet Crest, Ballantine Books, **1986**;
- Simon Conway **Morris**, *The Runes of Evolution*, Templeton Press, **2015**;
- Kary B. **Mullis**, *Dancing Naked in the Mind Field*, Vintage Books, **1998**;
- Erik A. **Petigura** andrew W. Howard and Geoffrey W. Marcy, *Prevalence of Earth-size planets orbiting Sun-like stars*, Proceedings of the National Academy of Sciences of the United States of America (PNAS), November **2013**;
- Nick **Pope**, *Open Skies, Closed Minds. For the first Time, a Government UFO Expert Speaks Out*, Pocket Books, Simon & Shuster, **1997**;
- Nick **Pope**, **2013**, http://www.nickpope.net/faq.htm;
- Kenneth **Ring**, Ph.D., *The Omega Project*, William Morrow and Co, New York, **1992**;
- Carl **Sagan**, *The Cosmic Connection* (1974), Anchor Press, Doubleday, **1980**;
- Carl **Sagan**, *Cosmos*, Random House, New York, **1980**;
- Rupert **Sheldrake**, *The Presence of the Past: morphic resonance and the habits of nature*, Times Books, New York, **1988**;
- Rupert **Sheldrake**, *Morphic Resonance: The Nature of Formative Causation*, Park Street Press, **2009**;
- Jean **Sider**, *Contacts supra-terrestres. Leurres et manipulations – Tome I (in French)*, Axis Mundi, **1994**;
- Jean **Sider**, *Contacts supra-terrestres, L'illusion cosmique – Tome II (in French)*, Axis Mundi, **1995**;
- Bernie S. **Siegel**, *Love, Medicine & Miracles*, Harper Collins, **1986**;
- Zecharia **Sitchin**, *Genesis revisited*, Avon books, New York, **1990**;
- Whitley **Strieber**, *Communion. A True Story*, Wilson & Neff, Inc., **1987**;
- Russell **Targ**, *Limitless Mind. A Guide to Remote Viewing and Transformation of Consciousness*, New World Library, **2004**;
- Kevin J. **Todeschi**, *Edgar Cayce on the Akashic Records*, ARE Press, **1998**;
- Jacques **Vallée**, *Passport to Magonia: From Folklore to Flying Saucers*, H. Regnery Co, **1969**;
- Jacques **Vallée**, *Dimensions: A Casebook of Alien Contact*, Ballantine Books, **1989**;
- Jacques **Vallée**, *Confrontations*, Ballantine Books, New York, **1991**;
- Jacques **Vallée**, *Revelations*, Ballantine Books, New York, **1992**;
- Jacques **Vallée** and Chris Aubeck, *Wonders in the Sky. Unexplained Aerial Objects from Antiquity to Modern Times*, Jeremy P. Tarcher / Penguin, **2009**;
- Peter D. **Ward**, Donald Brownlee, *Rare Earth: Why Complex Life Is Uncommon in the Universe*, Copernicus Books, **2004**;
- Lyall **Watson**, *Supernature, A Natural History of the Supernatural*, Hodder and Stoughton, **1974**;
- Stephen **Webb**, *If the universe is teeming with aliens... where is everybody? Fifty solutions to the Fermi paradox and the problem of extraterrestrial life*, Copernicus Books, **2002**;
- David **Wilcock**, *The Source Field Investigations*, Dutton, a division of Penguin Group, **2011**;

FURTHER READING FROM FLYING DISK PRESS
http://flyingdiskpress.blogspot.com/

UFOs OVER ROMANIA

DAN D. FARCAS PH.D.

PORTAL

A Lifetime of Paranormal Experiences

Adele Casales Rocha

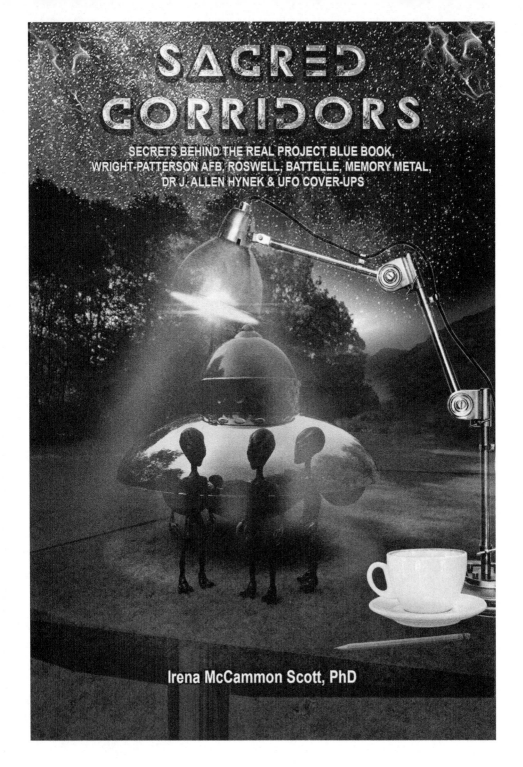

SACRED CORRIDORS

SECRETS BEHIND THE REAL PROJECT BLUE BOOK, WRIGHT-PATTERSON AFB, ROSWELL, BATTELLE, MEMORY METAL, DR J. ALLEN HYNEK & UFO COVER-UPS

Irena McCammon Scott, PhD

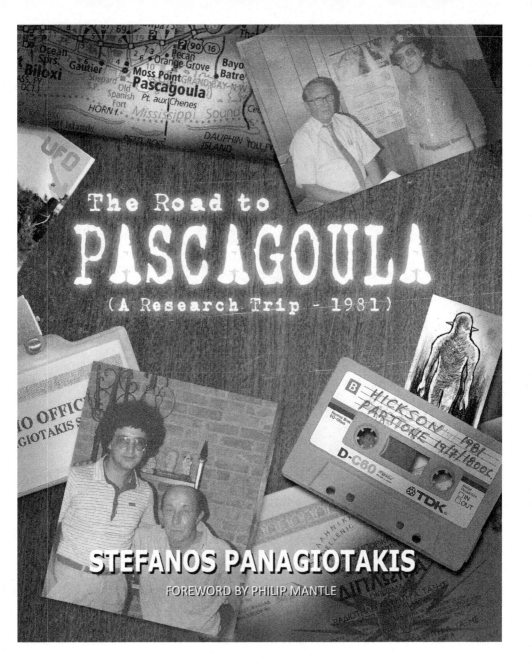

The Road to
PASCAGOULA
(A Research Trip - 1981)

STEFANOS PANAGIOTAKIS

FOREWORD BY PHILIP MANTLE

PASCAGOULA-THE CLOSEST ENCOUNTER

MY STORY
CALVIN PARKER

FOREWORD BY PHILIP MANTLE

THE
UFOLOGY
UMBRELLA

CLOSE ENCOUNTERS ARE NOT ENOUGH

JASON GLEAVES

PHILIP MANTLE

ONCE UPON A MISSING TIME

a novel of alien abduction

RUSSIA'S ROSWELL INCIDENT

And Other Amazing UFO Cases From The Former Soviet Union

By Paul Stonehill & Philip Mantle

Printed in Great Britain
by Amazon